The Sentimental Mode

The Sentimental Mode
Essays in Literature, Film and Television

Edited by JENNIFER A. WILLIAMSON,
JENNIFER LARSON *and* ASHLEY REED

McFarland & Company, Inc., Publishers
Jefferson, North Carolina

LIBRARY OF CONGRESS CATALOGUING-IN-PUBLICATION DATA

The sentimental mode : essays in literature, film and television / edited by Jennifer A. Williamson, Jennifer Larson and Ashley Reed.
    p.   cm.
Includes bibliographical references and index.

ISBN 978-0-7864-7341-0 (softcover : alk. paper) ∞
ISBN 978-1-4766-1450-2 (ebook)

1. American literature—20th century—History and criticism. 2. American literature—21st century—History and criticism. 3. Sentimentalism in literature. 4. American literature—English influences. I. Williamson, Jennifer A., 1978– editor of publication. II. Larson, Jennifer, 1977 July 4– editor of publication. III. Reed, Ashley, 1975– editor of publication.

PS228.S38S46 2014
810.9'384—dc23   2014001062

BRITISH LIBRARY CATALOGUING DATA ARE AVAILABLE

© 2014 Jennifer A. Williamson, Jennifer Larson and Ashley Reed. All rights reserved

No part of this book may be reproduced or transmitted in any form or by any means, electronic or mechanical, including photocopying or recording, or by any information storage and retrieval system, without permission in writing from the publisher.

On the cover: Mac Harshberger, *Untitled (Madonna and Child)* ca. 1924, woodcut, 14.7 × 10.2 cm. Gift of William W. Whitney (© Fine Arts Museum of San Francisco, courtesy the estate of Mac Harshberger)

Manufactured in the United States of America

McFarland & Company, Inc., Publishers
  Box 611, Jefferson, North Carolina 28640
    www.mcfarlandpub.com

Table of Contents

Preface 1

Introduction: American Sentimentalism from the Nineteenth Century to the Present
    JENNIFER A. WILLIAMSON 3

Doctor Jekyll and Mister Jim Crow: Medical Professionalism, Race and Postsentimentalism in *The Marrow of Tradition*
    BRIAN SWEENEY 15

Sentimental Satire in Anita Loos's *Gentlemen Prefer Blondes*
    LISA MENDELMAN 36

"Grimly sentimental": Pleasure, Trauma and Djuna Barnes's *Ryder*
    JULIE TAYLOR 56

"Violent and sentimental by turns": *Labor Defender*, Sentimentalism and the American Literary Left
    NATHANIEL CADLE 70

"You give a damn about so many things I don't": Hemingway's Gendered Sentimentalism in "The Snows of Kilimanjaro" and "The Short, Happy Life of Francis Macomber"
    MICHAEL T. WILSON 90

Sentimentalism and Celebrity Culture: Mae West as Novelist
    ANNE-MARIE EVANS 107

Swedenborgian Sentimentalism in John Rechy's *City of Night*
    MARÍA DEGUZMÁN 121

"Shame, thas a shame": The Anti-Sentiment of Sapphire's *Push* and *The Kid*
    ERICA D. GALIOTO 134

Profitable Sentiments: HBO's *The Wire* and Harriet Beecher
    Stowe's *Uncle Tom's Cabin*
        KRISTIN J. JACOBSON   151
Race, Religion and Sentimentalism in *Gilead* and *Home*
        ELIZABETH A. ELLIS   175
Madea's Middle Class: Sentimental Spaces in Tyler Perry's
    Madea's Family Reunion and *Why Did I Get Married?*
        ASHLEY REED *and* JENNIFER LARSON   190

About the Contributors   211
Index   213

Preface

The essays in this collection demonstrate that, despite the influence of realism, naturalism, modernism, and New Criticism, authors of the twentieth and twenty-first centuries continued to use nineteenth-century literature's sentimental forms and tropes in addition to developing political engagement through emotional, cross-boundary identification. In the twentieth and twenty-first centuries, the sentimental mode did not so much disappear as change, engaging with nineteenth-century tropes and ideals, combining them with emerging genres—as well as new media and technologies—and applying these multi-faceted perspectives to the cultural struggles of a new age. Authors of the twentieth and twenty-first centuries continue to struggle with sentimentalism's race, class, and gender ideals; however, sentimentalism's dual ability to promote these ideals and extend identification across them makes it an attractive and effective mode for political and social influence.

The analysis of twentieth- and twenty-first-century narratives contained within this collection reveals the ongoing use of sentimental expression that draws upon the mode's ability to instruct and influence readers through emotional identification. In the texts under discussion, sentimentalism appears as a key vehicle of political and social expression, just as it did in the nineteenth century; this more recent sentimentalism, though, operates in a supposedly "anti-sentimental" age—one that rejects the sentimental as feminized and embraces what may appear to be more masculine modes of naturalism, realism, and modernism. So, these twentieth- and twenty-first-century narratives employ aspects of the sentimental mode while simultaneously critiquing its failures by deconstructing nineteenth-century perspectives on race, class, and gender and the ways in which sentimental ideals promote these problematic perspectives. Many of the texts under discussion not only wrestle with the feminization of emotional expression, familial connection, and the domestic sphere, but also examine intersectional social codes and the ways in which race, gender, and class are co-encoded and simultaneously determinant.

Just as the sentimental genre cannot be defined by a strict, coherent plot structure or even a standard set of themes, the essays found in this collection interpret contemporary sentimentalism through a variety of means, including narrative structure, common tropes, and rhetorical moves. However, each of these essays demonstrates a continuation or variation of the sentimental mode, the foundation of which remains an examination of "self-in-society" and instructional emotional identification. Spanning from the very beginning of the twentieth century all the way to the first decade of the twenty-first, the texts and media under discussion show that sentimentalism is not only alive and well, but that it remains a national, expressive project at the core of American culture. An infinitely flexible mode, far from failing to capture American life, sentimentalism continues to embody the heart and struggle of the American people, from Socialist political action to debates over women's sexual power to the determination of masculine identity in a changing world to gay subcultures to racial identification and social change.

Together, these essays provide a range of perspectives, and a new vocabulary, for understanding sentimentalism past and present. They demonstrate not only the ways in which the tropes and ideologies of nineteenth-century sentimentalism are in force today, but also the ways in which these tropes and ideologies both shape and are shaped by contemporary experience and struggles for social change.

Introduction

American Sentimentalism from the Nineteenth Century to the Present

JENNIFER A. WILLIAMSON

Defining the sentimental novel or classifying sentimental fiction as a genre is more difficult than a twentieth-century reader might assume. Because of sentimentalism's association with nineteenth-century domestic fictions—and the frequent portrayal of tubercular young girls and religious conversion—addressing sentimental fictions as a group can mistakenly lead to the assumption that the genre names a coherent body of works that follow a common plotline and that sentimental writing is "bad" because it relies on overdetermined tropes and highly emotional scenes. In fact, even within nineteenth-century studies, there exists some debate about whether certain texts should or should not be classified as "sentimental fiction" because of the ways they challenge plot conventions associated with the large body of sentimental works. For example, Hawthorne excepted Fanny Fern's *Ruth Hall* from his general condemnation of women's writing and sentimental fiction because he was impressed by the text's style, writing to his publisher William Ticknor that he "enjoyed it a great deal. The woman writes as if the devil was in her, and that is the only condition under which a woman ever writes anything worth reading" (Person 24). Fern's novel occupies a tentative place within the canon of sentimental literature because although it includes sentimental scenes and tropes, it is not so focused upon the domestic as many sentimental texts, and it supports women's independent professionalization in the public realm.

Joanne Dobson, in her 1997 article "Reclaiming Sentimental Literature," advocates for a way to define and understand the genre that is based upon a literary analysis of textual structure rather than on cultural interpretation.

Although many narrative elements connect the novels produced within the sentimental genre, plot alone cannot define it. As Nina Baym has pointed out, there is a pattern of women's writing that extends beyond sentimental literature; similarly, writers of sentimental literature explored different plot formations in order to develop varied social commentaries that would trouble any critic seeking to classify the genre based solely on storyline. Sentimental literature can be difficult to define, but there is a distinct correlation among the texts, and recognizing this connection will help scholars to better understand how sentimentalism operates and to argue against the denigration that has occurred in the twentieth century by critics who dismiss sentimental texts for their emotionality, femininity, and "bad writing." Shirley Samuels has noted that sentimentality "appears not so much a genre as an operation or a set of actions within discursive models of affect and identification that effect connections across gender, race, and class boundaries" (6). Dobson meanwhile proposes a broader understanding of sentimental literature as a form of writing that "is premised on an emotional and philosophical ethos that celebrates human connection, both personal and communal, and acknowledges the shared devastation of affectional loss. It is not a discrete literary category [...] but rather an imaginative orientation characterized by certain themes, stylistic features, and figurative conventions" (266).

While the development of the individual and the self-in-society have long been recognized as significant (masculinized) themes of American literature, sentimental literature values and operates within a different social structure and instead "envisions the self-in-relation; family (not necessarily in the conventional biological sense), intimacy, community, and social responsibility are its primary relational modes" (Dobson, "Reclaiming" 267). In Dobson's reading, the core of the sentimental text "is the desire for bonding, and it is affiliation on the plane of emotion, sympathy, nurturance, or similar moral or spiritual inclination for which sentimental writers and readers yearn." Whereas traditional texts derive their tension from the possibility that individuality, freedom, and independent selfhood are threatened, the tensions of sentimental texts are created through the "[v]iolation, actual or threatened, of the affectional bond" which "leads to bleak, dispirited, anguished, sometimes outraged, representations of human loss, as well as to idealized portrayals of human connection or divine consolation" ("Reclaiming" 267).

One of the many contemporary criticisms levied against sentimental literature, most infamously by critic Ann Douglas, is that it is, plain and simply, "bad" writing. However, sentimental writing must be evaluated in light of its particular aims; such writing relied upon an idiom "designed to elicit feelings of empathy and concern, and whose language, like the language of realism, is intended to communicate meaning with minimal impediment" (Dobson, "Reclaiming" 268). The language is not so much "bad" as it is simple, conventional, and targeted to a general audience. Sentimental literature deliberately employs the familiar, using clear language to convey ideas while also drawing upon repeated, recognizable themes in order to make use of the social and cultural resonance an author expects a particular trope to hold for the reader. Rather than merely recycling flat, melodramatic imagery—as modern critics have accused—sentimental writers incorporate images and ideas that already possess deep cultural meaning for their audiences. Jane Tompkins argues that the familiar, stereotyped characters are not so much "defects" of writing as they are operations of "a cultural shorthand." Such characters as Little Eva, Ellen Montgomery, and Gertie Flint are not meant to be realistic representations but are instead "the carriers of strong emotional associations. Their familiarity and typicality, rather than making them bankrupt or stale, are the basis of their effectiveness as integers in a social equation" (xvi).

Despite sentimentalism's incredible popularity in the early- and mid-nineteenth century, by the late-nineteenth and twentieth centuries the term "sentimental" had become a label for melodramatic, flat representations that were deemed unrealistic, unsophisticated, and un-literary. Furthermore, calling a work "sentimental" was a way to judge it negatively as feminine—whether written by a woman or a man—because of its association with emotion and other traditionally feminized themes such as domesticity or religion. Thus, in broad strokes, critics dismissed both sentimental writing and feminized writing as non-literary and unsophisticated.

Throughout the twentieth century, nineteenth-century sentimental texts were largely dismissed or ignored, and contemporary writers strove to avoid association with the genre or the term. It wasn't until 1977, with the publication of Ann Douglas's *The Feminization of American Culture*, that scholars began treating sentimental culture and literature as a serious subject. However, Douglas offered only a negative assessment of sentimental fiction, arguing that the literature promoted women's submission, complicity, and withdrawal from the centers of political, economic, and cultural power in America.

It wasn't until the mid-eighties that scholars began to debate the social and political power of sentimentalism and sentimental texts. Tompkins—as well as other critics such as Phillip Fisher, Cathy Davidson, and Shirley Samuels—argued that sentimental texts were, in fact, demonstrating active and potentially radical engagement in the public sphere. Such texts emphasized domestic and religious principles in an effort to make inroads into avenues of cultural and social authority previously denied women altogether. Tompkins argues that sentimental novels rely on emotional appeals to generate sympathy in readers. This sympathy serves a key rhetorical function: engaging reader sympathy allows the text to generate compassion for its subjects and subject matter, so that sentimental scenes and characters promote emotional and moral education for the reader. Sentimental novels, then, attempt to teach readers to "think and act in a particular way" (xi). Such literature "has power in the world" that allows it to connect "with the beliefs and attitudes of large masses of readers so as to impress or move them deeply" (xiv). Thus, the function of the events and scenarios in the texts is "heuristic and didactic rather than mimetic, [since] they do not attempt to transcribe in detail a parabola of events as they 'actually happen' in society; rather, they provide a basis for remaking the social and political order in which events take place" (Tompkins xvii). Fisher, in *Hard Facts: Setting and Form in the American Novel* (1985), also argues that sentimental literature performs cultural work so effectively that the symbolic representations of the texts accomplish a cultural transformation by which "the unimaginable becomes, finally, the obvious" (8). Thus, the ideas—such as the recognition of the humanity of children, slaves, and prisoners—that sentimental fiction promotes become embedded in the broader culture and the work conducted by sentimentalism to develop those ideas is forgotten, making the literature today seem overdone and obvious.

Similarly, Davidson's *Revolution and the Word: The Rise of the Novel in America* (1986) demonstrated that sentimental fiction works within the confines of the legal doctrine of the *feme covert*, also known as coverture, the social and political practice by which women were rendered legally invisible and considered to be under the protection, guidance, and control of their fathers and, eventually, their husbands. Sentimental fiction reveals the social problems women experience under coverture, both illustrating the tragic failures that occur when male protection fails and offering potential remedies for women's empowerment. A focus on women's marriage choices and their consequences, as well as on women's sexual behavior, was also an examination of the social problems and conditions women experienced under coverture, their limited options, and the implications for women when family structure alters or fails. Samuels, in *The Culture of Sentiment: Race, Gender, and Sentimentality in Nineteenth-Century America* (1992), expanded the debate to include an understanding of sentimentality as a "national project" that extended beyond sentimental novels and pervaded all aspects of American society and national identity (3). Functioning as a set of rules for how to "feel right," sentimentality "is literally at the heart of nineteenth-century American culture," Samuels argues (5, 4). It is "a set of cultural practices designed to evoke a certain form of emotional response, usually empathy, in the reader or viewer" that enables it to produce or reproduce "spectacles that cross race, class, and gender boundaries" (4).

Once sentimentalism and the sentimental novel were established as legitimate fields of scholarly inquiry, numerous critics began to consider sentimentalism's cultural context and impact in the nineteenth century. Literary and cultural studies scholars took up the debate, studying sentimentalism in fiction, nonfiction, poetry, slave narratives, art, and rhetoric. Subsequent researchers examined sentimentalism in nineteenth-century family formation, social mores, religious beliefs, legal discourse, domestic economies, racial identity, and gender roles. Gillian Brown's *Domestic Individualism* (1990), Elizabeth Barnes's *States of Sympathy* (1997), Julia Stern's *The Plight of Feeling* (1997), Julie Ellison's *Cato's Tears* (1999), Lori Merish's *Sentimental Materialism* (2000), Paula Bennett's *Poets in the Public Sphere* (2003), and Laurent Berlant's *The Female Complaint* (2008) are among the numerous works that expand and extend the debates begun by Douglas and Tompkins.

Still, prevailing critical views hold that the twentieth century, with the rising influences of naturalism and realism, became increasingly hostile to the sentimental as a literary and political mode and that sentimentalism as an artistic and cultural practice all but disappeared. Realism, naturalism, modernism, and postmodernism seemingly set themselves in opposition to romanticism and sentimentalism, figuring the latter forms as feminized and as lacking qualities necessary to understand contemporary life and the modern individual. Sentimentalism came to be viewed as the product of a by-gone era. Twentieth-century writers often consciously sought to move away from highly structured, moralistic presentations of social and religious life and de-emphasized an individual's ability to enact social change through moral uprightness. Instead, modern authors tended to portray individuals with complex psychology who were subject to social and environmental forces that had overwhelming power to affect the course of their lives.

Realist and naturalist writers—such as William Dean Howells, Stephen Crane, Theodore Dreiser, Sinclair Lewis, and Frank Norris—developed a discourse of masculinity in which they styled themselves as objective observers of human nature; "acting as journalists or social-scientist investigators," they sought to re-brand sentimental and domestic writing as "too feminized for turn-of-the-century conditions" (Den Tandt 107). Such self-conscious rejection of sentimentalism "makes the pursuit of literary truth a gendered enterprise [as m]ale writers challenge discourses of conformity they regard as feminized" (Den Tandt 101). Many emblematic naturalist texts portray sentimental inauthenticity through parody or satire. For example, Norris's *McTeague* (1899) mocks sentimental representations of middle-class households and marriages, overtly linking monetary exchanges to social relationships and depicting grotesquely violent outcomes. Dreiser's *Sister Carrie* (1903) offers a naturalist version of *Charlotte Temple* by depicting an unrepentant, fallen woman who engages in prostitution and eventually rises to stardom; instead of being disgraced and punished by death, she discovers that her success will never lead to happiness. Another point of contention was realism's representation of female sexuality and desire, as authors displayed female "sexual behavior destructive to themselves and their surroundings. This context made the female protagonists' transgressions of sexual norms the benchmark of realistic radicalism" (Den Tandt 101). Realism directly challenged sentimentalism's focus on controlling female desires and channeling them toward socially acceptable avenues (as it also subtly acknowledged the risks and dangers of female sexuality). Instead, early naturalist novels offered a frankness about and fascination with female sexuality, often focusing on young women who engaged in prostitution or promiscuous relationships, leading Willa Cather to name them "lost lady narratives" (qtd. in Den Tandt 101).

By portraying their mode of writing as more real, more authentic, and more objective than sentimental, domestic, or romantic writing, and highlighting realism and naturalism's relationship to the social conditions of the new century, these writers argued that the sentimental novel no longer effectively captured either American experience or its cultural conditions. Despite realism and naturalism's need for a sentimental aesthetic to define themselves *against*, authors of these genres self-consciously argued that sentimentalism had no place in the modern era. They emphasized Darwinian, scientific, and objective analyses of social conditions over texts that depicted new world orders and Christian moral allegories. While sentimentalism helped solidify a developing middle-class culture, realism and naturalism capitalized on increasing urbanization and new social structures created by larger metropolitan cities, unrestrained capitalism, and tension between the middle and working classes.

Like proponents of realism and naturalism, critics of literary modernism view it as inherently anti-sentimental, not only rejecting the overtly moral and feminized novels of the previous era but also stressing the relationship between popular culture and high modern mandates. Despite its obsession with history and desire to show how the modern age had produced new ways of thinking and being in the world, modernist philosophy emphasized "a form of discourse that has no designs on the world. It does not attempt to change things, but merely to represent them, and it does so in a specifically literary language whose claim to value lies in its uniqueness" (Tompkins 125). By focusing on a work's aesthetic structure or impact and devaluing its message or social purpose, modernist literature contributed to a shift in the evaluation of literature in the twentieth century. According to modernist thinking, Tompkins observes, "works whose stated purpose is to influence the course of history, and which therefore employ a language that is not only not unique but common and accessible to everyone, do not qualify as works of art" (125). Under these new standards of artistic expression, sentimental literature's direct claims to moral and social influence as well as its lack of stylistic or linguistic experimentation became viewed as disappointingly unrealistic, obvious, and feminized—a perspective that persists today.

As an artistic movement intent on capturing the zeitgeist of the new era, modernism not only sought to embody the energies and experiences of the fast-paced, industrializing twentieth century but also worked to dismantle previous understandings of art, literature, and society that loomed large at the start of the new age. One of its direct targets was sentimental literature, which had adapted Enlightenment values of sensibility in the nineteenth century in order to shape the world through a feminized, religious, middle-class lens of Victorian mores. Avant-garde intellectuals worked to create a niche for themselves as true artists and thinkers, but in order to do so they had to topple the giants that had come before them and that had been embraced by the reading public.

In *Sentimental Modernism: Women Writers and the Revolution of the Word* (1991), Suzanne Clark argues that modernism's attack on sentimentalism enabled the movement to establish a new form of literary criticism that was intrinsically gendered and heavily dependent on the very thing it denigrated (34–35). In order to define itself as a significant literary movement, modernism needed the sentimental to provide an opposing system of values even as it held up true expression of human feeling as a test of its authenticity and of the efficacy of the aesthetics endorsed. By contrasting themselves with sentimental writers, modernists were able to establish themselves "as a discourse community, defined by its adversarial relationship to domestic culture. Multiple issues of class and gender, power and desire, were contained in this opposition to the sentimental" (Clark 1). Modernism created a gendered devaluation in which it "constituted itself by conflating the romantic with the sentimental and the popular. The private discourse of feeling and the public community of women, guardians of feeling, are, under modernism, both sentimental" (Clark 19). Yet, while modernism separated the low and popular from the high and inaccessible as indicators of artistic value, by the 1930s modernists and their critics had developed an interest in popular culture as an artistic subject, believing that the realities experienced by the masses were tangible and relevant to the current age. Common themes of daily life, advertising, and mass production appeared in visual art and literature, transformed from popular culture into high modern expression and experimentation. Michael Bell, in *Sentimentalism, Ethics, and the Culture of Feeling* (2000), observes that despite its criticism of the sentimental, "the modernist generation also continued the transformation of sentiment into an implicit criterion of true feeling, a development which even now largely escapes recognition whether in the common language of feeling or in the specialist practice of literary criticism" (160). The sentimental thus became "a short-hand for everything modernism would exclude, the other of its literary/nonliterary dualism" (Clark 9).

Feminist scholars and critics who sought to recover sentimental and domestic writing had to overcome the literary/nonliterary dualism set in place by modernism and supported by the New Critics. The narrative of nonliterary value—the view that sentimental writing in the nineteenth century lacked artistic value and could be judged only as an artifact of popular, trite women's culture—became such a dominant scholarly belief that twentieth-century authors all but turned away from sentimental forms and tropes, abandoning them under the censure of modernism's growing influence. Clark, however, has shown that sentimentalism was an integral part of modernism's development that could not be wholly left behind: "modernism rejected the sentimental, because modernism was sentimental. Modernism was still caught in a gendered dialectic which enclosed literature, making the text the object of a naturalized critical gaze" (7).

Addressing the role of politics in sentimental literature, critic Elizabeth Barnes avers that sentimental texts seek to subordinate democratic politics with a "politics of affinity, employing a method of affective representation that dissolves the boundaries between 'self' and 'other.'" In order to do this, sentimental texts teach "a particular way of reading both texts and people that relies on likeness and thereby reinforces homogeneity. In the sentimental scheme of sympathy, others are made real—and thus cared for—to the extent that they can be shown in relation to the reader" (*States* 4). Such a technique requires an interpretive structure that goes beyond the boundaries of the text and includes the reader, in fact requires identification between the reader and the text itself. As Davidson has shown, modern critics who are influenced by the New Critical model and who condemn the written style of the sentimental novel while ignoring the sentimental novel's historical and social context misunderstand the ways in which the original readers of the sentimental novel would have interpreted the text. She writes, "The sentimental novel spoke far more directly to the fears and expectations of its original readers than our retrospective readings generally acknowledge" (122).

Ignoring the ways in which the sentimental writing style constituted a direct appeal to readers and developed an emotional relationship between the text and its reading audience, this anti-reader stance places New Critics in strong opposition to the project of nineteenth-century sentimental literature, both as its authors directly stated and as the texts rhetorically operated, and ignores the ways in which style and structure work together to accomplish the particular aims of sentimental texts. Because New Critics sought ways to define "Literature," to differentiate the high from the low, and to claim and professionalize a method of critical evaluation that was objective and definitive, concentrating on the perceived flaws in sentimental literature's "intrinsic" properties allowed them to further define their own critical project. According to the New Critics and the critical schools that followed and were influenced by them, literary texts "such as the sentimental novel, that make continual and obvious appeals to the reader's emotions and use technical devices that are distinguished by their utter conventionality, epitomize the opposite of everything that good literature is supposed to be" (Tompkins 125).

Presently, critics and scholars do not recognize a coherent modern or twentieth-century sentimental genre, and most consider "sentimental fiction" a genre that belongs to the realm of the nineteenth century. The label "sentimental" has generally been used as "cultural shorthand" to dismiss a work perceived to be negatively feminine, flat, overwrought, or focused on religion. However, the sentimental mode has been deliberately employed throughout the twentieth century and has continued into the twenty-first, not only crossing social boundaries but appearing within a range of genres: from modernist fiction to Proletarian writing and photography to gay Latino writing to contemporary television.

As they adopt the sentimental mode, contemporary authors and scholars must both address the ways in which past forms of sentimentalism shaped America and acknowledge the ways in which it remains an effective means for influencing readers to initiate social change. The operation of sympathy endures as a relevant and powerful rhetorical mode, capable of extending identification across social boundaries and providing effective socio-political analysis in a manner comprehensible to the average reader. Just as in the nineteenth century, the twentieth- and twenty-first-century sentimental genre cannot be classified by a shared, circumscribed narrative structure or by the use of a precise set of tropes. Rather, what links contemporary sentimental texts and makes them a coherent and comprehensible mode is their analytical attitude toward sentimental tropes and their use of the sentimental aesthetic, which prioritizes a focus on sympathetic identification and an examination of familial and social relations—the self-in-society and all that entails. Twentieth- and twenty-first century sentimentalism, however, also maintains a self-consciousness about the genre, critiquing the mode even as it employs it, challenging tropes even as they are adopted and adapted. As the following essays show, sentimentalism is an adaptable and expandable mode that serves as a foundation for modern American culture and letters, but also encompasses the new and shifting sociocultural challenges of the new age.

WORKS CITED

Barnes, Elizabeth. *States of Sympathy: Seduction and Democracy in the American Novel.* New York: Columbia University Press, 1997. Print.
Baym, Nina. *Woman's Fiction: A Guide to Novels By and About Women in America, 1820–70.* 1978. Urbana: University of Illinois Press, 1993. Print.
Bell, Michael. *Sentimentalism, Ethics, and the Culture of Feeling.* Houndmills, Basingstoke, Hampshire: Palgrave, 2000. Print.
Bennett, Paula. *Poets in the Public Sphere: The Emancipatory Project of American Women's Poetry, 1800–1900.* Princeton, NJ: Princeton University Press, 2003. Print.
Berlant, Lauren. *The Female Complaint: The Unfinished Business of Sentimentality in American Culture.* Durham, NC: Duke University Press, 2008. Print.
Brown, Gillian. *Domestic Individualism: Imagining Self in Nineteenth-Century America.* Berkeley: University of California Press, 1990. Print.
Clark, Suzanne. *Sentimental Modernism: Women Writers and the Revolution of the Word.* Bloomington: Indiana University Press, 1991. Print.
Davidson, Cathy N. *Revolution and the Word: The Rise of the Novel in America.* 1986. New York: Oxford University Press, 2004. Print.
Den Tandt, Christophe. "American Literary Naturalism." *A Companion to American Fiction 1865–1914.* Ed. Robert Paul Lamb and G. R. Thompson. Malden, MA: Blackwell, 2005. 96–118. Print.
Dobson, Joanne. "Reclaiming Sentimental Literature." *American Literature* 69.2 (1997): 263–88. Web. 12 May 2011.
Douglas, Ann. *The Feminization of American Culture.* 1977. New York: Noonday Press/Farrar, Straus & Giroux, 1998. Print.
Dreiser, Theodore. *Sister Carrie.* 1903. New York: Oxford University Press, 1998. Print.
Ellison, Julie K. *Cato's Tears and the Making of Anglo-American Emotion.* Chicago: University of Chicago Press, 1999. Print.
Fisher, Philip. *Hard Facts: Setting and Form in the American Novel.* New York: Oxford University Press, 1985. Print.
Lang, Amy Schrager. *The Syntax of Class: Writing Inequality in Nineteenth-Century America.* Princeton, NJ: Princeton University Press, 2003. Print.
Matthews, Steven, ed. *Modernism: A Sourcebook.* New York: Palgrave, 2008. Print.
Merish, Lori. *Sentimental Materialism: Gender, Commodity Culture, and Nineteenth-Century American Literature.* Durham, NC: Duke University Press, 2000. Print.
Norris, Frank. *McTeague: A Story of San Francisco.* 1899. New York: Oxford University Press, 2000. Print.
Person, Leland S. *The Cambridge Introduction to Nathaniel Hawthorne.* Cambridge: Cambridge University Press, 2007. Print.
Rowson, Susanna. *Charlotte Temple: Authoritative Text, Contexts, Criticism.* 1791. Ed. Marion L. Rust. New York: Norton, 2011. Print.
Samuels, Shirley C., ed. *The Culture of Sentiment: Race, Gender, and Sentimentality in Nineteenth-Century America.* New York: Oxford University Press, 1992. Print.
Smith, Susan Belasco. "Introduction." *Ruth Hall: A Domestic Tale of the Present Time.* By Fanny Fern, ed. Susan Belasco Smith. New York: Penguin, 1997. xv–xlv. Print.

Stern, Julia A. *The Plight of Feeling: Sympathy and Dissent in the Early American Novel.* Chicago: University of Chicago Press, 1997. Print.
Tompkins, Jane P. *Sensational Designs: The Cultural Work of American Fiction, 1790–1860.* New York: Oxford University Press, 1985. Print.
Willis, Sara Payson [Fanny Fern]. *Ruth Hall: A Domestic Tale of the Present Time.* 1855. Ed. Susan Belasco Smith. New York: Penguin, 1997. Print.

Doctor Jekyll and Mister Jim Crow

Medical Professionalism, Race and Postsentimentalism in The Marrow of Tradition

BRIAN SWEENEY

[...] having [...] escaped from the Mr. Hyde of the mob, [he] now received the benediction of its Dr. Jekyll.—Charles Chesnutt, *The Marrow of Tradition*

[...] the hand of Henry Jekyll [...] was professional in shape and size: it was large, firm, [and] white [...].—Robert Louis Stevenson, *The Strange Case of Dr. Jekyll and Mr. Hyde*

Early in Charles Chesnutt's *The Marrow of Tradition* (1901), Major Carteret and his wife, Olivia, are discussing the care of their newborn son, Theodore "Dodie" Carteret, with "Mammy" Jane Letlow, the African American domestic who has loyally served Olivia's family since before the Civil War. Learning she will share responsibility for the child with a young African American nurse, a recent graduate of what she (Jane) describes as a "newfangle'" mission school, Mammy Jane is dismissive: "None er dese yer young folks ain' got de trainin' my ole mist'ess give me" (69). Olivia concedes that while the young nurse "does fairly well," her formal education is no substitute for the ties of mutual affection Jane has forged with her family over several decades: "I could hardly expect her to love the baby as you do" (69). Major Carteret agrees even more emphatically:

> Well, Jane [...], the old times have vanished, the old ties have been ruptured. The old relations of dependence and loyal obedience on the part of the colored people, the responsibility of protection and kindness upon that of the whites, have passed away forever. The young negroes are too self-assertive. Education is spoiling them, Jane; they have been badly taught. They are not content with their station in life [....] If all the colored people were like you [...] there would never be any trouble [70–71].

The young nurse, for her part, is repulsed by the ties of "reciprocal emotion"—"slavering" is her word for it—that fasten "[t]hese old-time negroes" to those by whom they had once been owned (71, 70). Renouncing their sentimental relation as emotional serfdom, perpetuating in the realm of affect a property relation no longer sanctioned by law, the nurse conceives of her connection to her employers in the impersonal, unsentimental language of contractual labor: "[T]hey gave her nothing but her wages, and small wages at that, and she owed them nothing more than equivalent service. It was purely a matter of business; she sold her time for their money. There was no question of love between them" (70). Against a paternalistic vision of mutual affection and obligation, the young, modern nurse sees herself as belonging to a dynamic, shifting, atomized society composed of radically autonomous individuals, mutually obligated not by fellow-feeling but by the contingent and impermanent terms of a contract.

The horrified repugnance with which Major Carteret greets a rising generation of black workers who feel little or no emotional attachment to the whites who employ them expresses a sentiment hardly unique to aristocratic Southerners pining for the *status quo ante bellum*. As Chesnutt knew, a belief in the increasing selfishness, ingratitude, and disloyalty of domestic workers—what came to be called "the servant problem"—united bourgeois whites across the United States in the late-nineteenth and early-twentieth centuries.[1] The oft-quoted March 16, 1880, journal entry in which a young Chesnutt wonders "why could not a colored man" produce a "far better book about the South than [...] Mrs. Stowe has written" less famously records Chesnutt's conversation about the servant problem with a white North Carolina bookseller (*Journals* 125). The bookseller, who had read a piece in *Harper's Magazine* on the obstreperousness of Irish servants up North, remarked to Chesnutt, "That's just the way it is getting to be down here. [...] You can't get a servant to hardly do anything." Chesnutt retorted, "[T]hat is one of the inconveniences that the rich have to suffer, that the poor are not troubled with. They do their own work and have no tyrannical servants to domineer over them" (*Journals* 126).

The *Harper's* article that inspired this exchange was one of many concerning the deteriorating relations between domestic workers and their employers printed in periodicals popular among the northern, liberal, white readership Chesnutt self-consciously courted in his authorial career.² In 1864, the prestigious, Boston-based *Atlantic Monthly*—a periodical to which Chesnutt later contributed several of his best stories—printed an article by Christopher Crowfield mourning the disappearance of the "mutual kindliness" in relations between American homemakers and their domestics. In a society in which "all are to be as free to rise and fall as the waves of the sea," writes Crowfield, workers, "infected with the spirit of democracy," have come to view domestic labor as at best a "stepping-stone" to more attractive and respectable employment (438, 439). It might surprise many readers to discover that "Christopher Crowfield" was a pseudonym used by Harriet Beecher Stowe, and that it was the author of *Uncle Tom's Cabin* who, in the fourth year of a bloody Civil War, was describing an upwardly-mobile lower class as "the great problem of [American] life" (437). But Stowe's hyperbolic view of the servant problem derives from a sentimental moral and social vision rooted in the writings of Adam Smith and other Scottish Enlightenment philosophers that saw the bourgeois household as both the fundamental unit of and the model for a cohesive, well-functioning society whose members were united by bonds of sympathy incubated within the home.³ As Philip Fisher writes, sentimental fiction sees "the family [as] the only social model for the relations between nonequal members of a society, relations based on dramatically different and unequal contributions to the group and equally dramatic and incomparable needs" (102). When, at the end of *Uncle Tom's Cabin* (1851), Stowe has George Shelby's at-long-last-emancipated slaves elect to remain perpetually on the Shelby plantation, declaring gratefully, "We don't want to be no freer than we are. [...] We don't want to leave the ole place, and Mas'r and Missis, and de rest" (446), it is an endorsement of a sentimental vision of relations between social nonequals that idealizes benevolent paternalism and grateful dependence.⁴

In the late-nineteenth and early-twentieth centuries, Stowe's sentimental vision of social relations had migrated to the nostalgic plantation fiction of Joel Chandler Harris and Thomas Nelson Page, which located that vision not in a post-emancipatory future but in an idealized, irrecoverable, pre-emancipatory past. Complaints about the ingratitude of modern workers constitute the flip side of such nostalgia, bespeaking a sensibility that Barbara Ryan describes as "postsentimental." Essentially reactionary, postsentimentalism *affirms* sentimental ideals of paternalistic and affectionate relations across lines of race and class, while nevertheless regarding those ideals as no longer fully *realizable* in the present due to the increasing self-interestedness of an upwardly mobile lower class (Ryan 136–137). From a postsentimental perspective, the social mobility of servants is particularly catastrophic, as it portends the destruction of the middle-class household and, by extension, the bourgeois social order that takes the middle-class household as its foundation and model.

Chesnutt referred to *The Marrow of Tradition* as his attempt to write an *Uncle Tom's Cabin* for the age of Jim Crow,[5] but the novel rejects the reactionary postsentimentalism into which Stowe's paternalistic vision had degenerated by the turn of the century and which regards the social aspirations of the (African American) lower class as a threat to American civilization (Chesnutt's rejection of this sensibility is clear from the fact that its primary spokesperson in the novel, Major Carteret, goes on to incite a racial massacre). Yet at the same time, Chesnutt's sensibility was too essentially bourgeois for him to side with the clinical impersonality of the business-like nurse who "sells her time" for money. In repudiating reactionary postsentimentalism, *The Marrow of Tradition* draws upon the rhetoric of professionalism to imagine a positive model of social mobility consistent with social responsibility, centered upon the black physician Dr. Miller, and defines this meritocratic, collectivist, and socially-responsible form of social striving over and against the figure of Captain McBane, a rapacious and unscrupulous capitalist and inveterate racist who promotes white supremacy and racial violence in the service of his narrow social and economic ambitions. But the novel's tentative endorsement of professionalist ideals over and against the threats of white supremacy and unbridled capitalism is complicated by the example of the self-serving professionalism of the white physician Dr. Price, as well as by Dr. Miller's professional crisis in the final chapters. While some critics view *Marrow* as ultimately repudiating a morally bankrupt professionalism in favor of a morality grounded in domestic womanhood, this essay argues that the novel tentatively endorses the professionalist sentiments of many elite African Americans of Chesnutt's generation, while at the same time expressing doubts as to the power of professionalism's ideals of meritocracy and public service to realize a more racially egalitarian bourgeois social order.

Professionalism and Populism in the Whites-Only Car

On November 10, 1898, in the city of Wilmington, North Carolina, more than 1500 white rioters took to the streets, stirred up by Democratic leaders who, by exploiting outrage over an anti-lynching editorial published in the town's black newspaper, stoked racial paranoia about "Negro domination" (Prather 23). The rioters terrorized and murdered black citizens; set fire to the offices of the black newspaper; forced the resignation of the white Republican mayor, other black and white members of the city government, and the entire police department (filling the vacancies with Democrats); and exiled prominent black and white Republicans from the city (Prather 37). Prior to the events of that November, Wilmington had been in the words of one historian "one of the best cities for blacks in the American South": more racially integrated than many Southern cities, its black population constituted a numerical majority and African American citizens held many public offices and owned many businesses (Prather 16–18). The massacre precipitated a mass exodus of African American residents, and by 1900 Wilmington was a white-majority city (Prather 37–38).

In September 1900, Chesnutt outlined the plot of a work of fiction to be based on the events, and his earliest notes reveal his intention to make the protagonist a young black doctor:

> Young colored man, educated, decides to settle in a Southern city, where he can be of more direct use to his people, personally as well as by example. He must be of some pursuit or profession, preferably medicine [...]A race riot breaks out, in which he suffers terribly [and] his child [is] killed [...] There is no redress and no hope of redress. The doctor prepares to leave the town. The child [...]of one of the chief promoters of the riot is taken suddenly and violently ill. There is only one white physician in the town who is capable of treating the case, which requires immediate attention, and this physician is out of town. The colored physician is called. He refuses; is persuaded, wavers, argues, yields, and saves the child's life ["Plot Notes," 212].

From the first, Chesnutt imagined that his fictional account of the Wilmington riot climaxing with the professional and personal crisis of a young black physician, torn between bitter grief and professional obligation when called upon to save the child of one of the riot's instigators. Critics have acknowledged that this juxtaposition of racial violence and professional dilemma gives professionalism an intensified thematic and figurative significance.[6] The black professional at the center of *The Marrow of Tradition* is Dr. William Miller, the grandson of slaves and the son of an industrious stevedore whose savings financed his son's education. Miller is a gifted physician who studied medicine in the United States and Europe before returning to the South to settle in his hometown of Wellington, North Carolina. There, he establishes a thriving medical practice, uses part of an inheritance to found a hospital, and makes plans to add a school for nurses and a medical college. He also starts a family: his wife, Janet, is the unacknowledged half-sister of Olivia Carteret (the daughter of Olivia's patrician father and a black housemaid whom he secretly marries), and they have a son of about six. Miller's professional accomplishments, social prestige, and conventionally respectable family life make him "one of [W.E.B.] DuBois's 'talented tenth' of Negro intellectuals who could absorb the highest values and professional skills of Western culture and use those for the uplift and betterment of their race" (Wideman 386). The philanthropic impulses that motivate Miller to remain in the South manifest his belief in his membership in the DuBoisian elect: "He had been strongly tempted to leave the South, and seek a home for his family and a career for himself in the freer North [...] or in Europe.... But his people had needed him, and he had wished to help them, and had sought [...] to contribute to their uplifting" (75).

Dr. Miller enters the novel as a passenger on a train traveling to Wellington from New York, where in a well-known scene he finds himself subjected to the laws of Jim Crow. Among the fellow passengers is an old friend and mentor, Dr. Alvin Burns of Philadelphia. By Dickensian coincidence, Burns, a white surgeon specializing in throat disorders, is traveling to Wellington to operate on a gravely ill Dodie Carteret. Burns and Miller sit together conversing until the train crosses the invisible line separating Maryland from Virginia, when the conductor approaches and, upon ascertaining that Miller is not Burns's servant—"The gentleman is not my servant," says Burns, "nor anybody's servant, but is my friend" (77)—explains that the laws of Virginia demand that Miller move to the colored car. An indignant Burns initially urges Miller to defy this "outrage upon a citizen of a free country," but Miller complies when the conductor threatens force (78). Miller, finding himself alone in the colored car, attempts to calculate how expensive it must be for the Southern railroads to provide separate accommodations for a solitary passenger. When he is eventually joined in the car by what he regards as "dirty, and malodorous" black laborers, he reflects that "these people were just as offensive to him as to the whites. [...] Surely, if a classification of passengers on trains was at all desirable, it might be made upon some more logical and considerate basis than a mere arbitrary, tactless, and [...] brutal drawing of the color line" (79, 82). Writing about the interplay of class and race in this episode, Walter Benn Michaels argues that Chesnutt has Miller object to the separate car law on essentially laissez faire grounds. According to Michaels, the point of the passage is that the less arbitrary, more logical social hierarchy that Miller seems to crave is "the one already in place before the train arrives in Virginia [...] Its method is economic—it divides the world not into black and white [...] but into first class and coach [....] And its logic is the logic of the market—you get what you are willing and able to pay for" ("Plots" 291). But Michaels's view that Miller argues against racial segregation on the grounds of its market inefficiency, thus affirming the superior rationality of market forces, completely discounts the significance of Chesnutt's choosing to make Miller a physician, and (therefore) a member of a profession that, for half a century, had been strenuously advocating for legal protections from a market economy it depicted as a hopelessly irrational mechanism for legitimately determining value.

A brief discussion of the professionalization of medicine reveals that the grounds of Miller's critique of the separate car law is not a belief in the rationality of the market but a commitment to a professionalist ideology that touted the virtues of meritocracy, standardization, and economic disinterestedness. During the heyday of Jacksonian populism, the field of medicine in the United States had been largely unregulated, with healers of all philosophical schools with widely differing degrees of medical experience and education competing in a relatively "open" market for patient-customers. Elite practitioners, disturbed by sectarianism and intense competition for patients, petitioned legislatures for the power to use licensing and certification to enforce uniform, high standards of medical practice and training, and to limit membership in the profession so as to prevent overcrowding and minimize competition. Reformers maintained that "the laissez faire of market capitalism was an inadequate policy for medical education and public health. There was no hidden hand in those realms that turned private interest into public benefit" (Haber 321). Because the best medical practices were not always the most profitable ones, and because medical knowledge often defied common sense, patients, it was argued, were not competent judges of a doctor's skill; only members of the profession itself, shielded from the pressures of the market and (therefore) able to override popular prejudice and folk beliefs, could make legitimate determinations of medical value and professional ability. Only an autonomous and sovereign medical profession with the powers of licensing and certification could elevate standards of medical care and guard the public against unscrupulous quackery and well-meaning ineptitude. Between the founding of the American Medical Association in 1847 and the turn of the twentieth century, many of the special privileges sought by professional reformers were gradually acquired, and a medical field which had once been relatively "open" became increasingly centralized, exclusive, and governed by institutionalized codes of ethics and practice.[7]

The success of professional reformers in eliciting political support for a more centralized and exclusive medical profession led inevitably to charges of elitism and monopolism. Critics complained that professionalization established a legally protected monopoly that homogenized the field while creating barriers to entry into the profession, serving the narrow economic interests of the emerging medical establishment while depriving "irregulars" of their livelihoods. In response to such charges, professionals adopted a lofty rhetoric of public service, touting the economic disinterestedness of the professional physician. The goal of professional reform, according to reformers, was not to artificially inflate wages, but rather to insulate doctors from the sordid pressures of market competition so as to enhance their ability to disinterestedly serve the public and advance medical knowledge. The adoption by many doctors of a "sliding scale" fee system based upon patients' ability to pay; the importance placed on *pro bono* work; and the commitment to initiatives to improve public health at the hypothetical cost (in market terms) of reduced demand for physicians' care all served to establish the medical profession's altruistic commitment to service and to justify its claim to special protections. In staking their claim to social prestige and professional autonomy on the promotion of a lofty ethical and social vision that looked beyond mere pecuniary interests, professional reformers took a rhetorical "stand against the depersonalization of mass markets and the egalitarianism of democratic politics" (Haber 350), and they portrayed the profession as an enlightened meritocracy of talent and virtue.

Many elite African Americans of Chesnutt's generation repeated the lofty rhetoric of professionalist reformers in urging talented blacks to enter the medical profession, despite the many obstacles to African American success in a field that remained segregated.[8] At the turn of the twentieth century, only a handful of black medical colleges existed in the entire United States, all of them located in the South. No medical colleges for black students existed in the North, and while African American students did intermittently gain admission to northern medical colleges, they were generally prohibited from interning at affiliated hospitals (Long 166–67). Moreover, many hospitals "denied admitting privileges to physicians of color, forcing them to leave patients who required hospitalization [...] at the entrance door," a practice that "affected [black] physicians' earnings, professional competency, and standing with patients" (Savitt 282). And given professional reformers' complaints about the intensity of internecine competition, many white physicians openly resented the entry of black doctors into what they perceived as an already overcrowded profession. The chronic exclusion of black doctors from numerous medical professional associations, including various regional chapters of the AMA, prompted the founding, in 1895, of the racially integrated National Medical Association (Long 167).

Despite such barriers to entry to the profession, by the turn of the twentieth century, many African Americans were working successfully as licensed physicians, many more aspired to the profession, and many black intellectuals promoted medicine as a field in which African American women and men could accrue social prestige and offer their fellow African Americans the abstract benefit of an inspiring example of social usefulness and the practical benefit of necessary medical care. Such endorsements of the medical profession often affirmed the premises of professionalist ideology. In 1898, W.E.B. DuBois told an audience at Fisk University,

> If ever a nation needed the gospel of health presented to them, it is the negro race, with its alarming death rate, its careless habits, its widows and orphans, and its sick and maimed. For the well trained physician, as distinguished from the quack, and the man who is too hurried to learn, there is a large and important work. The remuneration which a poor people can pay will not be large, but the chance for usefulness and far-reaching influence on the future of our race and country can scarcely be overestimated [836].

In depicting the medical profession as one which serves "widows and orphans" and in claiming that the reward medical professionals receive will not be primarily financial, DuBois affirms the medical profession's self-authorizing rhetoric of economic disinterestedness, social responsibility, and public service. Equally notable is DuBois's quite negative depiction of irregular physicians. One way the medical profession strove to reduce its numbers was to make a lengthy and arduous course of instruction a prerequisite to medical practice. While one effect of such requirements was to exclude aspiring doctors who lacked the means necessary to devote several years to their medical education, DuBois toes the professionalist party line by describing such disappointed would-be doctors as men who are "too hurried"—not too poor—"to learn." By making a virtue of the relatively unremunerative nature of the medical profession, and by depicting the chief barrier to a medical education as impatience rather than lack of means, DuBois endorses the professionalist view that distinguishes the professional from the irregular not only or even primarily on the basis of superior skill, but on the basis of superior virtue: the willingness to serve and to transcend pecuniary interest.

The Jim Crow car sequence of *The Marrow of Tradition* implicitly affirms the DuBoisian association of professionalization with racial uplift by depicting the separate-car law not primarily as a violation of Miller's rights as a citizen, much less (*pace* Michaels) as a barrier to the flow of capital, but as a violation of professional sovereignty. By dramatizing the moment when the car on which Burns and Miller are riding is magically transformed into a "white" car once it crosses an imaginary political boundary, Chesnutt depicts the separate car law as an irregular and aberrant parochialism, posing an unnatural barrier to the "natural" collegiality of the two professionals. By critiquing color prejudice on professionalist grounds, the episode affirms the cornerstone argument of professionalist reformers: that the sovereign autonomy of the medical profession to establish its own objective and uniform qualitative standards was essential to protecting American medicine from the vicissitudes of the market and the vagaries of regional backwardness. Racial prejudice, by this logic, comes to seem analogous to hydropathy or bloodletting: a parochial, outmoded idea to be swept away by the tide of standardizing and meritocratic professionalism.

If the collegiality of Burns and Miller exemplifies a vision of the medical profession as a color-blind meritocracy, Captain McBane represents the threats of parochial bigotry and unprincipled capitalism over and against which professionalist values were asserted. A member of the "poor-white class, to which, even more than slaves, the abolition of slavery had opened doors of opportunity," the social climbing, opportunistic, and (incidentally) one-eyed McBane uses political connections to enrich himself through unsavory means, securing for example a state contract for the use of convict labor (64, 65). McBane believes his wealth and white skin entitle him to power and position from which the lingering Old South class hierarchy bars him. Resentful of the continuing social and political influence of the old plantation class, McBane is even more horrified by the emergence of a black middle class (emblematized by William Miller), and so he opportunistically throws his lot in with the aristocratic Major Carteret and Colonel Belmont to conspire to overthrow Wellington's Republican leadership (supported by the city's black majority), restore his Democratic allies to power, and terrorize Wellington's black population into submission. His hope is to produce a new white racial solidarity that cuts across lines of class and will give him access to social privilege commensurate with his economic power. Jerry Letlow, the Carterets's servant and the grandson of Mammy Jane, astutely recognizes that McBane's aim is to realign Wellington's social and political life along crudely dichotomous racial lines: "[A]in' nothin' but po' w'ite trash nohow; but Lawd! Lawd! Look at de money he's got [...] 'Pears to me de bottom rail is gittin' mighty close ter de top. Well, I s'pose it all comes f'm bein' w'ite. I wush ter Gawd I wuz w'ite!" (66). And while the aristocratic Tom Delamere stands in for many members of his class when he is sickened and "annoyed" by "the presumption of this son of an overseer and ex-driver of convicts" (141), other prominent members of the aristocratic class, including Carteret, reluctantly make common cause with McBane, who continually seeks to compel them to realign their sympathies along racial lines. When one of his co-conspirators describes Dr. Miller as "a very good sort of negro" who doesn't "tread on any one else's toes" (199), McBane erupts: "That sort of nigger, though, sets a bad example [....] They make it all the harder to keep the rest of 'em down [....] I don't like smart niggers. [...] We'll run him out with the rest. This is a white man's country, and a white man's city, and no nigger has any business here when a white man wants him gone!" (199)

As Stephen Knadler argues, in dramatizing the process whereby a political alliance between the low-born McBane and his patrician co-conspirators is naturalized under the sign of "whiteness," *Marrow* reveals that "whiteness" has no essence but is "rather a performance mandated at particular historical moments for its political advantageousness and its suppression of other group identities such as class or ethnicity" (433–434). Fittingly, it is McBane himself whose complaint to the conductor leads to Miller's ejection from the white car, and the crudely dichotomous racial hierarchy McBane seeks to establish finds its visual counterpart in the white car sign that the narrative invites audiences to read in allegorical terms: "[A] large card neatly framed and hung at the end of the car, contain[ed] the legend, 'White,' in letters about a foot long, painted in white upon a dark background, typical, one might suppose, of the distinction thereby indicated" (77). As in the sign itself, McBane's ideal of racial whiteness requires for coherence the artificial "dark background" of an abjected blackness. It is telling that McBane, like Dr. Miller, enjoys the distinction of a title—"Captain"—but that his titles is, we are informed, a "polite fiction" (65): a self-conferred honorific derived from no external institutional power. Its self-conferred nature implies McBane's implicit rejection of the professionalist use of titles as signs of conferred authority, and thus a rejection of meritocracy in favor of a white supremacist social order in which power is self-authorizing. Unlike membership in a profession, theoretically (if not in practice) open to anyone who meets a set of objective standards applicable to all, whiteness is something one cannot earn, nor must one earn it. The one-eyed McBane dreams of a brutally rapacious social order in which all white men— but only white men—compete for dominance in an open market blind to distinction of talent or virtue—and in this country of the blind, the one-eyed McBane will be king.

Postsentimentalism, Sympathy and Professional Ethics

If turn-of-the-century America saw the emergence of a reactionary postsentimentalism that views an upwardly mobile (African American) working class as perilous to the social order, the opening chapters of *Marrow* draw upon the rhetoric of professional medical reformers to differentiate between a meritocratic and virtuous professionalism that reconciles individual aspiration with disinterested public service and the brutal scorched-earth capitalism of McBane, who dreams of a whites-only free market that consigns black Wellingtonians to the mudsill. But no sooner has this structure of oppositions been established than the unfolding of the plot raises doubts about the DuBoisian faith in professional ideals to promote African American social and economic advancement against both white postsentimentalism and the threat of an emerging white mobocracy.

Such doubts are raised early in the novel when Major Carteret refuses to allow Dr. Miller to assist Dr. Burns in the operation on Dodie Carteret. Burns vehemently protests Carteret's interference, depicting Carteret's color prejudice as a barbaric parochialism obstructing Burns's ability to execute his professional duties. Asserting the dignity of his "professional honor," Burns states that Miller's "color is not at all concerned" with his ability to act "in a strictly professional capacity," and claims that as a "matter of principle," his own professional judgment "must not give way to a mere prejudice" (88). Burns capitulates, however, after being falsely assured by the white physician Dr. Price that Carteret is motivated by personal animus rather than racial prejudice. Price's lie to Burns indicates that, for Price, racial loyalty trumps professional allegiance. Unlike the professedly "color-blind" Burns, Dr. Price cherishes the privileges his white skin confers, and his investment in racial whiteness is presented as symptomatic of his lax professionalism: "His claim of superiority to the colored doctor rested fundamentally upon the fact that he was white and Miller was not," a fact "for which he could claim no credit, since he had not made himself" (91). Price's eagerness to enjoy the privileges of a white racial identity he has not earned stands in stark contrast to the almost neurotic fastidiousness with which the professionalist Miller, conversing with Dr. Burns, distinguishes those traits for which he deserves praise from those he simply inherited: when Burns congratulates him upon looking "so well—and so prosperous," Miller replies, "I deserve no credit for either [...] for I inherited both health and prosperity" (74).

Dr. Price's later reluctance to prevent the lynching of Sandy Campbell, a black servant wrongly suspected of having murdered a white woman, confirms the hollowness of his professionalism. When Dr. Miller goes to his white colleague to ask for his help in defending the innocent Sandy against the irrational fury of the enraged mob, Dr. Price disingenuously invokes his professionalism as an excuse for inaction: "[T]his is no affair of mine, or yours. I have too much respect for myself and my profession to interfere, and you will accomplish nothing, and only lessen your own influence, by having anything to say" (162). Only after Sandy's employer, the patrician Mr. Delamere, sacrifices his sense of aristocratic honor for the sake of justice by swearing falsely to a trumped-up alibi for his innocent servant does Dr. Price risk his practice by testifying that in his professional judgment, a murder had not even been committed: the woman's death was likely due to shock (186). When the exonerated Sandy is released, the white mob that had gathered to lynch him now presses upon him its hearty congratulations: "With the childish fickleness of a mob, they now experienced a satisfaction almost as great as, though less exciting than, that attendant upon taking life [...] Sandy, having escaped from the Mr. Hyde of the mob, now received the benediction of its Dr. Jekyll" (186).

The allusion to Robert Louis Stevenson's Gothic novel associates the furious mob with primitive barbarity; more importantly, it figures its fury as a *layman*, while its more enlightened instincts are figured as the sacralized, degreed professional. But Hyde, of course, *is* Jekyll, while Jekyll is Hyde's public and respectable face, and in light of Price's contemptible withholding of exculpatory evidence, the allusion to Stevenson points up the subterranean continuity between the racial hatred of the mob and the putatively enlightened professionalism of Dr. Price. Given that the professional medical community made social responsibility the warrant for its claims to sovereign autonomy, Dr. Price's evasion of social responsibility undermines the ethical justification for the privileges he enjoys. In one passage in Stevenson's novel, Dr. Jekyll's hand is described as "professional in shape and size [...] large, firm, [and] white [...]" (54), and this casual identification of the professional with attributes of whiteness resonates with Dr. Price's view linking his privileged professional status to the privileges of whiteness. The self-serving behavior of Dr. Price lends credence to a populist antiprofessionalism that viewed professionals' rhetoric of public service as essentially performative, producing an illusory distinction between the disinterested professional and the appetitive mob that served the economic interests of the professional class.

While it is always possible to detach Dr. Price's personal failings from professionalism as such, and dismiss his venality as failed professionalism, Dr. Miller's failings in the final chapters cannot be similarly dismissed. If we accept Miller as Chesnutt's exemplar of the DuBoisian black professional, Miller's conduct during the climactic riot raises doubts about the power of professionalism to promote collective African American advancement and ground a more racially egalitarian social order. The riot brings Dr. Miller's entire professional and personal life to ruin: his six-year-old boy is killed by a stray bullet, and his hospital, "the fruit of old Adam Miller's industry, the monument of his son's philanthropy, a promise of good things for the future of the city," is burned to the ground, despite the efforts of a group of armed black laborers to defend it (234). These losses are so terrible that one is inclined to extenuate his professional failures during the riot. Yet, his behavior during the riot recalls Dr. Price's evasions of professional responsibility.

Consumed by panic over the fate of his missing wife and child, Miller repeatedly resists calls by black Wellingtonians that he provide leadership and service commensurate with his professional status and abilities. Miller refuses the invitation to join in armed resistance with the black laborers who go on to die defending his hospital, and, during his frantic search for his family, he refuses to aid the wounded: "[H]e came near running over the body of a wounded man who lay groaning by the wayside. Every professional instinct urged him to stop and offer aid to the sufferer; but the uncertainty concerning his wife and child proved a stronger motive and urged him resistless forward" (222). Only once does he "yield[ ] to professional instinct," stooping to the aid of an injured person who turns out to be Mammy Jane. In a final blow to the fantasy of benevolent paternalism, Jane is lying in the street just a few steps away from the Carteret home that, in the moment of crisis, offered her no protection; yet, the dying words of the loyal servant are "Comin', missis, comin'!" (226). In a particularly damning moment, Miller's own servant, Sally, believing she and Dr. Miller to be the only surviving blacks in Wellington, pleads with him for his protection, promising in exchange to work for him "fer nuthin', sir, all my bawn days" (220). The disturbing offer of Miller's terrified servant to, as it were, enslave herself to him in exchange for his protection (replicating the dynamic of paternalism and dependency that characterizes the Carteret household) underscores the social gulf Miller's professionalism has opened up between him and Wellington's larger African American community, and contrasts his enjoyment of social prestige with his failure of social responsibility that justifies that prestige. Moreover, even as he disclaims professional responsibility, he continues to derive benefits denied to other blacks due to his exceptional social standing as a black physician: briefly detained by a white rioter during his frantic search, Miller is preserved from violence due to the rioter's respect for his status as a physician.

When, in the final chapters of the novel, a shattered and grieving Miller finds himself unexpectedly entreated by Major Carteret, one of the riot's chief instigators, to save the life of his own son, the chronically sickly Dodie—Dr. Price, characteristically, has fled town at the first sign of trouble—the narrative's abrupt turn away from the larger canvas of social upheaval to a domestic tragedy built upon not one but two dead or dying children might be seen as a sudden swerve into sentimental territory: as though the novel, having laid bare the moral bankruptcy of Wellington's professional class, unexpectedly retreats into the ethics of sympathy it had previously associated with a paternalistic, reactionary postsentimentalism. As Philip Fisher observes, deathbed scenes involving children were central to nineteenth-century sentimental narratives because, as the "sudden, unexpected death" of a child was a "nearly universal" experience, such scenes facilitated sympathetic identification with a wide range of experiences of loss (109). Miller initially refuses Major Carteret's request that he tend to his gravely ill child, a refusal that shocks Carteret who had assumed that "professional ethics would require him to respond" (239), and it is Carteret, not Miller, who experiences an epiphanic moment of sympathetic identification familiar in sentimental narrative:

> In the agony of his own predicament,—in the horror of the situation at Miller's house,—for a moment the veil of race prejudice was rent in twain, and [Carteret] saw things as they were, in their correct proportions and relations,—saw clearly and convincingly that he had no standing here, in the presence of death, in the home of this stricken family [... H]e could not blame the doctor for his stand. [...] In Dr. Miller's place, he would have done the same thing [241].

Miller himself, however, is insensible to Carteret's appeals to sympathy and professionalism, and with Dodie's life hanging in the balance, a desperate Olivia Carteret comes to the Miller's home to plead for assistance. Olivia's appeal is explicitly sentimental in making family relation the basis for her claims upon the Millers' sympathy, as Danielson notes (85). "You know what it is to lose a child!" pleads Olivia, and her physical and vocal resemblance to her half-sister Janet leave even Dr. Miller "deeply moved" (243, 244). When Miller decides to leave the decision in his wife's hands, Olivia implores Janet with rhetoric that is even more intensely sentimental, calling Janet "sister," pleading for her child's life "for our father's sake," and offering Janet belated recognition of their kinship and acknowledging her right to the family name.

Olivia's language clearly implies a sentimental belief that their kinship will make it impossible for Janet to hold Olivia beyond the range of her sympathies. The strategy of her appeal recalls Elizabeth Barnes's discussion of the "peculiarly egocentric" character of a morality grounded in sympathy. In sentimental narrative, she writes, "sympathetic feeling" is evoked

> by making others appear related to oneself. Rather than teaching readers to appreciate difference, [sentimental texts] reinforce for readers the idea that recognition relies on likeness—that one is bound to love whatever or whomever appears most like one's own. [Sentimental narrative thus] intensifies the psychological link between humanity and homogeneity. [...] Whatever character(istic)s cannot be made to conform to the family image must remain excluded from sympathy, while those that are included must be represented in such a way that they prove familiar and thus identifiable [97].

Olivia's appeal to sympathy underscores her commitment to a postsentimentalism that presumes the moral priority of the bourgeois household and makes recognition of actual or potential family resemblance a precondition to moral obligation. Major Carteret's earlier complaints about the self-assertiveness of young, educated blacks demonstrated the complicity of this worldview with racial paternalism and a horror of the economic aspirations of the lower class.

By the logic of the novel, then, were the Millers to be swayed by this sentimental appeal, it would constitute an affirmation of a reactionary postsentimentalism that seeks to trap African Americans in a position of perpetual servility.

As it happens, many critics do interpret Janet's decision to accede to Olivia's desperate appeal marking a triumph of a specifically "maternal," "feminine," and "domestic" virtue. According to Stephen Knadler, "Chesnutt's hero [...] is less Dr. Miller than it is the black 'good mother'—Janet Miller" (436), while Susan Danielson claims that, professionalism having been revealed to be "inadequa[te as] a basis for social justice and healing," the novel substitutes an ethic of "compassion" that is "linked to [Janet's] capacity as a woman of feeling" which "infuse[es] the public world with the values of the private [and] the masculine world with the values of the feminine" (76, 87, 88).[9] And to be sure, Miller, by leaving the decision in the hands of his wife, described earlier in the novel as an "exhaustless fountain" of "sympathy" (92), admittedly seems prepared to borrow from his wife's stock of female domestic virtue in the time-tested manner of husbands in sentimental narratives, and Janet likewise seems to endorse a sentimental reading by announcing to the supplicating Olivia that she has "a heart to feel" (246).

But this conventionally sentimental affirmation of female sensibility and moral exemplarity does not tell the whole story, because Chesnutt has Janet explicitly derive her moral authority not exclusively or even primarily from reservoirs of compassion that are "naturally" hers as a woman, but from the social status and material comforts that are hers as the wife of a respected physician: "Now, when I have married a man who can supply my needs, you offer me back the money which you and your friend have robbed me of! [...] Now, when an honest man has given me a name of which I can be proud, you offer me the one of which you robbed me, and of which I can make no use" (246).[10] Janet's declaration denaturalizes and defeminizes her moral virtue and agency, making them originate instead in external professional institutional contexts within which Miller has conducted his public life. It is because of the social and economic benefits conferred by Miller's membership in the medical profession that Janet can reject Olivia's sentimental "bribe" of her father's name and thus disinterestedly offer Olivia the gift of her husband's professional skill. In this gesture, Janet not only rejects a postsentimentalism that idealizes domesticity and frets over the socially and morally corrosive effects of African American aspirations to the middle class, but moreover reaffirms a professional ethos that made special economic protections for the medical profession—protections that would limit competition and thus prevent the depression of doctors' wages—the precondition for disinterested professional virtue.

Flexner and the Limits of Meritocracy

By invoking her husband's professional status in acceding to Olivia's supplications, Janet pays tribute to professionalism's claim to disinterested social responsibility, but how are we to experience this tribute in the wake of Miller's professional failures during the riot? Are we to concur with her reaffirmation of professionalism, or see it as a naïve endorsement of an ideology that her husband has revealed, unbeknownst to her, to be hollow at its core? After Miller's failure to tend to the black victims of the white supremacist uprising, can his agreement to save the life of the offshoot of a powerful white family be viewed as personally and professionally redemptive, or as a capitulation to white authority in the name of professionalism? "[T]he future of your race," remarks Dr. Burns to Dr. Miller during their eventful train ride, "[...] is a serial story which we are all reading, and which grows in vital interest with each successive installment" (75), and to black intellectuals like W.E.B. DuBois, the medical profession seemed to hold out the promise that future "installments" in that narrative might tell of steady progress toward increased social, political, and economic equality.

The ambiguous conclusion of *Marrow*, if it can be read as an endorsement of professionalism, is hardly a ringing one, but—the ethics of sympathy having been rejected—it is not clear upon what other ethical or social grounds the novel imagines a more racially egalitarian Wellington might be built. Chesnutt had considered ending the novel with the Millers choosing to leave Wellington: having saved Dodie, Miller would have refused a grateful Major Carteret's offer of paternalistic protection, and the novel would have concluded with the poignant image of Miller departing for the North on "a Jim Crow car" ("Plot Notes" 213). But such a conclusion, however grim, would have made migration to the North a "way out" of a racial paternalism that characterized the thought of bourgeois whites throughout the United States. Instead, the novel leaves the outcome of the operation in doubt, and its final image is that of Dr. Miller preparing to climb a flight of stairs to Dodie Carteret's room, urged along by the words of a white doctor standing at the top: "There's time enough, but none to spare" (246).

In 1901, barriers to African American membership in the medical profession were daunting enough, but the next "installment" in the serial story of African American participation in the medical profession would be one of reduced opportunity and impaired credibility. 1910 saw the publication of a report on the state of medical education in North America, commissioned by the AMA's Council on Medical Education and written by Abraham Flexner, an archetypal Progressive Era educational reformer whom DuBois praised as "one of the great leaders of education in the United States" (1010). A pivotal document in the history of American medicine, the Flexner Report evaluated 155 North American medical schools, declared dozens of them substandard, and recommended reforms that "led to the uniform standards and courses of study in all U.S. medical schools [...] familiar today" (Long 158). Its verdict on black medical colleges was particularly damaging: "Of the seven medical schools for negroes in the United States, five are at this moment in no position to make any contribution of value. [...] They are wasting small sums annually and sending out undisciplined men, whose lack of real training is covered up by the imposing M.D. degree" (180–181). The report further questioned whether African Americans were truly suited to a physician's work, cautioning that "[a] well-taught negro sanitarian will be immensely useful; an essentially untrained negro wearing an M.D. degree is dangerous" (180). The result of the report was the closure of all but two of the black medical colleges then in existence: only Meharry Medical College and the medical program at Howard University survived Flexner (Savitt 259). Equally damaging, the report cast doubt upon the competence of the entire African American professional medical community, by suggesting that the majority of black physicians had received an inadequate education (Savitt 257).

With the publication of the Flexner Report, the American Medical Association, the foremost professional institution in American medicine, rationalized the segregated nature of American medicine on putatively objective, meritocratic grounds. While the Flexner Report was a decade away when *The Marrow of Tradition* first appeared in 1901, there is something prophetic of it in the novel's ambivalent commentary on the belief that the aims of medical professionalization might coincide with the object of African American advancement. Read in the shadow that the Flexner Report retrospectively casts upon the novel, that final tableau of a white doctor inviting Dr. Miller to join him at the top of the stairs might be read as a grim commentary on the illusory nature of the promise of racial uplift that some discerned in the rhetoric of medical professionalism. If *Marrow* draws upon the professional ideals of meritocracy and disinterested virtue to counter both the terror of aspirational blacks at the heart of white postsentimentalism and the emergence of a white mobocracy portended by the Wilmington riot, also present in the text is the suspicion that the meritocratic rhetoric of professionalism masked yet another institutionalization of white privilege—the suspicion that, in a Jim Crow America where the races were to be as separate as the fingers yet one as the hand, the hand of the professional was to be a white one.

Notes

1. On the servant problem, see Katzman 223–265; Ryan.
2. On Chesnutt's strategic courtship of northern white readers, see Brodhead 177–210.
3. See Smith's *Theory of Moral Sentiments* (1759), especially Part VI, Section ii, Chapter 1, "Of the Order in Which Individuals Are Recommended by Nature to Our Care and Attention," where sympathy is forged in the household and radiates outward to neighbors, colleagues, etc. (219–227).
4. On Stowe's racial paternalism, see especially Michaels, *Gold Standard* 101–112, and Brown 13–60.
5. In an October 8, 1901, letter to Washington, for instance, Chesnutt declares that *Marrow* was "by far the best thing I have done," and declares that his intention was to emulate Stowe by using "the form of a widely popular work of fiction [...] to win back or help retain the popular sympathy of the Northern people" for the "colored people" of the Southern states ("To Booker T. Washington").
6. As Susan Danielson observes, "Black medical professionalism provides [Chesnutt's] primary extended metaphor, evident in the casting of his central protagonist as a black physician, changing the name Wilmington to *Well*ington [...], and framing his novel with two medical emergencies" (76).
7. This account of the professionalization of U.S. medicine draws chiefly on Bledstein; Haber; Pernick; Savitt; and Starr.
8. For African American participation in medicine during the era of its professionalization, see Downs; Long; Savitt.
9. While Danielson concedes that Janet, in rejecting her family name, repudiates "the sentimental ties of family" (87), the terms in which she reads the novel are unmistakably sentimental in their affirmation of the separation of spheres, virtuous domesticity, and the moral exemplarity of women.
10. Todd McGowan, this essay suggests, underestimates the importance of Janet's invocation of her husband's name and of the material and social supports conferred upon her by structures of professional authority when he argues that Janet renounces in this scene all external, and in particular patriarchal, sources of authority in favor of the self-authorizing sovereignty of her individual will (70–71).

Works Cited

Barnes, Elizabeth. *States of Sympathy: Seduction and Democracy in the American Novel*. New York: Columbia University Press, 1997. Print.
Bledstein, Burton J. *The Culture of Professionalism: The Middle Class and the Development of Higher Education in America*. New York: Norton, 1978. Print.
Brodhead, Richard. *Cultures of Letters: Scenes of Reading and Writing in Nineteenth-Century America*. Chicago: University of Chicago Press, 1995. Print.
Brown, Gillian. *Domestic Individualism: Imagining Self in Nineteenth-Century America*. Berkeley: University California Press, 1990. Print.
Chesnutt, Charles. *The Journals of Charles W. Chesnutt*. Ed. Richard Brodhead. Durham, N.C.: Duke University Press, 1993. Print.
_____. *The Marrow of Tradition*. 1901. Ed. Nancy Bentley and Sandra Gunning. Boston: Bedford, 2002. Print.
_____. "Plot Notes." *The Marrow of Tradition*. By Charles Chesnutt. 1901. Ed. Werner Sollors. New York: Norton, 2012. 212–213. Print.
_____. "To Booker T. Washington." 8 October 1901. *"To Be an Author": Letters of Charles W. Chesnutt, 1889–1905*. Ed. Joseph R. McElrath, Jr., and Robert C. Leitz III. Princeton, NJ: Princeton University Press, 1997. 159–160. Print.

Danielson, Susan. "Charles Chesnutt's Dilemma: Professional Ethics, Social Justice, and Domestic Feminism in *The Marrow of Tradition*." *Southern Literary Journal* 41.1 (2008): 73–92. Web. 8 February 2013.

Downs, Jim. *Sick from Freedom: African-American Illness and Suffering During the Civil War and Reconstruction*. New York: Oxford University Press, 2012. Print.

DuBois, W.E.B. *Writings*. New York: Library of America, 1986. Print.

Fisher, Philip. *Hard Facts: Setting and Form in the American Novel*. New York: Oxford University Press, 1985. Print.

Flexner, Abraham. *Medical Education in the United States and Canada: A Report to the Carnegie Foundation for the Advancement of Teaching*. New York: The Carnegie Foundation for the Advancement of Teaching, 1910. Print.

Glazener, Nancy. *Reading for Realism: The History of a U.S. Literary Institution, 1850–1910*. Durham, NC: Duke University Press, 1997. Print.

Haber, Samuel. *The Quest for Authority and Honor in the American Professions, 1750–1900*. Chicago: University Chicago Press, 1991. Print.

Howells, William Dean. "A Psychological Counter-Current in Recent Fiction." *The North American Review* (December 1901): 872–888. Print.

Katzman, David M. *Seven Days a Week: Women and Domestic Service in Industrializing America*. Urbana: University of Illinois Press, 1978. Print.

Knadler, Stephen P. "Untragic Mulatto: Charles Chesnutt and the Discourse of Whiteness." *American Literary History* 8.3 (1996): 426–448. Web. 6 March 2013.

Long, Gretchen. *Doctoring Freedom: The Politics of African American Medical Care in Slavery and Emancipation*. Chapel Hill: University of North Carolina Press, 2012. Print.

McGowan, Todd. "Acting Without the Father: Charles Chesnutt's New Aristocrat." *American Literary Realism* 30.1 (1997): 59–74. Print.

Michaels, Walter Benn. *The Gold Standard and the Logic of Naturalism: American Literature at the Turn of the Century*. Berkeley: University California Press, 1987. Print.

———. "Plots against America: Neoliberalism and Antiracism." *American Literary History* 18.2 (2006): 288–302. Print.

Nelson, Dana. *National Manhood: Capitalist Citizenship and the Imagined Fraternity of White Men*. Durham, NC: Duke University Press, 1998. Print.

Pickens, Ernestine Williams. *Charles W. Chesnutt and the Progressive Movement*. New York: Pace University Press, 1994. Print.

Prather, H. Leon, Sr. "We Have Taken a City: A Centennial Essay." *Democracy Betrayed: The Wilmington Race Riot of 1892 and Its Legacy*. Ed. David S. Cecelski and John Hope Franklin. Chapel Hill: University of North Carolina Press, 1998. 15–42. Print.

Price, Kenneth. "Charles Chesnutt, the *Atlantic Monthly*, and the Intersection of African-American Fiction and Elite Culture." *Periodical Literature in Nineteenth-Century America*. Ed. Kenneth M. Price and Susan Belasco Smith. Charlottesville: University of Virginia Press, 1995. 257–274. Print.

Ruth, Jennifer. *Novel Professions: Interested Disinterest and the Making of the Professional in the Victorian Novel*. Columbus: Ohio State University Press, 2006. Print.

Ryan, Barbara. *Love, Wages, Slavery: The Literature of Servitude in the United States*. Urbana: University of Illinois Press, 2006. Print.

Savitt, Todd. *Race and Medicine in Nineteenth- and Early-Twentieth-Century America*. Kent, OH: Kent State University Press, 2007. Print.

Smith, Adam. *The Theory of Moral Sentiments*. Ed. D. D. Raphael and A. L. Macfie. Oxford: Oxford University Press, 1976. Print.

Sollors, Werner, ed. *The Marrow of Tradition*. By Charles Chesnutt. 1901. New York: Norton, 2012. Print.

Starr, Paul. *The Social Transformation of American Medicine: The Rise of a Sovereign Profession and the Making of a Vast Industry*. New York: Basic Books, 1982. Print.

Stevenson, Robert Louis. *The Strange Case of Dr. Jekyll and Mr. Hyde.* 1886. Ed. Katherine Linehan. New York: Norton, 2003. Print.

Stowe, Harriet Beecher. "House and Home Papers." *Atlantic* October 1864: 434–443. Making of America. Web. 3 February 2013.

———. *Uncle Tom's Cabin.* 1851–52. Ed. Jean Fagan Yellin. New York: Oxford University Press, 1998. Print.

Wideman, John Edgar. "Charles W. Chesnutt: *The Marrow of Tradition.*" *American Scholar* 42 (1972): 128–34. Rpt. Sollors, 381–390.

The writing of this article was supported by a Residential Fellowship from the Center for Citizenship, Race, and Ethnicity Studies (The College of Saint Rose). Thanks to those who attended my CREST talks as well as to Ashley Reed for their suggestions. In an earlier incarnation, the argument of this essay benefited incalculably from the guidance and critical insight of the members of my dissertation committee: Philip Gould, Kevin McLaughlin, Stuart Burrows, and Deak Nabers.

Sentimental Satire in Anita Loos's *Gentlemen Prefer Blondes*

LISA MENDELMAN

> Menck liked me very much indeed; but in the matter of sentiment, he preferred a witless blonde.—Anita Loos, "The Biography of a Book"

Anita Loos's euphemism for sex in her 1963 preface to *Gentlemen Prefer Blondes* invokes a long literary tradition of implicit physical intimacy. Juxtaposing mere "liking" with the alternative embodied by the "witless blonde," Loos does not exclusively redefine "sentiment" in terms of erotic desire. Rather, in this quip as in her 1925 bestseller, Loos's ironic rhetoric gestures toward and plays with sentiment's various nineteenth-century connotations. Pitted against Loos's cynical persona, the "witless blonde" evokes *Blondes*'s protagonist, a woman whose allure derives from apparent sincerity, sympathy, and naiveté, combined with the hint that she may not be as innocent or inexperienced as her exterior suggests.[1] What would it mean to treat Loos's ironic sentimentalism sincerely, as a revision rather than a rejection of the literary mode?

This essay reads *Gentlemen Prefer Blondes* as a sentimental novel, one that exemplifies the aesthetic category of "modern sentimentalism." As described below, modern sentimentalism reinvents the sentimental mode through experimental aesthetic practices, including, in Loos's epistolary "diary of a professional lady," stream-of-consciousness narration, dialectical writing, and an extensive use of irony. Invoking the logic of this aesthetic category, this essay argues that *Blondes* is not simply a satire of a nineteenth-century sentimental novel in which a working-class girl from Arkansas becomes an author and a Hollywood actress through her sympathy, understanding, and moral "reverance [sic]" (Loos, *Blondes* 53). Rather, as *Blondes* establishes, satire and its related technique of irony can be sentimental. This essay presents a theoretical and historical context for a reading of *Blondes*'s sentimental satire. It then details *Blondes*'s revised sentimental plot, heroine, and community, and highlight intersections between its rendering of Jazz Age femininity, female sexuality, and labor and the contemporaneous cultural discourse about these topics.[2] In each of these capacities, *Blondes* reflects the evolving sensibilities and aesthetic interests of the modernist period and demonstrates the enduring relevance of sentimental feeling therein.

Sentimentalism and Satire

My use of the term "sentimental" refers to a structure of feeling that characterizes subjective emotion as a source of individual knowledge and potential interpersonal connection.[3] "Sentimentalism" refers specifically to the literary mode that reproduces this subjective emotional emphasis in its aesthetic detail and other formal choices. While acknowledging nineteenth-century associations with emotional excess, religious morality, and domestic femininity, my definitions aim to identify continuities between earlier sentimental aesthetics and the transformations of the sentimental mode in a period famous for its disavowal of the sentimental. My definitions also challenge the idea that sentimental feeling necessarily affirms itself—that sentimentalism validates the power of "right feeling" to empathically connect individuals, produce good liberal subjects, and rebuild the world in its own moral-ethical image.[4] This essay argues that the aesthetics of sentimental feeling need not be nearly as affirmative or connective as critics often suggest.[5]

This thinking calls for less of a departure than a return to eighteenth-century understandings of sentimentalism. In his 1795 essay *On the Naïve and Sentimental in Literature*, Friedrich Schiller describes the literary mode as the manifestation of a distinctly modern consciousness, "the result of the attempt to restore the substance of naïve emotion even under the conditions of reflection" (16). For Schiller, sentimental literature is born out of the lack of "correspondence between [an author's] feeling and his thinking which existed in reality in the first state, [and] now only exists as an ideal," "here in the state of culture where that harmonious co-operation of his whole nature is merely an idea" (39). The sentimental mode reflects this intellectual, emotional, and sensory dis-integration and necessarily results in a satiric or an elegiac treatment. Schiller writes:

> A poet is satirical when he takes as his subject the distance from nature and the contradiction between reality and the ideal [...] he can accomplish this seriously and with emotion as well as jokingly and with merriment, according to whether he lingers in the area of the will or in the area of the understanding. The former occurs by means of castigating or pathetic satire, the latter by means of jocose satire [43].

Unlike sentimentalism's later associations with hyperbolic emotion and sympathetic contagion, Schiller's "laughing satire" and its "mockery" require "the constant avoidance of passion," as "the comic writer must avoid pathos and always entertain the understanding" (43–48).[6] Indeed, the "goal" of the author as well as the reader of sentimental satire is "to be free of passion, to look always clearly, always calmly around him and into himself, to find everywhere more chance than fate and to laugh more over absurdity than to rage or to weep over malice" (46). For Schiller, the sentimental mode is one of reflective critique and aesthetic instruction, as it imagines relating to the world through the unified sensual and emotional experience that he calls "naïve." Schiller's sentimentalism thus emerges from and instantiates a detached, self-witnessing sensibility. Schiller's sentimental aesthetics are also, as Kevin Newmark notes, fundamentally negative: the literary mode embeds impossibility within its register, as it aspires toward a reunified sense and sensibility that will never be achievable except as an aesthetic ideal.[7]

Insisting as much on the limited power of emotion as on feeling's centrality in the aesthetic encounter, Schiller's theory provides an historical precedent and a theoretical framework for the sentimental dynamics of *Gentlemen Prefer Blondes*. Like Schiller, this essay does not argue that all satire is sentimental. Rather, it contends that these literary modes have common affective qualities that mean that satire can be sentimental. Attending to how the aesthetic categories associated with these literary modes overlap and at times collaborate promises to enrich an understanding of sentimental aesthetics. In its focus on a single modernist-era novel, this essay does not purport to answer Elizabeth Maddock Dillon's observed "relentless question of whether or not [sentimentalism] is any good" (497). As June Howard and Jessica Burstein suggest, the judgmental slant with which sentimentalism has often been read—as good or bad writing or ideology—has led to an "undermin[ing of] the analytic value" of the category and a "misunderstanding [of] both the artists and the period" in which it is authored (Howard 63; Burstein 228). Concentrating on *Blondes*'s aesthetics, this essay argues that sentimentalism participated in modernist-era aesthetic innovation in more thoroughgoing ways than we have yet understood.

Modernism's antipathy toward sentimentalism has been well documented, if perhaps retrospectively codified and overemphasized.[8] As Suzanne Clark summarizes, "The term *sentimental* marks a shorthand for everything modernism would exclude, the other of its literary/nonliterary dualism" (9, emphasis in original). Even as reappraisals of the period's cultures of feeling have challenged the concept of a modernist/sentimental divide and identified sentimental sensibilities within the modernist canon, much of this criticism maintains sentimental*ism* as a conservative, formulaic aesthetic category that recapitulates nineteenth-century practices.[9] By this logic, sentimentalism's discursive, rhetorical styles are incompatible with modernist formalism. This logic also affectively differentiates sentimentalism and modernism, suggesting that the former affirms feelings that the latter suspects are inauthentic, naïve, coercive, or no longer relevant. Jonathan Greenberg asserts, "Complementary to satire is the affective excess, often called sentimentality, that modernist satire aims to avoid, denounce, or expose" through "various stances—restraint, irony, aloofness, ridicule, aggression—[that] challeng[e] the perceived inauthenticity of sentimental feeling or moral sentiment" (xiv, 46). Greenberg positions modernist satire on an axis that intersects with sentimentality's "affective excess," but his essay suggests that the intersection he identifies may be a continuum rather than a single plot-point, in aesthetic form as well as affective tenor. As *Blondes* establishes, satiric treatments of sentiment can be less extreme than the "cruelty" and "sadistic or anarchic desires" of Greenberg's cohort, and can regulate emotion without a complete disavowal of it (xvi, xiv). Indeed, *Blondes* demonstrates that it is altogether possible to generate an ironic sensibility and embed a suspicion of emotion within the aesthetics of sentimental feeling.

This discussion of *Blondes*'s modern sentimentalism and the feelings it affirms and critiques hinges upon the argument that irony can be sentimental. While observing irony's moral and ethical dimensions, scholars typically examine its epistemological, semantic dynamics, rather than its affective component.[10] However, as Linda Hutcheon argues, irony's "evaluative attitude," often referred to as "tone," is crucial to communicating and appreciating what is meant by what is said (11). Thus, as Hutcheon details, a wide range of feelings are potentially intended and produced by irony, from "derisive disparagement" to "detachment," anger to affection (38). This essay proposes that these feelings inform the "intuitive" dynamics that Wayne Booth attributes to irony's cognitive processing. As Booth describes, irony's "building of amiable communities" involves "the predominant emotion [...] of finding and communing with kindred spirits" (13, 28).[11] Booth emphasizes intellectual affiliation, but his "amiable communities" have an affinity with the "intimate public" that Lauren Berlant identifies in twentieth-century sentimentalism. As Berlant writes, "what makes a public sphere intimate is an expectation that the consumers of its particular stuff *already* share a worldview and emotional knowledge that they have derived from a broadly common historical experience" (viii, emphasis in original). In the case of *Gentlemen Prefer Blondes*, irony structures an intimate public based on an experience of vague understanding, an amiable community bound by uncertain intimacy.

Anita Loos's Sentimental Aesthetics

Dubbed "The Soubrette of Satire" for the hundreds of Hollywood films she authored in the 1910s, Anita Loos was no stranger to satire or sentimental narratives when she wrote the first "Lorelei" sketch that ran in *Harper's Bazar* in March 1925.[12] According to Loos's later accounts, the initial sketch was written as a joke intended only for H. L. Mencken, to "poke fun at his romance" with the latest in a series of "stupid little blondes" (*Kiss* 191). Although "it hit close to home and was an intrusion on his sentimental life, he suggested that the manuscript be published"—though not in Mencken's own *American Mercury*, because, Loos claimed he told her, "I don't dare to affront my readers. Do you realize, young woman, that you're the first American writer ever to poke fun at sex?" (*Kiss* 191). Despite the "intrusion" on one of Mencken's numerous "sentimental" lives, Loos published the piece, which led to five monthly installments in *Harper's*.[13] The sketches were revised and published by Boni & Liveright as *Gentlemen Prefer Blondes* in November 1925, and the book sold out the day of its release. Regardless of the veracity of her retrospective origin narrative, Loos's anecdotes mirror her text's emphasis on the cultural imbrications of sex, sentiment, and irony—and their combined value in the American literary marketplace.[14]

Loos's ironic sentimental rhetoric has generated near-paradoxical interpretations dating back to *Blondes*'s initial publication. Suggesting that the novel's affective depth would go unappreciated, William Faulkner wrote to Loos, "you have played a rotten trick on your admiring public.[...] [M]ost of them will be completely unmoved—even your clumsy gags won't get them—and the others will only find it slight and humorous" (qtd. in Blom 39). As Faulkner anticipated, the implications of the novel's aesthetics have indeed divided Loos's readers, producing what Susan Hegeman calls an "indecision about the generic status of *Blondes* [in which] there is an impulse to see the book either as a satire of '20s morality, as a thinly disguised tragedy, or as a combination of the two: a tragedy problematically dressed up as satire" (526). Perceiving a similar schism, Faye Hammill concludes, "The primary difference between the admiring and the critical reads of *Gentlemen Prefer Blondes* is that the former consider Loos as an ironic and perceptive commentator on mass culture and the latter see her as an emanation from the culture and a producer of its commodities. In fact, Loos's novels are self-consciously both products and critiques of American popular culture" (75).

These apparently incompatible readings collectively support Booth's argument that "unstable ironies tend to dissolve generic distinctions," primarily because there is no suggestion that the irony leads "to some final point of clarity" and instead inspires a "series of further confusions" (233, 241). *Blondes*'s multifaceted appeal derives precisely from its lack of clarity and its sustained confusion. For literary critics, this emphatic ambiguity enables the novel to be read in collaboration with any number of scholarly interests, from modernism to Marxism, feminism to vernacular humor.[15] Without attempting to resolve the novel's inherent tensions and reduce or ignore its complexity, this essay proposes that readers can also appreciate some of *Blondes*'s innovations through a sentimental lens. Indeed, sentimental discourse and its implicit values are the currency that fuels many of the novel's previously discussed economies, including its sexual, linguistic, material, and cultural-capital structures of exchange.[16]

Blondes's *Sentimental Satire*

Blondes's sentimental narrative details the story of Lorelei Lee, whose unflagging belief in "fate" and upwardly-mobile "ambishions" propel her from working as a mandolin player and a stenographer in Little Rock, Arkansas, to Hollywood, New York, and Europe, where she meets and marries "the famous Henry Spoffard, who is the famous Spoffard family, who is a very very fine old family who is very very wealthy" (76). Chronicled in Lorelei's vernacular, the trajectory of this marriage plot and its apparently chaste romance adopt the tropes and discourse of a sentimental "education," wherein intellect, morality, sympathy, and emotional integrity explicitly trump the physical exterior that is implicitly Lorelei's biggest asset. Like many sentimental protagonists, Lorelei is seemingly intuitively, though not unconsciously, aware of the value of sentiment. As her account of Henry's refined wealth and "very very strong morals" suggests, Lorelei appreciates the "Prespyterian" "senshurer's" potential to reward her with the triumphs of many nineteenth-century sentimental novels, including upper-class social status, financial security, and intimate connection (78). As she reports:

> So then Henry said that when he looked at all of those large size diamonds he really felt that they did not have any sentiment, so he was going to give me his class ring from Amherst College instead. So then I looked at him and looked at him, but I am to full of self controle to say anything at this stage of the game, so I said it was really very sweet of him to be so full of nothing but sentiment [101].

In this economy, "sentiment" means nothing—in terms of immediate material value and the cultural capital of conspicuous consumption, and everything—in terms of intimate investment and the cultural capital of social position. Unlike Henry, Lorelei seemingly appreciates the layered "game" of sentimentality from the outset, such that she successfully exchanges the term's various meanings for one another, becoming an author, a Hollywood actress, and a high-society bride, who is "very happy myself because, after all, the greatest thing in life is to always be making everybody else happy" (123).

Despite its obvious ironies, *Blondes*'s hyperbolic happy ending does not undermine sentimental satisfaction. In the final pages of the novel, the now-married Lorelei makes a sentimental appeal to Henry, and then follows through with it, albeit by her own notions of improvement and moral education. As she tells him, "I wanted our life to mean something and I wanted to make the World a better place than it seemed to have been yet" (120). Her solution to this impulse is a decidedly contemporary, American source of meaning and global impact: Hollywood film production. Thus, Henry's wealth and his attachment to Lorelei and to moral reform lead to a conclusion in which several structures of desire collapse into one: Lorelei prompts him to open a film studio to make "pure" films for her to star in, which are authored by her apparent lover, who "is happier than anyone else, because of all the understanding and sympathy he seems to get out of me" (120, 123). It is arguably unclear who receives the novel's sentimental education—Henry and his family, who are "all delighted" by the immediate, material, consumer sentiments of Lorelei's film studio "[b]ecause it is the first time since the war that [they] have had anything definite to put their minds on," or Lorelei, who comes to appreciate the financial and social value of Henry's sentiment many times over (120). For all of these characters, Hollywood and consumer culture not only promise, but also seemingly provide, a version of the community, affiliation, financial gain, and upward mobility that often figure as byproducts of sentimental connection. Replacing World War I as a collective object of national patriotism, Hollywood inspires a certain vague sense of belonging that is apparently more than adequate. Thus, Lorelei determines, "I really think I can say good-bye to my diary feeling that, after all, everything always turns out for the best" (123). Lorelei's aphorism may be naïve, but the novel bears it out.

While satirizing the sentimental trope of a neatly resolved ending and an accompanying moral lesson, *Blondes* offers a different satisfaction to the reader: the ability to appreciate the novel's layered ironies and thereby join the "amiable community" of other readers. Accepting this ironic resolution and joining this community, however, requires tolerating quite a bit of ambiguity. While Loos's authorial position is one of critique, Lorelei's first-person narrative perspective, in diary entries that appear to be stream-of-conscious, renders the target of that critique ambiguous. As Mark McGurl writes, "Lorelei's 'unreliability,' arising not from duplicity but from stupidity, may be intended to place author and reader in a position of intellectual superiority to the story's narrator. [...] And yet this 'pathos of distance' hovers remarkably close to a stream of discourse that continues to solicit the reader's identification and sympathy" (107). Lorelei's phonetic verisimilitude and its suggested lack of formal education predispose the reader to an ironic, if sympathetic, distance from Lorelei and an intellectual identification with Loos. However, this same narrative style prohibits a stable interpretation of Lorelei and of Loos's intent and thus undermines a secure or singular alignment with either figure. Lorelei's speech patterns, for example, obscure as well as reveal her intelligence, recurrently challenging the reader's assumptions about intellect and sophistication, and thus also making Lorelei available for intellectual identification, rather than pity. In contrast to McGurl, who reads Lorelei as a "moron" whose "simplicity, innocent avarice and guileless guile seem to enable her triumph over the series of predatory males who patronize her," this essay argues that Lorelei's simplicity looks suspiciously like dissemblance (107–108).

Although Lorelei may appear to be an example of Wyndham Lewis's modernist "child-cult," her expressed naiveté clearly supports more than a little conscious manipulation (qtd. in McGurl 110). She deploys "self controle," fakes illness, determines "what kind of conversation to use on" people, and, in the novel's most elaborate economic exchange, manages to obtain, sell, steal, and then resteal a diamond tiara (79). Last but certainly not least, Lorelei seems to have shot, and been acquitted for shooting, her former boss, when she discovered him with a girl "famous all over Little Rock for not being nice": "I had quite a bad case of histerics and my mind was really a blank and when I came out of it, it seems that I had a revolver in my hand and it seems that the revolver had shot Mr. Jennings" (25). Lest readers miss the displacement of agency, "Mr. Jennings became shot" by the gun that seems to have been in her hand (25). Reinforced by retrospective distance several times over (Lorelei belatedly relates the long-ago trial in the context of running into her former prosecuting attorney), the narration and its ironic distance ameliorate as much as they accentuate the anecdote's disturbing potential: it is unclear whether Mr. Jennings died, whether Lorelei's assertion that "he was not the kind of a gentleman that a young girl is safe with" qualifies her action as self-defense, or whether her temporary "histerics" translate into any feelings or other awareness about the incident (24). Thus, even in a moment that directly challenges the reader's identification with or sympathy for Lorelei, Loos's narration resists a definitive reading. This instability, coupled with the narration's ironic humor, sustains the hovering pathos that McGurl describes. As the shooting anecdote exemplifies, this hovering phenomenon derives less from Lorelei's apparent stupidity or simplicity than from the inability to determine just what is going on underneath the surface of her narration.

The novel's other characters reinforce this shifting sympathy, offering assessments that contradict one another and indeed even contradict themselves, but that always articulate Lorelei's desire according to their own wishes. Her cynical, "unrefined" counterpart Dorothy suggests that Lorelei is a gifted performer best suited for "a part that only had three expressions: Joy, Sorrow, and Indigestion" (122). Her former prosecuting lawyer reverses his original opinion upon further contact: "He said he always thought that I only used my brains against gentlemen and really had quite a cold heart. But now [...] it seems that he really is madly in love with me because he did not sleep a wink since we became friendly" (27–31). None other than the father of psychoanalysis, the "very very sympathetic [...] Dr. Froyd, [...] looked at me and looked at me, [...] seemed very very intreeged at a girl who always seemed to do everything she wanted to do," and then pronounces her "quite a famous case" for her apparent lack of inhibition (90). Freud's response to Lorelei reinforces the dynamics at work with the other characters: he apparently falls for her superficial appeal (suggested by all of his "looking") while also idealizing her interiority according to his own standards (an absence of repression or neurosis). Regardless of how superficial Freud's response seems to be, his clinical interpretation—and indeed the readers' own—desires a version of the understanding and interpersonal connection associated with the sentimentality it rejects: he sees what he wants to see, and determines that Lorelei feels what he wants her to feel.

Taking Lorelei's verbal habits at face value, her intent and agency are seemingly unclear to her as well. Her heavily qualified narration, in which she "seem[s] to be thinking practically all of the time," expresses a provisional relationship to her own thoughts and feelings that does not entirely seem to be a performance (3). Her refrain—"I really do not seem to care"—accompanies an awareness that feelings can be misleading, as men can "make you feel quite good about yourself and you really seem to have a delightful time but when you get home and come to think it all over, all you have got is a fan" (32, 55). The irony of this particular linguistic economy, of course, is that ignorance and intelligence bear an uncanny resemblance, and straightforward communication undermines, rather than facilitates, a sense of intimacy. Lest readers treat her diary as a transparent representation of her subjective experience, Lorelei highlights her selectivity, telling a suitor and then Freud "things that I really would not even put in my diary" (11, 90). Indeed, Lorelei's narration is an explicit performance from the seventh entry: "I am taking special pains with my diary from now on as I am really writing it for Gerry" (12). This indecipherable combination of reliability and unreliability, sincerity and manipulation, naiveté and knowledge, mean that any given analysis of Lorelei's interiority can be reversed or undone. Lorelei thus functions as a remarkably malleable object for others' projection—an act of identification or disidentification that is always sentimental (motivated by an emotional wish).

Lorelei can be read as a naïve character whose simplicity provokes various longings and desires, including jealousy, anger, disdain, disgust, and disparagement. She can be read as a performing modern subject, eliciting an identification that comes with its own host of sympathies and aggressions. Alternatively, the reader can identify or sympathize with Lorelei's various "gentlemen friends," her friend Dorothy, or any of the other characters that refract her ironically powerful, ambiguous affect, some of whom no doubt prefer the pleasure of not knowing what she really means. Additionally, readers can disidentify with all of the characters and affiliate with Loos and other readers or, as McGurl suggests, hover between these various responses. In some ways, the more Lorelei's intent is scrutinized, the less clear it becomes—a logic that is crucial to *Blondes*'s sentimentalism: Lorelei's appeal involves not thinking too hard and enjoying the uncertain intimacy and vague understanding her narration and its irony generate, rather than pitching into the vertiginous interpretive project of determining what she means or thinks. If this insistence on the pleasures of surface reading formulates part of Loos's critique, it remains unclear whether thinking too much or thinking too little is her target. The reader's ability to appreciate all of these ironies structures a connection with Loos, with other readers, and perhaps with Lorelei, that is akin to the connections within the novel, an experience of mutual understanding predicated on ambiguity.

Lorelei's position as a sentimental heroine reflects not only these gender-neutral dynamics of modern subjectivity, but also the specific dynamics of a contemporaneous femininity that alternately demands innocence and knowledge, agency and passivity, sincere feeling and ironic detachment. In her interactions with other characters as well as her narration, Lorelei's success comes from her ability to maintain the intrinsic contradictions of this femininity—to appear naïve while clearly manipulating at least some of this appearance, to be an indirect agent of unclear ambition, and to remain utterly opaque when it comes to her emotional interiority. Scholarly treatments of Loos's novel often associate Lorelei with 1920s femininity and the decade's icon of young white womanhood, the flapper. Several also note *Blondes*'s depictions—and linkage—of female sexuality and female labor. This essay emphasizes the sentimental dynamics at work in these conflated concepts in the novel, as well as in the Jazz Age culture it reflects.[17]

In many ways, the iconic flapper extends the ambivalent sentimentality of her predecessor, the New Woman, who was and still is frequently characterized as coolly pragmatic and rational at best, calculatingly unfeeling at worst.[18] Although distanced from the New Woman's progressive activism and her first-wave-feminist agenda, the flapper is often depicted as equally unemotional, particularly when it comes to sex (a shift no doubt related to the popularization of birth control and the free love movement in the 1910s and early 1920s). In a 1922 *New York Times* article, Virginia Potter, the President of the New York League of Girls Clubs, lauds the flapper as a "modern young girl" who "looks life right straight in the eye; she knows just what she wants and goes after it, whether it is a man, a career, a job, or a new hat" (O'Leary 49). Potter's description of the "newest woman" and her "fierce intensity" suggests an unsympathetic quality to the flapper's self-absorbed pursuits, in which every desire functions according to consumer-driven market logic (49). In the same article (and noting that she is too busy to know any flappers, let alone participate in the fad), actress Doris Keane pronounces the flapper to be the singular antidote to American sentimentalism:

> I think the flapper is the one hope of our stage today. Day in, day out, here in America the public get fed—and fed up—with pap—sugary, sloppy, sentimental plays; drama for the eight-year-old mind, I call it. The flapper won't stand for it, she passed that stage long ago. While her elders emote and all weep all over the place she laughs. Hers is not a nervous, hysterical laugh, either. Heaven forbid! No! It is a superior, supercilious chuckle betraying the right amount, just the fashionable amount, of amusement [49].

The flapper's evolved, dispassionate relationship to emotion, Keane suggests, will be her contribution to American literature. In its pitch-perfect modulation according to the current fashion, the flapper's detached "amusement" undoes historical constructions of hyperbolic, over-emotional, and neurotic femininity. The flapper's ongoing performance scripts a condescending distance from expressive emotion, a self-regulation that renders her interiority utterly opaque to her audience.

Although these descriptions of the flapper, her material ambitions, and her affective opacity clearly echo some of Lorelei's characteristics, she (like

Keane) does not identify as one. As in Lorelei's retelling of when "the bullet went in Mr. Jennings lung," her femininity is constituted indirectly, through disidentification, deflection, disavowal, and other negations (90). She tells Henry's mother, "I did not seem to like all of the flappers that we seem to have nowadays because I was brought up to be more old fashioned" (94). Identifying as a "more old fashioned girl," Lorelei maintains the material and physical interests associated with the flapper by behaving according to a traditional femininity of understanding, sympathy, naïve emotion, matrimonial desire, and sexual passivity. *Blondes* suggests that, far from being at odds with each other, old-fashioned sentimentality in fact undergirds new constructs of femininity—indeed, being "so old fashioned that I was always full of respect for all of my elders" and their version of femininity is precisely what produces Lorelei's modern appeal (94). She appears to be naïve and sincere for the characters—men and older women—who desire a femininity of naiveté and sincerity, while also appearing ironically detached and ambitious enough for the characters—Dorothy, her maid, her gay male peers—who desire a femininity of intellect, cynicism, and self-interest. To the extent that these desires often contradict themselves (i.e., a simultaneous demand for both sexual knowledge and virginal inexperience), Lorelei's opacity allows her to sustain these near-paradoxical mandates, to evince a femininity of unclear intelligence, agency, sexual desire, professional ambition, and sentiment itself.

As in Loos's prefatory quip about the sentiment of the witless blonde, *Blondes* capitalizes on sentimentalism's connections to bodily sensation and emotional experience, and the ambiguous overlap between this implied physical and emotional activity. Lorelei's "sympathetic" interactions with her "gentlemen friends" occur in the name of "friendship" and "education," wherein Lorelei and her "nice," "understanding" friends "always seem to want to improve my mind and not waste any time" (6–7). This sentimental discourse suggests that Lorelei has sex, or at least promises sex, in return for jewelry and other material goods. Through this rhetoric, Hegeman writes, "The narrative prolongs the erasure of sex to such an extent that sex becomes its central preoccupation"—a comment that applies to a number of nineteenth-century sentimental romances, in which the marriage plot is fundamentally constructed by and around linguistic omissions of physical and sexual desire (534). One reading of *Blondes*'s linguistic economy would simply replace affective connection and platonic desire with sexual connection and erotic desire. However, the novel does not allow such one-to-one translation: there is no explicit reference or revealing detail to indicate that any sex occurs whatsoever and, as Sarah Churchwell observes, the implications of Lorelei's vocabulary are not stable.[19] Thus, Churchwell argues, "[t]he object of Loos's satire is not only sex, but also euphemism itself" (149). Although certainly an object of satire, Loos's euphemisms serve several additional, important purposes. As Catherine Keyser notes, the "loose and baggy syntax, malapropisms, euphemisms and misspellings obscure both [Lorelei's] body and the events she describes" (65). Offering very little physical detail, Lorelei's narrative voice is, ironically, quite disembodied. Emphasizing and obscuring Lorelei's body and her actions, *Blondes*'s sentimental discourse reflects a femininity that both accentuates and deemphasizes sexuality.

As Keyser suggests, sex is not the only activity potentially euphemized by *Blondes*'s language; all of Lorelei's labor is effectively obscured. Although Lorelei concludes the novel as an author and an actress, she achieves this professional success without naming either vocation as her goal. As she writes on the first page, "It would be strange if I turn out to be an authoress" (3). Asserting that her early career as a mandolin player required too much work, Lorelei prefers the "recreation" of authorship: "Writing is different because you do not have to learn or practise and it is more tempermental because practising seems to take all the temperment out of me" (3, 5). Casting her decision to write as alternately calming and healthfully agitating, Lorelei's explicit goal remains her "romantic ideal" of matrimony, a desire that aligns her with the majority of working women in the 1920s, who were predominantly young, single, and in the workforce only until marriage (98). Operating within this professional economy, Lorelei's seeming exchange of sex for money echoes contemporaneous debates about working women, as advocates as well as critics of a gendered minimum wage cautioned against the "loss of virtue" women would be driven to with or without such protection. In an argument that anticipates the Supreme Court's 1923 ruling on the unconstitutionality of a minimum wage for women, an Arkansas judge wrote:

> I am unwilling to say that woman's health of virtue is dependent upon financial circumstances so as to justify the State in attempting to regulate her wages. Her virtue is without price in gold. She may become the victim of her misplaced affections and yield her virtue, but sell it for money—no. When she falls so low as that it is only from the isolated helplessness of her shame and degradation [qtd. in *A Woman's Wage* 49].

Invoking the tropes of a seduction plot—including victimhood, misplaced affections, and yielded virtue—as an explanation for prostitution, the judge's language illuminates the enduringly sentimental conceptions of sex, work, and femininity from which Loos's "professional lady" emerges.

For Lorelei, as for Loos's reader, sentimental language and tropes suggest many different things (including sex) without committing to them—a suggestibility that both Lorelei and Loos cash in on for their constructions of community. As Burstein notes, "sentiment involves certain cognitive operations based on the imagination of connections" (247). In the diamond tiara exchange, Lorelei collaborates with Dorothy to acquire, and then reacquire, the coveted object from two men hired to get it back to its original owner, the wife of one of her "gentlemen friends." Lorelei concludes, "We all seem to understand one another because, after all, Dorothy and I could really have a platonick friendship with gentlemen like Louie and Robber. I mean there seems to be something common between us" (72). This apparent understanding forms an alliance against a bulwark of old money, morality, and conservative femininity—a woman who wears long skirts, large hats, and is "unrefined" enough not to know the difference between real diamonds and paste (60). Accordingly, Lorelei and Dorothy "thank" the men "for all of [their] hospitality. Because it is the way all the French people like Louie and Robber are so hospitable to we Americans that really makes Paris so devine" (73).

Importantly, this "platonick" affective community is just as underwritten by implicit sexuality as Lorelei's potentially non-platonic friendships. Louie and Robber are, the novel suggests, gay lovers: "I mean Louie is always kissing Robber and Dorothy told Louie that if he did not stop kissing Robber, people would think that he painted batiks" (68). Watching the two men interact, Lorelei determines, "[e]ven if it is unusual for an American to see a French gentleman always kissing his father, I really think it is refreshing and I think that we Americans would be better off if we American fathers and sons would love one another more like Louie and Robber" (70). Thus, the "common" something between the two women and the two men seems to be not only the mutual desire for wealth, an appreciation for material goods, and a class-based alliance against dated social mores, but also their common sexual desire for men. As in its Hollywood ending, *Blondes*'s community is no less structured by shared desires, recognition, and values than other imagined kinships—its collaborations and affinities simply formulate collectivity in terms that differ from the traditional nineteenth-century novel.

But are these collective values anything other than financial and self-interested? For as frequently as she has been identified as a gold-digger, Lorelei does express desires and care for others that cannot be traced to money. She apparently misreads the affection between Louie and Robber, but, inadvertently or otherwise, she communicates a liberal wish for the social acceptance of varying expressions of love. Critics have also noted Lorelei's and Dorothy's commitment to mutual advancement and highlighted Lorelei's supportive, if condescending, treatment of her black maid Lulu, whose included commentary identifies her as an ironic, intelligent interlocutor.[20] Time and again, Lorelei attempts to "reform" Dorothy, and she consistently follows through on her belief that "I really think that there is nothing so wonderful as two girls when they stand up for each other and help each other a lot" (79, 58).

Lorelei's relationship with Lulu, however, is more problematic. Sympathetic to Lulu's "very sad life" of extramarital affair and divorce, Lorelei promises her a career for life and appreciates Lulu's affection: "I mean I really believe she could not care any more for me if she was light and not colored" (20). Determining Lulu's depth of feeling according to her skin-color, Lorelei recognizes her not by race but rather by skin-tone. In other words, Lorelei not only manipulates appearances, she responds to superficial distinctions as well. These affectively-charged surfaces include the bodies that are implicitly central to *Blondes*, as well as the language Lorelei carefully edits: "I nearly made a mistake and gave her a book by the title of 'The Nigger of Narcissus' which really would have hurt her feelings. I mean I do not know why authors cannot say 'Negro' instead of 'Nigger' as they have their feelings just the same as we have" (13). Again, the implications of Loos's irony are unclear—is she critical of Lorelei's naïve fantasy that language has the power to correct or restructure social inequality or critical of the racism embedded in her pseudo-universalism ("they have their feelings just the same as we have")? Is she critical of Joseph Conrad's title and in agreement with Lorelei? Is she critical of the American publishing house that changed Conrad's title for the first printing of his novel on this side of the Atlantic?[21] *Blondes* does not provide an answer.

As these suspended criticisms indicate, Loos's novel is not about resolving its irony or appreciating some consistent ironic joke. Indeed, much as the narrative runs on vague understanding and uncertain intimacy, *Blondes* provokes this uncertainty in its reader: the experience of being in on the irony but not quite sure what it implies. If this unstable irony produces a discomfiting sense of inadequacy or a desire for greater certainty, *Blondes* equally invites readers to appreciate that the joke is not as simple as it looks, to recognize that their interpretive strategies and expectations might be part of the problem, and to enjoy the ironic pleasures of this knowledge. Regardless of how a given reader responds to these aesthetics, *Blondes* ably demonstrates that sentimentalism and the feelings it induces can be far from simple. Therein lies part of its enduring appeal.

Coda: Blondes's *Amoral Lessons*

Blondes equally develops an ironic version of the moral instruction historically associated with sentimental literature. While a number of Loos's contemporaries and early critics failed to appreciate the crucial ironic distance between Loos and her protagonist, dismissing both women as depthless and imitative, Carl Van Vechten was among those who appreciated Loos's innovative aesthetics and her version of modern sentimentalism in particular.[22] In his review of the novel, Van Vechten asserts, "[i]n the first place, [*Gentlemen Prefer Blondes*] ranks as a work of art. [...] Not once, in spelling, phraseology, or point of view, does [Loos] depart a hair's breadth from the mental attitude of her subjective heroine. This, in itself, may be considered a feat." Having explicitly identified Loos's talent, Van Vechten assumes a seemingly different tone in the remainder of his review. Adopting Loos's rhetorical irony, Van Vechten enumerates the "salutary lessons" to be learned from the "profound book":

> As a warning to young men, pointing out the danger of encountering high-power blondes in New York, the value of this sociological work cannot be overemphasized. Indeed, I would suggest that every father, whose son nurses any intention of leaving home for a great city, should insert a copy in his offspring's carpet-bag, and I am convinced that it would be an excellent plan for sons to protect their papas in the same generous manner. If papa doesn't need the advice he will enjoy the text anyway.
>
> The book should be kept out of the hands of women of all ages, particularly wives of butter and egg men. They are worried enough about blondes as it is, and one glance at a single page of Miss Loos's tract is likely to impress them with the advisability of keeping daddy under lock and key from thenceforth. No more business excursions to the great city will be permitted, nor will papa be allowed to take long automobile rides for his health.
>
> There are further salutary lessons to be derived from an inspection of Miss Loos's pregnant pages. Travellers to Europe will learn to their horror that traps are set for unsuspecting Americans in the homes of English duchesses. When it is generally known that Bessie and Uncle Ed are usually invited to spend week-ends at Windsor for the purpose of selling them something in the old family manor, it is to be expected that the pair will be a little more shy about accepting these tempting invitations.
>
> I am inclined to believe, indeed, that "Gentlemen Prefer Blondes" will be more epoch-making, will have more far-reaching effects on American life, than any book which has appeared here since *Uncle Tom's Cabin*. Already, I hear, it has driven three hitherto successful gold-diggers to seek honest employment.[23]

Comparing the novel to one of the enduring touchstones of sentimental American literature, Van Vechten engages the same ironic sentimental aesthetics that Loos employs, emphasizing the moral lessons embedded in the feelings the novel produces in its various readers—enjoyment, generosity, worry, horror, shyness, suspicion. As in the novel itself, the majority of these feelings and Van Vechten's asserted "aesthetic and ethical value of the volume" are underwritten by the implicit sexuality of "Miss Loos's pregnant pages." Also as in Loos's novel, the layered implications of Van Vechten's review destabilize its ostensible criticism, inviting a range of contradictory interpretations. Just how ironic is Van Vechten? To what extent does his irony indicate praise or denigration? Is his initial admiration of the novel just as tongue-in-cheek as his subsequent claims of aesthetic and ethical value?

Thus, Van Vechten's review replicates *Blondes*'s version of sentimentalism, a version in which irony emphasizes connection and understanding at the same time as it destabilizes them. Grounded in imagined connections of shared knowledge and ironic humor in which the victim is uncertain and potentially multiple, Van Vechten's and *Blondes*'s sentimental aesthetics are contingent upon ambiguity.[24] This ambiguity produces a perpetual relativism that does not destroy morality so much as qualify it, reminding readers, as Booth says of irony, "to say *both-and*, not *either-or*, when we see that people and works of art are too complex for simple true-false tests" (ix). Indeed, any moral or political meaning a reader would project onto the irony would be based on her own desires—which would, of course, make her just as naïve as the characters who perceive Lorelei's feelings according to what they want her to feel. Ironizing Lorelei's critical self-consciousness as well as the naiveté or intelligence readers would project onto it, *Blondes* reminds readers of their own desires for the sentimental fallacies of simplified connection and definitive moral and literary structures. Equally generating and ironizing a critical self-consciousness in its reader, *Blondes* offers a sentimental education in the pleasures and discomforts of modern feeling.

Notes

1. The parallel between Mencken's preferred "witless blonde" and Loos's protagonist is reinforced by *Blondes's* oft-repeated origin story, as addressed later in this essay. In this retrospective comment, and with a wink and a nod, Loos implies that Mencken's preferences were not uniformly intellectually rigorous, progressive, or adherent to the "disdain of sentimental weakness" he attributed to "aesthetic sensibility" (Mencken 33). As *Blondes* bears out, sentimentalism has an enduring appeal and genuine traction in the modernist period, even with a modernist tastemaker who would reject the sentimentality of those around him. For an overview of Mencken's perspective on masculinity, femininity, and sentimentality, see *In Defense of Women* (1918). In tone as well as subject matter, this ironic-yet-seemingly-honest text reads as a fantastic counterpart to *Blondes*.

2. The space of this essay prevents a detailed discussion of the alternatives to this particular version of "Jazz Age femininity," but there are certainly key racial and class dynamics at stake in this performance of gender. Sentimentalism emerged as a white, middle-class genre, and *Blondes* fulfills this generic expectation of race and class. The novel is by and about a white woman and, while the majority of its female characters work, the protagonist—a former stenographer whose expenses (including a black maid) are now paid by her various suitors—embodies a complicated version of middle-class femininity, as her labor is inspired by a desire for status-oriented commodities.

3. This definition invokes Raymond Williams's concept of a "structure of feeling," which Williams describes as a "deliberately contradictory phrase [...] it is a structure in the sense

that you could perceive it operating in one work after another which weren't otherwise connected—people weren't learning it from each other; yet it was one of feeling much more than of thought—a pattern of impulses, restraints, tones, for which the best evidence was often the actual conventions of literary and dramatic writing" (159).

4. As Burstein summarizes, "Virtually all modern critics engaging the subject share the premise that the sentimental is fundamentally connective. These forms of communion involve descriptions of a responsive dynamic that binds a sentimental text to the bodily presence of its reader; the relation between an author and her readers (often taking the form of a text's political efficacy); a community of readers produced by the circulation of a sentimental text; the workings of sentimental identification within the text; or the ideology of the sentimental at the level of cultural form, producing, it is maintained, connectedness of sociality in its loosest form" (226).

5. This consideration of the connective dynamics of sentimentalism is indebted to Berlant's ongoing study of twentieth-century sentimentalism and Burstein's argument about the dissociative sentimentalism of Mina Loy's and Dorothy Parker's poetry.

6. For an overview of scholarship on nineteenth-century sentimentalism, see Howard. For a discussion of the phenomenology associated with nineteenth-century sentimental literature, see Sanchez-Eppler.

7. As Newmark writes, "Schiller's own understanding of the aesthetic state was already less *naively* anachronistic and more *sentimentally* prudent than the contemporary ideologies that have ensued from it. To the extent that Schiller insisted that the aesthetic state was and could only be an ideal, it already emphasized a measure of negativity in its own theorization and understanding of beauty" (196, emphasis in original).

8. For a summary of modernism's antipathy to sentiment, see Clark. For an attention to the critical codification of this phenomenon, see Greenberg. For a discussion of the cultural and critical trajectory of sentimentalism across several centuries, including the modernist period, see Bell.

9. Recent discussions of feeling in modernist literature include Altieri, Bell, Burstein, Greenberg, and Nieland.

10. See Booth and Burke.

11. Booth's description of the "community of believers" specifically refers to the aesthetic he calls "stable irony." While this essay identifies *Blondes* as a work of "unstable-covert-local" irony within Booth's taxonomy, it argues that *Blondes*'s unstable irony simply introduces instability *into* the sensibility that binds Booth's "amiable community," perhaps because its implied meanings are still "local" rather than "infinite."

12. This appellation comes from Julian Johnson's 1917 *Photoplay* article of the same title.

13. In 1930, Mencken married author, professor, and suffragette Sara Haardt after a tumultuous seven-year courtship—a timeframe in which he was also romantically linked to at least two other women, silent film actress Aileen Pringle and writer Marion Bloom. For a history of this tumultuous decade in Mencken's romantic life, see Martin.

14. Various scholars have questioned the veracity of Loos's oft-retold origin story. As Barreca, Hegeman, and Hammill note in their commentary on Loos's manipulation of her public persona, Loos's *performance* of this particular narrative is revealing in and of itself.

15. For readings that detail *Blondes*'s relationship to modernist discourse, see McGurl; feminist and Marxist perspectives, see Hegeman; vernacular humor, see Tracy.

16. While many of these readings touch upon the interrelated nature of the novel's economies, for extensive treatment of *Blondes*'s sexual economics see Blom and Hegeman. For readings of *Blondes*'s "vernacular modernism" and particular attention to its language, see Everett, Frost, and Tracy. For a reading of *Blondes*'s material economy, see Churchwell. Finally, for readings of *Blondes*'s circulation of cultural capital, see Hammill and McGurl.

17. Churchwell, Hammill, and Hegeman are among the critics who detail Lorelei's sexuality and discuss her obscured labor.

54   The Sentimental Mode

18. The New Woman appeared, as Patterson asserts, in many, often paradoxical, "incarnations—degenerate, evolved type; race leader or race traitor; brow-beating suffragette, prohibitionist, mannish lesbian, college girl, savvy professional woman, barren spinster, club woman, lady drummer, restless woman, wheelwoman, or insatiable shopper—represent[ing] a complex response to an emerging, feminized conception of modernity" (16). Nearly all of these characterizations keep emotion at arm's length.

19. See Churchwell, 148–149.

20. For discussion of feminist criticism on Lorelei and Dorothy, see Barreca, xvii. For a brief treatment of Lorelei's relationship with Lulu, see McGurl, 206*n*31.

21. For a detailed description of *The Nigger of Narcissus*'s publication history on both sides of the Atlantic and in serialized as well as novel form, see Hawthorn.

22. As noted earlier, the critical debate that surrounds *Blondes* dates back to its reception. Two oft-quoted examples of the extremes: while Edith Wharton called it "the great American novel," Wyndham Lewis identified Lorelei as Loos's (and middle-class America's) tragic victim, asserting that Loos "makes fun of the illiteracy, hypocrisy, and business instinct of an uneducated american flapper-harlot for the benefit of the middle-class public who can spell [...] and Miss Loos arrives at this by affecting to be her victim ('told from the inside' method)" (qtd. in Hammill, 59–60).

23. From Van Vechten's review, "Fast and Loos." Reprinted by permission from the Carl Van Vechten Trust.

24. This construction of the pleasurable ambiguity of ironic humor invokes a range of critical theory, including Freud's work with jokes and its suspended/delayed-victim phenomenon, in which, as Keyser notes, "play with language permits the critical aims of the joke to land without immediately alerting its target" (5). For more attention to this doubleness of humor and its diagnostic implications for "specific problems of modernity" in Loos's work and other modern magazine writers, see Keyser.

Works Cited

Altieri, Charles. *The Particulars of Rapture: An Aesthetics of the Affects*. Ithaca, NY: Cornell University Press, 2003. Print.

Bell, Michael. *Sentimentalism, Ethics, and the Culture of Feeling*. New York: St. Martin's, 2000. Print.

Berlant, Lauren. *The Female Complaint: The Unfinished Business of Sentimentality in American Culture*. Durham, NC: Duke University Press, 2008. Print.

Blom, T. E. "Anita Loos and Sexual Economics: *Gentlemen Prefer Blondes*." *Canadian Review of American Studies* 7.1 (1976): 39–47. Print.

Booth, Wayne. *A Rhetoric of Irony*. Chicago: University of Chicago Press, 1974. Print.

Burke, Kenneth. *A Rhetoric of Motives*. New York: George Braziller, 1950. Print.

Burstein, Jessica. "A Few Words About Dubuque: Modernism, Sentimentalism, and the Blasé." *American Literary History* 14.2 (2002): 227–254. Print.

Churchwell, Sarah. "'Lost Among the Ads': *Gentlemen Prefer Blondes* and the Politics of Imitation." *Middlebrow Moderns: Popular American Women Writers of the 1920s*. Ed. Lisa Botshon and Meredith Goldsmith. Boston: Northeastern University Press, 2003. 135–64. Print.

Clark, Suzanne. *Sentimental Modernism: Women Writers and the Revolution of the Word*. Bloomington: Indiana University Press, 1991. Print.

Douglas, Ann. *The Feminization of American Culture*. New York: Farrar, Straus, and Giroux, 1977. Print.

Everett, Barbara. "The New Style of *Sweeney Agonistes*." *Yearbook of English Studies* 14 (1984): 243–263. Print.

Fleissner, Jennifer. *Women, Compulsion, Modernity: The Moment of American Naturalism.* Chicago: University of Chicago Press, 2004. Print.
Frost, Laura. "Blondes Have More Fun: Anita Loos and the Language of Silent Cinema." *Modernism/Modernity* 17.2 (2010): 291–311. Print.
Greenberg, Jonathan. *Modernism, Satire, and the Novel.* Cambridge: Cambridge University Press, 2011. Print.
Hammill, Faye. *Women, Celebrity, and Literary Culture Between the Wars.* Austin: University of Texas Press, 2007. Print.
Hawthorn, Jeremy. "Lookalikes: Conrad and the Denial of Human Individuality." *Conrad First: The Joseph Conrad Periodical Online,* 2006. Web. 1 March 2013.
Hegeman, Susan. "Taking Blondes Seriously." *American Literary History* 7.3 (1995): 525–554. Print.
Howard, June. "What is Sentimentality?" *American Literary History* 11.1 (1999): 63–81. Print.
Hutcheon, Linda. *Irony's Edge: The Theory and Politics of Irony.* London: Routledge, 1994. Print.
Johnson, Julian. "The Soubrette of Satire." *Photoplay* (July 1917): 27–28, 148. Print.
Kessler-Harris, Alice. *A Woman's Wage: Historical Meanings and Social Consequences.* Lexington: University Press of Kentucky, 1991. Print.
Keyser, Catherine. *Playing Smart.* New Brunswick, NJ: Rutgers University Press, 2010.
Loos, Anita. "The Biography of a Book." In *Gentlemen Prefer Blondes.* 1963. New York: Penguin, 1989. xxxvii-xlii. Print.
_____. *Gentlemen Prefer Blondes.* 1925. New York: Penguin, 1989. Print.
_____. *Kiss Hollywood Good-by.* New York: Viking, 1974. Print.
Maddock Dillon, Elizabeth. "Sentimental Aesthetics." *American Literature* 76.3 (2004): 495–523. Print.
Martin, Edward A. *In Defense of Marion: The Love of Marion Bloom and H. L. Mencken.* Athens: University of Georgia Press, 1996. Print.
McGurl, Mark. *The Novel Art: Elevations of American Fiction after Henry James.* Princeton, NJ: Princeton University Press, 2001. Print.
Mencken, Henry Louis. *In Defense of Women.* New York: Alfred A. Knopf, 1918. Print.
Newmark, Kevin. *Irony on Occasion: From Schlegel and Kierkegaard to Derrida and de Man.* New York: Fordham University Press, 2012. Print.
Nieland, Justus. *Feeling Modern: The Eccentricities of Public Life.* Urbana: University of Illinois Press, 2008. Print.
O'Leary Margaret. "More Ado About the Flapper." *New York Times Book Review.* 16 April 1922: 49. Web. 15 October 2012.
Patterson, Martha. *Beyond the Gibson Girl: Reimagining the American New Woman, 1895–1915.* Urbana: University of Illinois Press, 2005. Print.
Sanchez-Eppler, Karen. "Bodily Bonds: The Intersecting Rhetorics of Feminism and Abolitionism." *Representations* 24 (Autumn 1988): 25–59. Print.
Schiller, Friedrich. *On the Naïve and Sentimental in Literature.* 1795. Trans. Helen Watanabe-O'Kelly. Manchester: Carcanet New Press Limited, 1981. Print.
Tracy, Daniel. "From Vernacular Humor to Middlebrow Modernism: *Gentlemen Prefer Blondes* and the Creation of Literary Value." *Arizona Quarterly* 66.1 (2010): 115–143. Print.
Van Vechten, Carl. "Fast and Loos." Unpublished rev. of *Gentlemen Prefer Blondes,* by Anita Loos. TS. Dated November 1925. Accessed in the Carl Van Vechten Papers. The Henry W. and Albert A. Berg Collection of English and American Literature, The New York Public Library. Astor, Lenox and Tilden Foundations. 13 September 2011. Rev. subsequently published, under same title, in *Book Review* 1:20 (January 1926). Reprinted by permission from the Carl Van Vechten Trust. Print.
Williams, Raymond. *Politics and Letters.* New York: Verso, 1981. Print.

"Grimly sentimental"

Pleasure, Trauma and Djuna Barnes's Ryder

Julie Taylor

In a letter to T. S. Eliot, who he thought had a little too much time for Djuna Barnes, Ezra Pound proffers a bitchy limerick about the author of *Nightwood* (1936):

> There once wuzza lady named Djuna
> Who wrote rather like a baboon. Her
> Blubbery prose had no fingers or toes;
> And we wish Whale had found this out sooner [*Selected Letters*, 286].[1]

With its satiric depiction of a soft, flabby, and indulgent textual corpus, Pound's limerick dramatizes a well-established narrative about the "high" modernism associated with the "men of 1914." After the insights of Andreas Huyssen, it is standard to view modernism as a movement that gained cultural coherence from its repudiation of all that it deemed fleshly, feminine, emotional, commercial, and slavishly generic; as a poetics committed to being "austere, direct, free from emotional slither" and "harder and saner" than the literature of the nineteenth century (Pound, *Literary Essays*, 12). From her fondness for the eighteenth-century almanac to her flirtations with Chaucerian verse, the King James Bible and the Jacobethan revenge tragedy, Djuna Barnes's oeuvre is characterized by a perverse and promiscuous intertextuality that confounds the dichotomies implied by Pound. And in her first novel, *Ryder* (which appeared briefly on the American bestseller list upon its publication in 1928), Barnes's intertexts include nineteenth-century sentimental fiction, a genre which appears to epitomize the "anti-modern" characteristics enumerated above.

But if modernist authors and critics alike have historically overemphasized the gulf between sentimental and modernist aesthetics, any explanation of Barnes's work as a simple revival or continuation of the sentimental project poses further problems. In *Sentimental Modernism*, Suzanne Clark understands the work of Djuna Barnes as an example of the continuing occurrence of sentimental values—including an appeal to feeling and progress and an "allegiance to maternal and comforting forms"—within literary modernism (38). While "feeling" in its most capacious sense is indeed crucial to Barnes's modernism, her queer fictions are dramatically opposed to the inherent value of such notions as "progress" and the "maternal and comforting." The tropes and effects of the sentimental novel are neither unthinkingly absorbed nor ruthlessly satirized in Barnes's modernism.[2] Rather, Barnes offers a modernist reading of this "outmoded" form through which we may appreciate the full complexity and ambivalence of these tropes and effects. In the case of *Ryder*—a digressive, semi-autobiographical chronicle of the polygynous and abusive Wendell Ryder and his family—Barnes's anti-moralistic treatment of the mixed feelings attending sexual trauma is in fact powerfully related to her generative reading of the sentimental novel.

Barnes's ambivalent relationship to nineteenth-century sentimentalism is suggested in *Ryder*'s first clear reference to the genre in a chapter entitled "Tears, Idle Tears!" In *The Rise of Silas Lapham* (1885), William Dean Howells, that famous enemy of sentimental fiction, satirically fabricates a novel called *Tears, Idle Tears*, which Tom Corey sums up as "a famous book with ladies. They break their hearts over it" (217). While Barnes's chapter of the same name includes some of Howell's satirical bite, it significantly revises his denigration of sentimental novels and their emotional female readers. *Ryder*'s "Tears, Idle Tears!" deals with the separation of two family members (Amelia and her sister Ann as Amelia prepares to leave England for America and marriage to Wendell Ryder): a common scene in the sentimental fiction dominating the United States's literary market between 1840 and 1880. In one sense, Barnes indeed suggests the weaknesses of sympathetic identification in the sentimental tradition. She mocks sentimental narrative strategies by reducing Ann's concern for her sister to hysterical catastrophizing and by encouraging the reader to maintain a satirical distance from the frequent displays of weeping. Yet the scene fails, importantly, to replicate Howells's sexist dismissal of the value of tears. While Barnes pokes fun at the clichéd language of sentimental tradition ("There, there, my poor dear, you can be sure of nothing but death and rent-day, and it never rains but it pours, and it were better never to have been born [...] and it's better late than never" [44]), she also suggests a female resistance in such scenes, staging the subversive potential of female affection as a counter to the reproductive demands of the family. Ann's care for her sister involves an implicit critique of patriarchal dominance: "a place for everything and everything in its place! Tis what has ruined the lives of all women since the first came up out of a man with his rib sticking in her side!" (44). The sisters argue and laugh as well as cry in their farewell: through Barnes's modernist reading, dispute, difference of opinion, and affective ambivalence are all witnessed within the sentimental scenario.

Writing in 1942 to her friend and literary champion, the novelist Emily Coleman, Barnes reflects upon her work's imbrications with the sentimental, and suggests a belief that this maligned discourse is never quite as far away as one might like:

> I started out grimly sentimental—which is silly. Now I would wish nothing better than to write logically & without emotion. Quite impossible for me, of course. I even find in Shakespeare too great a sweetness. I know of no writer as mean as I would be! Proust, amid his icicles, drips sentimentality [...] to be impersonal one has also to be emotional—one should not be kicked too much, not too much beaten—or the very body that would revolt finally lies still.

While Barnes is perfectly aware that it is every serious modernist's stated imperative to reject the sentimental, she also reflects on the impossibility of such a rejection. For the body that "revolts" is also a body that feels, and so her "mean" and "impersonal" modernism requires that the body can still move and be moved. "Grimly sentimental" is indeed a pertinent term for the uses to which, in *Ryder*, Barnes puts the conventions of this unfashionable literary genre. As a form of fiction that deals with traumatic childhood events (including death, illness, separation from family members, and abuse by adults) and emphasizes an embodied form of reading, the sentimental novel is a crucial cultural resource for reading *Ryder*. *Ryder* details possibly autobiographical early trauma in a style better characterized as bawdy than earnest or melancholy and is a text that celebrates affective ambivalence as it refuses to submit that feeling must follow narrative in a logical or predictable fashion.

Through her reading of the sentimental novel, Barnes suggests that affect often precedes narrative as well as moral clarity and highlights the traces of pleasure that might be found in even the most painful and traumatic scenarios—in particular the crucial sentimental scenario of the dying young girl. While *Ryder* overturns explicitly moralizing narratives of the virgin's death, it also suggests the ways in which the sentimental novel was, in its adumbration of the complexities of feeling, more radical than its contemporary readers might have supposed. Barnes's reading of nineteenth-century fiction might therefore be seen as a form of processing, akin to the trauma response itself, by which the complexities of the earlier texts are *retrospectively comprehended*.

Just as the sentimental genre helps Barnes to write about childhood trauma, the model of belatedness that characterizes traumatic experience indeed describes her "witnessing" of this earlier literary tradition.[3]

Barnes alludes to the quintessential sentimental scenario of an "innocent" young girl's death in Chapter 27, when the Ryders' grandmother, Sophia, reading aloud to her family, excises the "harrowing" demise of "little Emily":

> "Ah, ah, indeed, here little Emily gives up the Ghost," said Sophia, and turned to the next chapter. But that night, Julie on her breast, she read the death scene by the light of a round kerosene lamp, going word for word over the harrowing details, Julie's eye going over, too, but slowly, "and here," said Emily, "take the needle from me, it is too heavy!" and she closed her sweet violet eyes and breathed no more—And the darkness pulled at the lamp and at Julie and tore her away from her beloved while yet she lay upon her breast [122].

Specifically, this scene would seem to allude to Louisa May Alcott's *Little Women* (1868–9), where the exemplary invalid Beth March must eventually give up on her sewing because she can no longer lift the needle. But more crucially, Barnes focuses on the sentimental tableau of the virgin's death to suggest the particularity of the reading experience. Sophia skips the death scenes because Wendell weeps "like a woman," fulfilling the stereotypical role of the over-emotional, self-indulgent (and feminized) reader of sentimental fiction (122). But for Julie, the death scene is significantly affecting and the identification intense: she is "pulled" and "torn" by reading of Emily's death. In *Ryder*, reading is the means by which Julie comes to know and process her own trauma. Equally, by (re)reading the sentimental novel, by "witnessing" it through her own sentimental performance, Barnes allows readers to see its strangeness as a form in which sex, death, trauma, and childhood become queerly connected. Through her engagement with this narrative trope in particular, Barnes suggests both the limitations of sentimental ideology *and* its subversive potential; its rigid moral dimensions *and* the destabilizing feelings and attachments it provokes.

The young girl's death takes centre stage in *Ryder*'s Chapter 24—entitled, importantly, "Julie Becomes What She Had Read"—in a scene that will be crucial to this essay. Here the young Julie (often interpreted as a figure for the author herself) has a traumatic but obscure dream about the death of another young girl. What Julie appears to have been reading is, significantly, the sentimental fiction of the nineteenth century. Indeed, Arabella Lynn, the dying girl in Julie's dream, recalls in name Gabriella Lynn, the heroine and narrator of Caroline Lee Hentz's sentimental bildungsroman, *Ernest Linwood* (1869). The dream has been interpreted psychosexually, and Julie, partly because of what we know about Barnes's own childhood, is understood to have been the victim of incestuous abuse by her father, Wendell.[4] Indeed the chapter ends with Julie awaking to find her grandmother weeping and begging Wendell not to strike his daughter, whom he has heard "deriding [him] greatly" (110). While, for reasons that will become apparent, it is problematic and indeed impossible to extract a straightforward incest narrative from the dream, the affective tableau of "Julie Becomes What She Had Read" communicates, in all of its complexity and ambivalence, the experience of sexual trauma.

In nineteenth-century sentimental fiction, the death of the virgin is generally depicted less as a trauma and more as a beautiful and redemptive episode. In a exemplary scene from what is surely *the* exemplary sentimental novel, *Uncle Tom's Cabin*, Harriet Beecher Stowe's Little Eva assures her family and friends that they too can become angels and gives them the "long, golden brown curls" she has cut from her head, before dying peacefully with a "high and almost sublime expression" on her face (294; 303). The death of the equally innocent and virtuous Beth in *Good Wives* (1869), the second volume of *Little Women*, is depicted in similarly satisfying terms. None of Barnes's characters display such absolute innocence, and Arabella's need to ask forgiveness before death, requesting that her mother leaves her "to my solitude, that I may set my soul to its most necessary order" might be read as a parodic nod to a genre where such dying virgins never need to try to be good, but whose innocence is presented as "natural" through virtue of its effortlessness (107). When the narrator asks that the "dear reader" pause to consider if Arabella's death is not for the best because "What foul demon might have weakened that structure had it reared into full womanhood?" the tone is deeply ironic (108).

This irony does not necessarily stem from the fact that Arabella has already been sexually abused, as Anne Dalton suggests, but relates equally to Barnes's critique of any moral scheme that might encourage the reader to privilege childhood innocence above all else. And both the conventional victim position of the incest narrative and the apparent moral scheme of the sentimental tradition are complicated through the syntactic and semantic parallels with Chapter 17, "What Kate Was Not," and Arabella's shared physical characteristics with Wendell's mistress, Kate Careless. The repeated refrain "Is this not she [...]?" echoes the earlier repetition of "Might Kate-Careless not have been [...]?" and similar images are used to consider the characters of both the worldly Kate-Careless and the apparent Julie-figure, Arabella (106; 88). Both Kate and Arabella have an "aureole of curls," and Arabella's angelic status echoes Kate's ironic description as a possible "symbol of virginity" who is "adored and honored and revered as only angels are revered, honored and adored for their unity of pale locks" (106; 89). By confusing the figures of virgin and whore,

Barnes critiques the manipulative practice of engaging sympathy through moralistic characterization.

The narrative obscurities and moral ambivalence that characterize *Ryder* would indeed seem to set it apart from the sentimental tradition, where a specific emotional response to coherent narratives of pain and suffering is posited as the moral ideal. The most famous example of this link between sympathy, story, and morality is, of course, Stowe's entreaty for an emotional yet rational response to her representation of slavery in *Uncle Tom's Cabin*: "There is one thing that every individual can do,—they can see to it that *they feel right*" (452). In contrast, Barnes's ambivalence about events and characters suggests an attempt to avoid a fixed moral orientation toward the representation of trauma. However, it is through a focus on affective ambivalence that Barnes also suggests that this "moral and proper repertoire of feelings" might be just one side of the sentimental coin (Hendler 2). For although Little Eva's death serves to reify and celebrate childhood innocence, it is also emblematic of the ways that pain and pleasure cohabit the pages of sentimental fiction and serves as a reminder that affective reading practices invited by the sentimental novel might be at odds with its supposed didactic purpose. Barnes's modernist reading of the sentimental novel allows readers to witness that readers have always found enjoyment in apparently traumatic scenes and that childhood, as realized by Stowe and others, is a rather queer state.

Ann Douglas has famously suggested the not insignificant pleasure of Eva's "essentially decorative" death scene (4). Douglas claims that Eva's sainthood is "there to precipitate our nostalgia and our narcissism," encouraging a self-indulgent response in her readers, who "bestow on her that fondness we reserve for the contemplation of softer emotions" (4). For Douglas, the Little Eva plot also provides "historical and practical preparation for the equally indispensable and disquieting comforts of mass culture" (4). The description of Eva's death chamber is indeed a gloriously kitsch celebration of purchasable pleasures, providing an aspirational shopping-list for the materially-minded reader:

> The windows were hung with curtains of rose-colored and white muslin, the floor was spread with a matting which had been ordered in Paris, to a pattern of [St Clare's] own device, having round it a border of rose-buds and leaves, and a centre-piece with full-blown roses. The bedstead, chairs, and lounges, were of bamboo, wrought in peculiarly graceful and fanciful patterns. Over the head of the bed was an alabaster bracket, on which a beautiful sculptured angel stood, with drooping wings, holding out a crown of myrtle-leaves. [...] The graceful bamboo lounges were amply supplied with cushions of rose-colored damask, while over them, depending from the hands of sculptured figures, were gauze curtains similar to those of the bed. [...] In short, the eye could turn nowhere without meeting images of childhood, of beauty, and of peace [291–2].

Stowe not only sets the scene for religious martyrdom and childhood innocence preserved, but her eye for interior design and color co-ordination provide aesthetic and sensual pleasure to the reader. As tragic early death meets with a heady consumerist desire, the reader delights while weeping for Eva.

The interior décor in "Julie Becomes What She Had Read" is decidedly less appealing. Instead of Eva's roses, myrtle, and matching marble vases, Arabella descends the stairs "past the potted, odoriferous cyclamen" (106). This rather shabby interpretation of the sentimental scene is perhaps one of Barnes's more directly satirical statements about the genre, providing a bathos that critiques Stowe's glamour. Pleasure in this otherwise distressing scene is located rather differently, but Barnes does offer a more generous and generative reading of the material pleasures of the sentimental death scene in Chapter 14, "Sophia's Last Will and Testament." Here, Sophia's instructions for her burial function as a re-reading of the Victorian obsession with the aesthetics of death. Sophia (herself a Victorian) wants to be buried in fine jewelry, beside a photograph of her husband dressed as a Moorish noble and she in a "basque with shoulder-knots of lace and brazil braid" (79). She describes in detail the coffin she has chosen, noting its materials and dimensions, and requests: "About, upon and around the coffin, a fretwork, chiseled deep, representing calyx, stamen and pistil, and neatly disarranged closed books, with a frieze at head and foot, portraying the convolvulus at hazard with the hawk" (78). Sophia's clear delight in such preparations reflects the morbid pleasure in death found in Victorian literature and the specific obsession with flora, costume, and furnishings found in sentimental fiction.

However, through Barnes's repetition of this trope, the queerness of the Victorian obsession can be fully "read." "Calyx, stamen and pistil" relate specifically to the reproductive function of flowers, and so emphasize the gendered and sexual undertones of flora in nineteenth-century death scenes. In Eva's death chamber, flowers are used to symbolize an unrealizable innocence, but Barnes's reading suggests that they might actually function as signifiers of the sexuality they are anxiously called upon to disavow. The connections between sex and death are further emphasized by Sophia's plans to be buried with her husband in a sexual pose.[5] The specifics of this are unclear because of the censor's asterisks, but the excisions suggest the bawdy implications of the scene. Thus the pleasure attributed to death scenes acquires a specifically sexual frisson, with Barnes's exaggerated emphasis making clear what Stowe perhaps knew all along: that death can be made sexy.

The confluence of sex and death, pain and pleasure, is more radically and literally incorporated into the reworking of sentimental tropes in Julie's traumatic dream. In this sense, Barnes's reading of the genre allows readers to see both the rich ambivalence of sentimental tropes and the inadequacies of any moralizing narrative of sexual trauma, which cannot take into account such ambivalences. Julie's distress in the scene is clear as she suffers "the tortures of the damned [...] in all ages, all times and all bindings," and she undergoes the kind of dissociation often associated with traumatic experience: "And starting from her bed in a wide-eyed somnambulic sleep, she walks the floor, her groping hand playing madly over the features of the host that is her sleeping self, within that thrall" (107). Yet sensual pleasure and warmth is suddenly offered in juxtaposition to these images of distress: "All is snatched up again and leans, all voluptuous sixteen, from the flowery casement, her young bosom warm to the warm sun" (109). Warmth and pleasure intensify in an image that need not be decoded psychosexually, but rather suggests, through a language of movement and temperature, a feeling of sexual climax: "Down she looses her hair as though it were the molten sluices from the gorger parapet melting in the noonday heat, flooding the garden, covering the roses with a web of brightness" (109).

The unexpected eroticism of sentimental scenarios has recently been explored by Marianne Noble, who considers how the Calvinist association of violence with love governs understandings of sexuality in this context. While she claims that Eva's "passing is not tinged with the erotic. Rather, fantasies of wounding appear to be most fully eroticized in *Uncle Tom's Cabin* when projected onto suffering *black* bodies," Noble understands Eva's death as a "blissful reintegration with totality" and, furthermore, recognizes fundamental connections between sentimentality and masochism (138, emphasis in original):

> Like masochism, sentimentalism can be read, broadly, as a quest for a state of union, or plenitude. And like masochism, sentimentalism describes a world in which pain is an avenue toward achieving that desired state of oneness. When providential theories of pain are read in the context of sentimental affirmations of sympathetic suffering, the result is an implicit link between pain and a mystical pleasure of transcendent union [62].

The mixture of pleasure and pain that Noble reads as paradigmatic of sentimental fiction (but would nevertheless remain unacknowledged, one assumes, by nineteenth-century readers) is rendered explicit in Barnes's reworking of the genre, in which erotic suffering *is* projected onto the bodies of young girls. Barnes's witnessing of the mixed feelings relating to sexuality in sentimental culture is, crucially, linked to her representation of the affective ambivalence of sexual trauma: the sentimental novel therefore becomes an appropriate medium for acknowledging the combination of pleasure and pain relating to Julie's experience.

Barnes's re-reading of the sentimental novel not only emphasizes the potential for eroticism within scenes of suffering, but also allows readers to appreciate the queer consequences of the genre's focus on sympathetic identification. Chapter 24's equal concern with the identification provoked by reading and the question of inter-familial eroticism points to the potentially unstable and unsettling qualities of sympathy implied by sentimental writers but only fully articulated in recent literary criticism. In *States of Sympathy: Seduction and Democracy in the American Novel,* Elizabeth Barnes argues that in popular American narratives of the eighteenth and nineteenth centuries the post-revolutionary and antebellum family serves as the model for social and political affiliations: "In American fiction and nonfiction alike, familial feeling proves the foundation for sympathy, and sympathy the foundation of democracy" (2). Yet crucially, sympathy proves that feeling cannot be controlled, hence the preoccupying theme in American literature of the "distinction between licit and illicit love, exemplified in a score of stories about incest and seduction" (E. Barnes 3). "Far from subverting the goals of national union," Barnes writes,

> incest and seduction represent the logical outcome of American culture's most cherished ideals. In holding up the family as a model for socio-political union, sentimental rhetoric conflates the boundaries between familial and social ties. The result is a confusion of familial and erotic attachment: one learns to love those to whom one already feels related [E. Barnes 3].

Through its focus on inter-familial eroticism in a sympathetic scenario, *Ryder* reiterates and elucidates a trend in sentimental fiction, indicating the potential proximity between familial and sexual love.

Furthermore, besides witnessing the incestuous elements of sentimental narratives, *Ryder* picks up larger trends relating to the complex acts of sympathetic identification found in the popular literature of the previous century. Elizabeth Barnes writes that "if sentimental literature attempts to teach us anything, it is that psychological boundaries are permeable and that 'selfhood' is a distinctly relational construct" (76). The unstable and relational notion of selfhood is explored throughout *Ryder*, but is brought to the fore in Barnes's treatment of the affective ties between Julie and Arabella. Sympathy in sentimental culture is, Hendler argues, "an emotional response to reading or seeing an expression of another's feelings. It is thus at its core an act of identification" (3). Hendler identifies two strands of sympathetic identification in sentimental scenarios: as the reader is asked to feel *like* the protagonist "in a way that maintains a degree of difference between subject and object of sympathy" she is also asked to feel *with* the protagonist, to partially "submerge his or her identity and experience in the emotions of the fictional figure in order to transform partial sameness into identity" (5). Hendler claims that the experience of sympathy is a potential threat to identity because, "even in its most conventional manifestations," it is "predicated on a loss of self; it is in some sense depersonalizing" (123). This "depersonalized" sympathy is shared by Barnes's model of affect, which suggests that emotional engagement with a text has always already involved a degree of confusion about the distinction between subject and object. While Barnes's more radical model of subjectivity means that her representation of feeling depends on an even less reified distinction between self and other, her modernist reiteration allows the reader to reflect on the complexities inherent in the sentimental form.

In sentimental literature, sympathetic identification has a specifically moral element and works on the basis of a clear distinction between good and bad. Elizabeth Barnes claims that sentimentality can be defined by the intention "to both represent and *reproduce* sympathetic attachments between readers and characters," with sentimental narratives offering examples of sympathetic bonding in their storylines as models for the readers' own response (5, emphasis in original). This relates to the concept of "feeling right" because sympathetic identification with a "good" character always seems to lead to moral improvement for the sympathizer. Elizabeth Barnes gives a famous example of this in Senator Bird's "awakening of sympathy" in *Uncle Tom's Cabin*, but the sentimental canon includes such genre-defining examples as Katy's relationship with Cousin Helen in Susan Coolidge's *What Katy Did*, the March sisters' reaction to Beth's illness and death in *Little Women,* and Gabriella Lynn's identifications with her dying servant and her mother in *Ernest Linwood* (E. Barnes 94). Yet in *What Katy Did*, Coolidge suggests some of the complexities of the sentimental tradition through her self-reflexivity about the generic trope of the good invalid. The "very, very good" Cousin Helen has an imaginative significance for Katy and Clover before they meet her: they "played Cousin Helen" and imagined her to look "something like 'Lucy' in Mrs Sherwood's story [...] with blue eyes, and curls, and a long, straight nose. And she'll [...] lie on the sofa perfectly still and never smile, but just look patient" (94–5). Coolidge threatens to explode the myth of the "saintly invalid" when Cousin Helen fails to have blonde curls or even to look very ill, yet ultimately conforms to the generic convention of creating a figure for Katy's sympathetic identification (96). As "half an angel," Helen serves as a role model for Katy, teaching her how to be a good invalid, and Katy's identification in turn serves as a model for the reader (105). Julie's identification with the *im*perfect Arabella in *Ryder* offers a repetition-with-a-difference of this sympathetic model.

Julie's reading provokes identification through feeling, and such feeling, her "suffering the tortures of the damned [...] in all ages, all times and all bindings," serves as a guide for Barnes's reader (106). Julie suffers as many, with many, suggesting an empathy that goes beyond the ordinary boundaries of subjectivity and identification, based on a loosening of the distinctions between self and other and between text and world. As a reader, Julie's self and her feelings are shaped in response to the text. In *Ryder*, different affective threads need not be untangled to create coherent subjects and narratives: such discontinuities in narrative and subjective coherence do not make for an affectively impoverished reader because Barnes's avoids links among factual information, consistent characterization, and the representation of trauma. In *Empathic Vision: Affect, Trauma, and Contemporary Art*, Jill Bennett notes the isolation of affect from character in early Deleuze and claims that:

> The value of Deleuze's notion that affect is produced as intensity, by formal means rather than by narrative, is that it allows us to understand affect as something other than an emotional response to character, and thus to address the limitations of a narrative organization that contains affect within certain corporeal and moral boundaries [31].

The different characters and "figures" of *Ryder* (and Barnes indeed erodes the distinctions between the two) relate to each other and to the text in a highly ambiguous manner, preventing narrative and moral clarity without reducing affect.

Affect seems to go beyond corporeal boundaries in the dream described in Chapter 24. Dalton's psychosexual decoding of such images as the flooding of the valley and the fattening of the fig tree is persuasive; yet, the description of a sudden and violent storm could also be read in terms of its affective weight. Indeed, an affective reading is not only in line with the advice, voiced by the narrator of *Ryder*'s first chapter, that we should "reach not beyond the image" (3), but also coheres with comments made a few lines earlier which suggest that feelings may be transferred into the wider world: "Does not everything wear a muted aspect this bright spring morning? The very flowers hush their noisy trembling, the trees move no bough, and the birds warble but falteringly" (108). Here the world is read through certain affective states that stick to and change the world. Bennett has suggested the value of attending to Veena Das's claim that "trauma is not something immaterial that happens to the individual, leaving the world unchanged—rather it has a palpable extension within the world" (49). That the material world is perceived and even shaped through affect further distances the trauma depicted in the chapter from individual characterization, psychology and, implicitly, auto/biography.

Although affects are not always bound to subjects who are already defined in the text, affect can be a way of shaping the subject, of defining her contours. Feeling is certainly designated as an embodied activity by *Ryder*, but the bodies that feel do not always have the status of clearly defined characters within the novel. The traumatic experience in Chapter 24 is represented in the language of touching and feeling. The physical sensation of touch is the means by which one is touched emotionally, and movement is the means to being moved. Julie's identification works not on the basis of hermeneutic inquiry, and there is no drive to discover the facts of Arabella's narrative. Rather, it is through a vocabulary of movement and spatial positioning that the many selves of Julie feel with another body: "Julie Grieve Ryder, Julie in multitude, follows that little body to the grave. It is Julie now lying on her bed, it is Julie snatched up and flung down into the market place, where they are selling Jesus for a price" (109).

Similarly, *self*-identification is seen to work on the basis of feeling, not knowing. Arabella's panicked touching of her own face from an external perspective not only conveys her fear and distress, but also suggests how these affects are brought into being—through feeling itself: "And starting from her bed in a wide-eyed somnambulic sleep, she walks the floor, her groping hand playing madly over the features of the host that is her sleeping self, within that thrall" (107). Such feeling of feeling, the sensation of sensation, brings the representation of affect in the chapter outside the order of teleological narrative where emotional identification works on the basis of a psychological understanding of motive, cause and effect.

While in sentimental fiction the virgin's peaceful and redemptive death is generally seen from the perspective of the loving family, Arabella's death is a traumatic event registered at the level of the body's sensations. That the death is in itself touching is suggested because it is described *as a touching*: "death's unpeopled army had laid its icy hand upon her heart" (108). Death becomes not so much a narrative conclusion but a particular affective state, an intensification of one affect at the cost of others: "The frail mould that but a moment gone housed a thousand impulses now holds but the long impulse of death!" (108). The image of a "frail mould" of impulses suggests a body that is a living and changing theatre of affect, where different affects may co-exist or one may dominate. Because the trauma of the chapter is not conveyed through a narrative of cause and effect, where readers feel for a character because of the events they encounter, Julie becomes the agent of pure affect: "It is Julie all horror, and terror, and great history. She becomes the shudder of the condemned. Her feet are all soles turned up, and her hands all backs for agony. Every man's heart is in her mouth, the bowels of the world kennel in her belly. Echo and its voice, screaming the scream incredible, comes homing to her throat" (109). The emphasis on the body, but a body that goes beyond the boundaries of subjectivity, is suggested by the combination of figural and physical and individual and collective body parts. Like an exaggerated version of the sentimental reader, for whom the tears of another sympathetic witness within the text provide a cue for her own weeping, Julie is moved, or affected, by affect.

Julie's bodily identifications with Arabella provide a model for reading *Ryder*. Such a mode of reading, Barnes suggests, might challenge the moralistic aspects of the sentimental genre while honoring and indeed opening up some of its significant complexities. Barnes turns to the nineteenth-century sentimental novel precisely because, in her reading, it becomes a genre that enables her to express the full complexities of traumatic experience. But it might be equally said that the logic of belated understanding that characterizes the trauma response—the way in which trauma is experienced only through repetition in the present—provides a description of Barnes's own relation to the sentimental genre. Through her modernist witnessing, Barnes simultaneously reads and rewrites the sentimental novel, at once finding and producing the queer complexities of this apparently outmoded, anti-modern, and conservative form.

Notes

1. "Whale" is Pound's nickname for Frank Morely of Faber & Faber, who edited *Nightwood* with Eliot.

2. Clark's inclusion of Barnes in her *Sentimental Modernism* goes against the grain of most Barnes criticism. Beginning with James Scott's 1976 reading, Barnes's attitude toward the sentimental in *Ryder* has been summarized as broadly parodic and antagonistic. Louis Kannenstine refers to digressive tendencies that halt the "forward movement" of *Ryder*'s plot, and which enable Barnes to signal "the death of the social or domestic novel of generations that had dominated the nineteenth century" (36). Daniella Caselli astutely notes Barnes's complex relationship to the sentimental in *Nightwood* in her claim that, in this novel, "anti-sentimentality is also surrounded, tainted, and infected by the sentimental" (Caselli, 176). Caselli understands *Ryder*, however, in opposition to the nineteenth-century novel, noting, for instance the "sentimentality and the realism savagely mocked in Anna de Grier's letters coveting Austen-like parsonages" (199). And Ann Edmunds, whose work has done much to expand the complex relations between modernism and sentimentalism, describes *Ryder* as an "(anti-) domestic" novel where "grotesque attachment to the ideals of polygamy, promiscuity, idleness, and freethinking at once parodies and overturns inherited conventions of sentimental domestic fiction" (40).

3. The notion of belatedness is key to psychoanalytic understandings of trauma, from Freud's early insight that "*hysterics suffer mainly from reminiscences*" to recent work by the psychoanalytic critic Cathy Caruth (Freud, 7, italics in original). Caruth indeed emphasizes the "central Freudian insight into trauma, that the impact of the traumatic event lies precisely in its belatedness, in its refusal to be simply located, in its insistent appearance outside the boundaries of any single place or time" (8–9).

4. The fullest elaboration of such a reading is found in the work of Anne Dalton, see below.

5. Diane Warren writes that Sophia's will is "at once radical and conservative": because while she expresses her desire to be buried in a sexually intimate pose she does so in "the clichéd language of sentimental fiction" (52). This essay suggests that such a tension is already present within sentimental fiction itself.

Works Cited

Alcott, Louisa May. *Little Women, or Meg, Jo, Beth, and Amy*. Ed. Anne K. Phillips and Gregory Eiselein. New York: Norton, 2003. Print.
Barnes, Djuna. Letter to Emily Coleman. 28 December 1942. Djuna Barnes Papers, Special Collections, University of Maryland Libraries. Series II, Box 3, Folder 18. Print.
_____. *Ryder*. Normal: Dalkey Archive Press, 1990. Print.
Barnes, Elizabeth. *States of Sympathy: Seduction and Democracy in the American Novel*. New York: Columbia University Press, 1997. Print.
Bennett, Jill. *Empathic Vision: Affect, Trauma, and Contemporary Art*. Stanford: Stanford University Press, 2005. Print.
Caruth, Cathy, ed. *Trauma: Explorations in Memory*. Baltimore: Johns Hopkins University Press, 1995. Print.
Caselli, Daniela. *Improper Modernism: Djuna Barnes's Bewildering Corpus*. Farnham, UK: Ashgate, 2009. Print.
Clark, Suzanne. *Sentimental Modernism: Women Writers and the Revolution of the Word*. Bloomington: Indiana University Press, 1991. Print.
Coolidge, Susan. *What Katy Did*. London: Puffin Classics, 1994. Print.
Dalton, Anne B. "Escaping from Eden: Djuna Barnes' Revision of Psychoanalytic Theory and Her Treatment of Father-Daughter Incest in *Ryder*." *Women's Studies* 22.2 (1993): 163–79. Print.
Edmunds, Susan. *Grotesque Relations: Modernist Domestic Fiction and the U.S. Welfare State*. Oxford: Oxford University Press, 2008. Print.
Freud, Sigmund. *The Standard Edition of the Complete Psychological Works of Sigmund Freud*. 24 vols. Vol II. Ed. James Strachey. London: Hogarth Press, 1955. Print.
Hendler, Glenn. *Public Sentiments: Structures of Feeling in Nineteenth-Century American Literature*. Chapel Hill: University of North Carolina Press, 2001. Print.
Hentz, Caroline Lee. *Ernest Linwood; or, The Inner Life of the Author*. Gloucester: Dodo Press, 2007. Print.
Howells, William Dean. *The Rise of Silas Lapham*. New York: Penguin, 1986. Print.
Kannenstine, Louis F. *The Art of Djuna Barnes: Duality and Damnation*. New York: New York University Press, 1977. Print.
Noble, Marianne. *The Masochistic Pleasures of Sentimental Literature*. Princeton, NJ: Princeton University Press, 2000. Print.
Pound, Ezra. *Literary Essays of Ezra Pound*. Ed. T. S. Eliot. London: Faber & Faber, 1954. Print.
_____. *Selected Letters of Ezra Pound, 1907–1941*. Ed. D. D. Paige. London: Faber & Faber, 1971.
Scott, James B. *Djuna Barnes*. Boston: Twayne, 1976. Print.
Stowe, Harriet Beecher. *Uncle Tom's Cabin*. 1851–52. Ed. Jean Fagan Yellin. Oxford: Oxford University Press, 1998. Print.
Warren, Diane. *Djuna Barnes' Consuming Fiction*. Aldershot: Ashgate, 2008. Print.

An earlier version of this essay appeared in Djuna Barnes and Affective Modernism *(Edinburgh University Press, 2012). Reprinted with permission.*

"Violent and sentimental by turns"

Labor Defender, *Sentimentalism and the American Literary Left*

NATHANIEL CADLE

In the October 5, 1907, issue of *Industrial Union Bulletin*, which briefly served as the official publication of the Industrial Workers of the World (IWW), editor A.S. Edwards declared that the IWW had finally freed itself from "sentimentalism and bourgeois reaction" at its third annual convention, marking "a distinct advance in an understanding of the philosophy and structure of the [labor] movement" (qtd. in Brissenden 210–11). Although Edwards was referring to the organizational culture of the IWW rather than to literary aesthetics, his conflation of "sentimentalism" and "bourgeois reaction" anticipates a major concern of writers, publishers, and critics of proletarian literature during the 1930s. Already in 1907, Edwards, speaking on behalf of the IWW—an organization that soon would develop close ties to *The Masses* and the other more politically radical "little" magazines of the 1910s and 1920s—registered a desire to abandon sentimental modes of discourse because of their perceived association with bourgeois values and thus their inappropriateness for addressing working-class issues.[1]

Thirty years on, however, writers and critics who had been associated with *The Masses* and its various descendants continued to bemoan the presence of sentimentalism in much proletarian literature. In 1936, James T. Farrell, a frequent contributor to *New Masses*, derided what he called "the school of revolutionary sentimentalism," which he dismissed as "anti-rational to the core" and "a literature of simplicity to the point of obviousness, and even of downright banality" (21). Just one year later, Claude McKay, who had coedited *The Liberator* in 1922, complained of some Leftist critics' tendencies of preferring "sentimentality above intellectuality in estimating proletarian writing and writers" (111). Far from having "advanced" beyond sentimentalism, as Edwards had asserted, American writers on the Left felt the need to continue disavowing it—a rhetorical move that paradoxically called attention to sentimentalism's persistent appeal (as a mode of writing) to many producers and consumers of proletarian literature. To be sure, both Farrell and McKay criticized sentimentalism on aesthetic ("banality") rather than political grounds ("bourgeois reaction"), but they shared with Edwards a concern that sentimental modes of discourse were too simplistic for addressing complex problems, which required "philosophy" and "intellectuality" instead.

None of these writers was constructing straw men. Sentimentalism remained an extremely popular mode of representing working-class issues and promoting the Socialist cause throughout the first four decades of the twentieth century. Socialist writers Upton Sinclair and Ernest Poole, whose respective novels *The Jungle* (1906) and *The Harbor* (1915) were bestsellers, have been dismissively described as "often sentimental" (Hart and Leininger 552).[2] In the 1930s, Farrell and McKay were responding to a particular critical position that explicitly advocated the use of sentimentalism by first-time writers of proletarian literature. Both Farrell and McKay identified Michael Gold, McKay's former coeditor at *The Liberator* and a founding editor of *New Masses*, as the most important representative of this position—and with good reason. In his famous essay "Go Left, Young Writers!"—which appeared in the January 1929 issue of *New Masses* (and from which this essay borrows its title)—Gold held up "the goal of a proletarian literature in America," characterizing that literature as "sensitive and impatient" and "violent and sentimental by turns" (4). In other words, in contradistinction to Edwards, Farrell, and McKay, Gold identified sentimentalism as a valid literary mode for representing working-class conditions, lives, and values. Moreover, Gold went on to exemplify this approach in his own writing, most notably in his influential novel *Jews Without Money* (1930). As Walter Rideout observes in his classic study of radical American fiction, "Gold's chief talent is the ability to tell brief tales in the rhetoric of intense emotion, an emotion that is always on the verge—and frequently well beyond the verge—of diving into sentimentality" (151). Rideout quickly goes on to reinscribe the presumed opposition between sentimental and "serious" proletarian literature by contrasting Gold's talents with those of a leading representative of high modernism: "*Jews Without Money* [was] sentimental, [but] *The 42nd Parallel* was [not]; in fact, what made John Dos Passos's fifth novel so impressive was in large part its combination of technical brilliance and sardonic objectivity. Here was concrete, published proof that when a writer 'went Left,' he did not need to sacrifice his art" (155).

The distinction between sentimentalism, which by implication Rideout does not consider technically brilliant, and more "serious" modes of writing was never as clear-cut within the American literary Left as Farrell, McKay, and Rideout would have their readers believe. On the contrary, this essay contends that Gold was more accurate in identifying sentimentalism as one among several modes that Leftist American writers could (and did) employ, depending on context, audience, and ultimate aims. Analysis of the radical periodicals of the period, which Gold's status as an editor of both *The Liberator* and *New Masses* underscores, provides a fuller understanding of the range of literary modes available to American writers on the Left as well as of the degree to which supposedly "serious" writers, such as Dos Passos, engaged the sentimental mode when doing so suited their purposes. After all, while contributors do not always necessarily agree with the content that their editor chooses to include in a particular issue of a magazine, it is worth noting that the masthead immediately above Gold's "Go Left, Young Writers!" in the January 1929 issue of *New Masses* listed both Dos Passos and McKay (not to mention Sherwood Anderson, Eugene O'Neill, Upton Sinclair, and Edmund Wilson) as "Contributing Editors," implying, if not explicitly establishing, their agreement with Gold's essay.

Yet it was not in the pages of *New Masses* that sentimentalism emerged as a particularly useful mode of writing for the American literary Left. In the September 1930 issue of *New Masses*—only twenty months after the first appearance of "Go Left, Young Writers!"—Gold backed away considerably from his earlier position regarding sentimentalism. This time, he advocated the "technical precision" of what he called "proletarian realism" over the use of "sentimentalities" or "melodrama" ("Notes of the Month" 5).[3] Rather, this essay examines the use of sentimentalism for immediate and highly specific purposes in the pages of *Labor Defender*, including its use by such noted contributors as John Dos Passos, Upton Sinclair, and Theodore Dreiser. The space that *Labor Defender* provided these and other writers to engage the sentimental mode constitutes an important, yet largely ignored, intersection of sentimentalism, modernism, and Leftist discourse in the United States during the 1920s and 1930s, and it reveals the diverse range of venues and modes of writing that magazines of the period afforded Leftist American writers.

In his insightful study of *The Masses* in *The Public Face of Modernism*, Mark S. Morrisson provides historical context for understanding the range of periodicals that American writers on the Left had at their disposal for addressing important issues. Morrisson attributes the decline of *The Masses*, probably the most influential of the politically radical "little" magazines of the 1910s, not to its infamous struggles with the U.S. Postal Service following the passage of the Espionage Act in June 1917, but rather to its editors' own inability to reconcile their heterodox commitment to cultural pluralism with their increasingly orthodox Socialist politics. Even before the Espionage Act became a reality, Morrisson claims, *The Masses* had

> aimed at some kind of integration of oppositional discourses, from politics to literature and art in what might be called a counterpublic sphere. But [...] the issue of identity, especially the multiple determinants of class, race, and ethnicity, made the magazine's move from the progressivist melting pot ideal of the prewar years to an early version of the pluralism of the twenties so problematic that the magazine was forced to simplify itself and dogmatically choose *an* identity—class—to override all others [201].

Its commitment to pluralism had made *The Masses* aesthetically eclectic and vibrant, with writers and artists employing "a number of textual and pictorial strategies": free verse and imagist poetry, more conventional dialect writing, and even playful manipulation of what Morrisson calls "the sentimental vocabulary of popular magazines" in many of *The Masses*'s cartoons (180–81). Such eclecticism, however, carried with it the constant threat of fragmentation, a danger that, according to Morrisson, the editors of *The Masses* could not stave off indefinitely without enforcing greater political orthodoxy and aesthetic uniformity among their contributors, as they did when they launched *The Liberator* in 1918.

Morrisson is perhaps a little too quick, however, in identifying a straight genealogy from *The Masses* through *The Liberator* to *New Masses*. When Morrisson refers to a "gradual transformation of a heterodox and exuberantly challenging magazine like the *Masses* into the final Communist party-owned *New Masses* by the 1930s" (171), he risks eliding a somewhat more complicated history as well as the continued legacy of the various "textual and pictorial strategies" he identifies, including the sentimental mode explored here, in the magazines of the American Left during the 1920s and 1930s. In point of fact, the official heir of *The Liberator* was *Workers Monthly*, which resulted from a merger of *The Liberator*, *Labor Herald*, and *Soviet Russia Pictorial* in 1924. *New Masses* was launched in 1926, partly in response to *Workers Monthly*'s hard-line stance and partly in response to its relative lack of interest in literature.[4] Of course, the presence of Michael Gold and other figures associated with *The Masses* and *The Liberator* helped to create a sense of continuity between those magazines and *New Masses*, but Gold and his staff clearly made an effort at persuading readers of that continuity: the masthead above Gold's essay in the September 1930 issue announces the "Fifth Year of the New Masses" and the "Twenty First Year of the Masses."

The point here is not that *New Masses* was not a descendant of *The Masses* and *The Liberator*, but rather that it was one descendant among several. Morrisson's narrative of fragmentation is therefore even more accurate and helpful than he directly asserts. The collapse of *The Masses* and the subsumption of *The Liberator* into *Workers Monthly* gave rise to a number of Leftist magazines with varying degrees of affiliation with the Communist Party USA (CPUSA), which was founded in 1919. Furthermore, these periodicals had their own particular objectives and modes of discourse: *Workers Monthly* and its direct descendant *The Communist* (renamed 1927) served as the CPUSA's chief theoretical publication, where party leaders could denounce Trotsky or discuss the "Negro question"; *New Masses* served as the chief literary magazine of the Left and, as the above quotations of Gold indicate, became an important site for debating the most appropriate forms of fiction and poetry for reaching and representing the working classes; and *Y.C.L. Builder* and other magazines advised readers on more practical issues, such as creating effective leaflets and recruiting new members. Each of these magazines can be viewed as carrying on the legacy of *The Masses* in various ways—and not least because many of the writers and artists who contributed to *The Masses* contributed to these other magazines as well. Thus the competing strategies or modes that Morrisson claims resulted in the fragmentation of *The Masses* lived on in its various "fragments," the subsequent magazines of the American Left.

As suggested above, it was in *Labor Defender*, the official publication of the International Labor Defense (ILD), that sentimentalism survived and retained its greatest viability as a mode of discourse for Leftist American writers. Formed in 1925 to provide "legal aid, moral and financial support" to "all workers who are being persecuted by the capitalist government and various other agencies of the employing class, for their participation in the class struggle" (ILD 10), the ILD was the U.S. branch of International Red Aid and is probably best known for defending Sacco and Vanzetti and the Scottsboro Boys.[5] Published monthly from January 1926 to December 1937, *Labor Defender* existed mainly to draw attention to the various efforts of the ILD and to raise funds for those activities.

Outlining the goals of the ILD and *Labor Defender* in the magazine's first issue, James P. Cannon, who served as the first executive secretary of the ILD, promised that the magazine would "carry illustrated stories of all current cases of persecution of the workers in this and other countries, and [would] attempt to revive the interest of the labor movement in the more than one hundred men who are now confined in the various prisons of the country because of their activity in behalf of the workers" (7). More specifically, Cannon declared that the magazine's chief aim would be to "build up communication and bonds of solidarity between those in prison and individuals and organizations thru the I.L.D. taking upon themselves the responsibility to provide funds for the prison comforts and necessities of prisoners as well as to look after the needs of their dependents" (7). The ILD's ability to provide funds to prisoners and their dependents, however, relied heavily upon the generosity of the readers of *Labor Defender*. Underscoring this reality, the advertisement on the back cover of that same January 1926 issue (Figure 1) asks readers to participate in the ILD's "$5-a-Month Pledge Fund." Such calls for participation in the ILD's fund drives would become a recurring motif throughout *Labor Defender*'s run. In May 1928, for instance, Rose Karsner, Cannon's wife, appealed to "members of the International Labor Defense everywhere, and especially those in the anthracite region," to "do their utmost to help raise the necessary funds with which to accomplish [...] the fight to free [Sam] Bonita and his comrades" (101). And calls for new or renewed subscriptions to *Labor Defender* dominated back covers of the magazine well into the 1930s.

This reliance upon the generosity—or "bonds of solidarity," as Cannon put it—felt by its readers helps to explain why sentimentalism was an especially appealing mode of writing for contributors to *Labor Defender*. In order to elicit from its readers such tangible "bonds of solidarity" as monetary donations, the magazine's editors and various contributors consistently strove to engender feelings of compassion for the sufferings of the people they wrote about, and compassion, Philip Fisher points out, is "the primary emotional goal of sentimental narration. Compassion exists in relation to suffering and makes of suffering the primary subject matter, perhaps the exclusive subject matter, of sentimental narrative" (105).

More precisely, *Labor Defender*'s editors and contributors engaged in what Rebecca Wanzo calls sentimental political storytelling. Reaffirming the relationship between compassion and sentimentalism, Wanzo emphasizes the political ends toward which the representation of certain forms of suffering can be mobilized:

> In the United States, the logic that determines who counts as proper victims has historically been shaped by sentimental politics—the practice of telling stories about suffering bodies as a means for inciting political change. Sentimental political storytelling describes the narrativization of sympathy for purposes of political mobilization. It is key if people want to mobilize sympathy and have what I call affective agency—the ability of a subject to have her political and social circumstances move a populace and produce institutional effects [3].

Wanzo is particularly interested in how *certain* "images of suffering African Americans become iconographic examples of noble suffering" and thus elide

Figure 1. The back cover of the inaugural January 1926 issue of *Labor Defender* advertises the ILD's "$5-a-Month Pledge Fund" (*People's World*, Chicago, published with the permission of the Wolfsonian–Florida International University, Miami Beach).

other "representations of suffering blacks" that are deemed less likely to produce such political mobilization (18)—a concern to which this essay will return later. For now, the point is that Wanzo's concept of sentimental political storytelling enables readers to approach the use of sentimentalism in *Labor Defender*—and potentially elsewhere among the writings of the American literary Left—not as an aesthetic failure or an inability on the part of the magazine's contributors to break free from bourgeois modes of writing, but rather as a strategy for achieving specific political goals in a particular context. Through their use of sentimentalism, *Labor Defender*'s editors and contributors attempted to instill in their readers enough compassion for "class" prisoners that those readers would be moved to contribute monetarily to the ILD's efforts to overturn unfair convictions.

A case in point is the way *Labor Defender* represented Tom Mooney. Mooney had been convicted of the 1916 Preparedness Day bombing on the basis of perjured testimony and other questionable evidence, and thanks in large part to his connections to William "Big Bill" Haywood and other early leaders of the IWW, he became a *cause célèbre* in the Leftist periodicals of the 1920s and 1930s.[6] Importantly, however, each magazine represented Mooney and his case differently. Perhaps no clearer example of those differences—and perhaps no clearer example of the extent to which *Labor Defender* relied upon the conventions of sentimentalism—can be found than in the images that appear in Figures 2 and 3. Figure 2, a drawing of Mooney by Hugo Gellert, appeared alongside Gold's "Notes of the Month" in the September 1930 issue of *New Masses*. Both Gellert's drawing and the caption that accompanies it emphasize Mooney's optimism and heroism: Gellert portrays him as square-jawed and smiling, and the caption labels him a "courageous fighter" who still celebrates May Day despite having served thirteen years in prison. Figure 3, on the other hand, is a photograph of Mooney that accompanied an essay by Upton Sinclair in the October 1928 issue of *Labor Defender*. In contrast to Gellert's heroic depiction of Mooney, this photograph focuses the viewer's attention

Figure 2. Hugo Gellert's optimistic and heroic portrait of Tom Mooney appeared alongside Michael Gold's "Notes of the Month" in the September 1930 issue of *New Masses* (Mary Ryan Gallery, New York).

Figure 3. The October 1928 issue of *Labor Defender* reprinted this photograph of Tom Mooney bidding farewell to his mother before entering San Quentin State Prison (*People's World*, Chicago, published with the permission of the Wolfsonian–Florida International University, Miami Beach).

not on Mooney but on his mother, whose face literally obscures her son's as they bid farewell to one another. The iron bars of San Quentin behind them unsettle what should be a tender, domestic scene between a mother and her son, and this juxtaposition underscores the state's unfair disruption of their family. By reprinting this photograph alongside Sinclair's essay, entitled "California: Land of Orange Groves and the Frame-up," the editors of *Labor Defender* clearly wished to elicit the reader's compassion—for Mooney's mother as well as for Mooney himself.[7] To what political ends the reader's sympathy was being mobilized becomes clear in Sinclair's call for "protest meetings" and "public demonstrations" on Mooney's behalf: "To let [unjustly imprisoned] men out would be to admit the crime which was committed against them," Sinclair explains, neatly reversing the roles of criminal and victim, "and the only way the criminals can be moved is by making them realize that keeping their victims locked up is bad advertising" (203).

Mooney, who was probably the most famous political prisoner in the United States during the 1920s and 1930s, essentially became *Labor Defender*'s poster child. As Richard H. Frost observes, "Virtually every issue of [...] *Labor Defender* contained a Mooney news item or photograph. Mooney became a member of the ILD national advisory board" (444).[8] Like other prisoners the

ILD supported, Mooney also wrote letters that were published in the magazine. Cannon had highlighted the "department [known as 'Voices from Prison'] specially devoted to letters from those who are behind the bars in the interests of labor" as "one of our most prized features" (7), but Mooney's contributions to the magazine far exceeded those of any other prisoner who corresponded with *Labor Defender*. Mooney had served as circulation manager of the San Francisco-based weekly *The Revolt* in the early 1910s and thus probably had a better understanding of the needs and expectations of periodicals than most of *Labor Defender*'s other prisoner-correspondents. Indeed, the fact that the magazine sometimes published Mooney's essays separately from the "Voices from Prison" department suggests how much the editors of *Labor Defender* valued his writing and how much in tune with the editors' aims Mooney was. His evocatively titled "The Prison Hell-hole of California," which appeared in the January 1929 issue, employed the same sentimental juxtapositions between what should be pleasant domestic routines and the ugly indifference of prison life that his photograph in the October 1928 issue did.

Giving an account of his daily activities, Mooney describes being "compelled by the 'gun-bulls' [guards] to submerge his [slop-]bucket so deeply in the trough that his hands become wet with dirty water in which hundreds of buckets have been rinsed" and complains of having to consume "mouldy bread and chicory coffee, served out of filthy buckets and by inmate waiters whose coats and aprons are so dirty they no longer resemble white" (6). An anonymous introduction to Mooney's essay underscores the unwholesomeness of the life Mooney was forced to lead in prison, noting that "Mooney works long hours and at very hard work for a sick man" and that "should Mooney die in San Quentin Prison there is every possibility that his body would be desecrated [...] for experimental purposes" (6). This sense of outrage at the potential "desecration" of Mooney's body by medical students after his death, which has little bearing on his living conditions or the working conditions of the proletariat, is surprising to find in a Leftist periodical and only makes sense as a purely sentimental appeal to readers.

It is precisely the presence of such sentimental appeals that makes *Labor Defender* so important to our understanding of the full range of discursive modes and contexts available to American writers on the Left. Many of the most prominent writers and intellectuals associated with the CPUSA during the 1920s and 1930s contributed pieces to—or were otherwise involved with—*Labor Defender*. T.J. O'Flaherty, Max Shachtman, J. Louis Engdahl, and Joseph North served as editors of the magazine at various times, and Michael Gold, Scott Nearing, William L. Patterson, and Whittaker Chambers contributed occasional articles. In an essay for the May 1928 issue, for example, Gold included the piteous living conditions of political prisoners among the list of things he thinks of on May Day: "I think of the gloomy dungeons of the world where sit our prisoners. [...] The sun is not allowed to shine into the cells of our comrades in prison" (108). By November 1932, Chambers, John Dos Passos, Hugo Gellert, Maxim Gorki, and Josephine Herbst were listed as "Contributing Editors." That all of these people were simultaneously contributing to *New Masses*, *The Communist*, and other CPUSA-affiliated periodicals—and, more to the point, that *Labor Defender* could serve as a very different but still meaningful site of publication for them—demonstrates the "dialogic" capacities that Sean Latham and Robert Scholes attribute to magazines: "Periodicals [...] create and occupy typically complex and often unstable positions in sometimes collaborative and sometimes competitive cultural networks" (528–29). *Labor Defender* in particular reveals the unexpected importance of sentimentalism to the American Left, thereby destabilizing, yet also enriching, our understanding of the diversity of writing within their network of publications.

* * *

Labor Defender arguably reached its peak of literary vibrancy as well as cultural and historical significance during the latter half of 1931. From June through December of that year, the magazine became an important venue for some of the writers associated with the National Committee for the Defense of Political Prisoners, especially John Dos Passos and Theodore Dreiser, who served as its chair. What drew these writers to *Labor Defender*—and what energized the magazine more generally—was almost certainly the magazine's coverage of the Scottsboro Boys' trials and the plight of the Kentucky coal miners who were involved in the so-called Harlan County War.[9] By the end of 1931, in fact, these two sets of events were presented to readers of *Labor Defender* as convergent, and that perceived convergence gave many of the magazine's articles during this period a sense of urgency that was sometimes missing from earlier and later issues. In a November 1931 article entitled "The Bended Knee or Clenched Fist? Mooney—Harlan—Scottsboro," Joseph North, who would go on to edit *New Masses*, emphasized this convergence and coupled it with the ILD's longer-standing support of Tom Mooney. Identifying Mooney, the Scottsboro Boys, and the Harlan miners as the three "major case[s] before the eyes of the American masses today," North prophesied that "the winter of 1931 will be the outstanding winter of struggle. [...] It is precisely in this time that the working-class must win the freedom of their class-war martyrs—Mooney—the Harlan miners—the Scottsboro Negro boys" (210, 221).

Labeling Mooney, the Harlan miners, and the Scottsboro Boys "martyrs," of course, invokes the overtly religious rhetoric of sentimentalism, but the articulation of the specific injustices they faced into a larger pattern of "class-war" points to a more pressing issue that several Leftist periodicals attempted to address in the early 1930s. As Barbara Foley notes, the CPUSA and its various organs were particularly concerned at the time with "the role of American blacks in the revolutionary struggle":

> The American party's endorsement of the 1928 Comintern position provided the impetus for unprecedented levels of antiracist activity. [...] During the Third Period, the party initiated aggressive campaigns against lynch terror and for black/white workers' unity in the Jim Crow South[, including] the party's vigorous campaign in defense of the Scottsboro boys. [...] By 1934, [...] there were 1,000 Communists in Alabama, 95 percent of them black. The Birmingham ILD had 3,000 members, and the Birmingham CP was several times larger than the local NAACP [174, 177].

Thus when North ended his article by calling for, among other things, "greater activity among the Negro masses" (221), he was seizing an opportunity provided by the Scottsboro Boys' plight to correct what, in its report on its fourth national convention, the ILD itself had called "its failure to pay the necessary attention to the persecutions of the Negro workers and to recruit these most oppressed workers into the I.L.D." (ILD 6–7). *Labor Defender*'s reliance upon a discursive mode that had already proven effective for promoting white sympathy for black suffering, most notably in *Uncle Tom's Cabin*, made it a particularly attractive site of publication for Leftist American writers interested in addressing the issues that the Scottsboro Boys' trials raised.

As noted above, however, Rebecca Wanzo draws attention to the forms of black suffering that are *not* represented by sentimental political storytelling in favor of those that are. "In the Civil Rights Era in the twentieth century," Wanzo argues, "nonviolent African Americans modeled patient suffering subjects subjected under Jim Crow laws, and they became the twentieth-century standard-bearers for articulations of idealized suffering bodies in political rhetoric through the widespread circulation of their struggles in photography and television" (18). In the case of the Scottsboro Boys, their extreme youth—"The Oldest Is Not Yet 20," a fundraising advertisement on the back cover of the May 1931 issue declared (Figure 4)—and the willingness of some of their mothers to be photographed (Figure 5) no doubt helped to make them more appealing "suffering subjects" to *Labor Defender*'s editors, contributors, and readers than any number of other imprisoned or lynched African Americans.

Moreover, the resemblance between the fundraising advertisement for the Scottsboro Boys' defense and the advertisement above it for a subscription drive for *Labor Defender* itself (also Figure 4) suggests that the magazine did

WHITE AND NEGRO WORKERS!

9 YOUNG NEGRO WORKERS
(The Oldest Is Not Yet 20)
FACE THE ELECTRIC CHAIR
In SCOTTSBORO, ALABAMA

THEY ARE SENTENCED TO BURN ON JULY 10.
WILL YOU LET THEM BE LEGALLY LYNCHED?
THE SOUTHERN BOSSES WANT TO LYNCH THEM!
PROTEST — FIGHT — FREE THEM!
RUSH FUNDS FOR LEGAL EXPENSE AND MASS PROTEST!

INTERNATIONAL LABOR DEFENSE
80 East 11th Street, Room 430, New York City

I demand the freedom of the nine young Negro boys who face legal lynching. I am contributing to the fund to fight for their freedom, the following amount $ ....

Name
Address
City

WILL HER BOYS BE LYNCHED?
A Birmingham mother, Mrs. Wright, mother of 2 of the Scottsboro boys, is in the North struggling to save her sons.

Above: Figure 4. Proximity and similarity of design link the magazine's subscription drive to the ILD's fundraising drive for the Scottsboro Boys' defense on the back cover of the May 1931 issue of *Labor Defender* (*People's World*, Chicago, published with the permission of the Wolfsonian–Florida International University, Miami Beach).

not avoid the same problem that, according to Mark S. Morrisson, *The Masses* failed to resolve: the tendency to allow class identity to subsume all other forms of identity (169–70). Indeed, in an article preceding Joseph North's in the November 1931 issue of *Labor Defender*,

Left: Figure 5. This photograph of the mother of Andy and Roy Wright, two of the Scottsboro Boys, appeared alongside John Dos Passos's article "Scottsboro's Testimony" in the July 1931 issue of *Labor Defender* (*People's World*, Chicago, published with the permission of the Wolfsonian–Florida International University, Miami Beach).

black writer Eugene Gordon bewailed the fact that "the Negro has developed race consciousness instead of class consciousness" (208). Regardless of these implications, the trials of the Scottsboro Boys did initiate a particularly rich period in *Labor Defender*'s run in terms of the literary prominence of its contributors. The remainder of this essay will concentrate on their contributions to the magazine.

Notably, the publication of articles by such "serious" authors as Dos Passos and Dreiser had little apparent effect upon the style or tone of *Labor Defender* during this time. On the contrary, both Dos Passos and Dreiser engaged sentimentalism productively and, for the most part, sincerely when they wrote for the magazine, indicating that *Labor Defender*'s preferred discursive mode shaped their own contributions. For example, in his first essay about the Scottsboro Boys, which appeared in the June 1931 issue, Dreiser invoked the need for sympathy by noting its historical absence in the treatment of black Americans in the United States: "The Negro as well as the white, before the law, should be treated with understanding, and liberality. Through no fault of their own, a century or two ago, some of them were drafted as slaves by the white powers and yet that, instead of evoking sympathy, has produced belittlement and hatred" ("Dreiser on Scottsboro" 108). In order to produce that sympathy, Dreiser and other members of the National Committee for the Defense of Political Prisoners, including Lincoln Steffens, Malcolm Cowley, John Dos Passos, Waldo Frank, Hugo Gellert, and Josephine Herbst, signed "An Open Letter to the Governor of Alabama," which appeared opposite Dreiser's essay in the June 1931 issue. The letter registered the signers' "protest in regard to the recent event at Scottsboro," which they characterized as "a lynching concealed in the forms of law" (109).

The letter's chief rhetorical strategy, however, involved a direct appeal to Governor Benjamin M. Miller—and any other white reader—to imagine his own children in the Scottsboro Boys' position and thereby to identify with the Scottsboro Boys' parents and their lack of power to intervene in this injustice: "Your own children, Governor Miller, or the minor sons of any influential white family of Alabama, would not be submitted to this kind of 'justice' in an Alabama court, and no state in this union has a right to speak of justice as long as the most friendless Negro child, accused of a crime, receives less than the best defense that would be given its wealthiest white citizen" (109). By forcing Miller and other white readers to confront their own position of privilege, which was based on race, the letter invited them to feel compassion for "friendless Negro child[ren]," such as the Scottsboro Boys, who had little access to good legal defense.

This relatively straightforward use of sentimental rhetoric by Dreiser and the National Committee for the Defense of Political Prisoners was typical of these writers' contributions to *Labor Defender*. In fact, the only notable subversion of the magazine's sentimentalism occurs in Dos Passos's July 1931 essay on the Scottsboro Boys, "Scottsboro's Testimony," wherein he unexpectedly and ironically invoked pity for the "poor whites" who were responsible for the miscarriage of justice. Directly addressing his readers, Dos Passos claimed, "You have to realize how physically and emotionally undernourished and starved the small tenant farmers, the small storekeepers, the jellybeans and drug-store loafers who make up the lynching mobs are, to understand the orgy or righteousness and of unconscious sex and cruelty impulses, that a lynching lets loose. The feeling of superiority to the Negro is the only thing the poor whites of the South have got" (131). Apparently, the editors of *Labor Defender* felt the need to counterbalance this use of irony because, alongside Dos Passos's essay, they printed a photograph of the mother of two of the Scottsboro Boys (see Figure 5 above) and a note appealing "to all workers and sympathizers to rush funds for the defense of the youths" ("Scottsboro's Testimony" 131). The inclusion of this photograph—of a person Dos Passos's essay does not mention—served to remind those readers who might miss Dos Passos's irony of the proper subjects of their sympathy.

If the editors of *Labor Defender* were making a point by undercutting Dos Passos's use of irony, then Dos Passos seems to have taken it to heart because he eschewed irony altogether when he turned his attention to the "poor whites" who made up the bulk of the Harlan County miners.[10] In his December 1931 article "The American Standard in the Mines," Dos Passos exhibited the same concern for the corrosive effect of repressive atmospheres upon domestic conditions that the magazine displayed in its representations of Mooney's life in prison:

> We heard the same story in Pineville, in Harlan Town, in Straight Creek, in Evarts; children without clothing to get through the winter, children unable to go to school because their parents couldn't dress them properly, without shoes, who hadn't tasted milk in months; men, women and children crowded into company shacks without water or sanitation, into shacks so cranky and tumbledown that they make not the slightest pretense of keeping the weather out [234].

Dreiser, whose essay "I Go to Harlan" immediately preceded Dos Passos's article in the same issue of *Labor Defender*, similarly focused on these poor living conditions and their effect upon the miners' children: "Then we went off into the mining camps themselves, and witnessed for ourselves the conditions against which the miners are protesting. Their state is deplorable. Shacks for houses, polluted water, potatoes and beans to dine on every night. In one village I discovered that deaths among the children from starvation last summer was [sic] four to seven a week" ("I Go to Harlan" 233). This sort of suffering, Dos Passos reasoned, could not fail to elicit the reader's compassion: "The coal mine workers are desperate; they face a winter of starvation and disease that any man with the imagination to feel in the least the sufferings of his fellow men will shudder to think of" ("American Standard" 234). Echoing the magazine's stated goal of engendering "bonds of solidarity," as James P. Cannon worded it, between its subjects and its readers, Dos Passos ended his article hopefully by envisioning "a new wave of solidarity" that such feelings of compassion might create, and in keeping with the magazine's frequent fundraising efforts, the editors appended a note to the end of Dos Passos's article calling for "every worker and sympathizer to speed funds to the Prisoners' Winter Aid Campaign of the I.L.D." ("American Standard" 234).

It is perhaps telling that, when Dreiser, Dos Passos, and other members of the National Committee for the Defense of Political Prisoners published *Harlan Miners Speak* in 1932, they acknowledged the ILD's role in "center[ing] possible attention and so modify[ing] if not dispel[ling] some of the ills being suffered by the miners" (4), but they largely abandoned the sentimentalism favored by *Labor Defender*. Instead, *Harlan Miners Speak* exemplified and literalized the commitment to reportage that Paula Rabinowitz identifies at work in many of the writings of the American literary Left (78). Most of the book is taken up by affidavits and other testimony the miners provided themselves: at 138 pages (out of a total of 348), the longest chapter by far is entitled "The Miners Speak for Themselves." Rather than producing compassion for the miners by telling stories about their suffering, then, *Harlan Miners Speak* recorded those stories in the miners' own words and, in one of the "explanatory paragraphs" attributed to Dos Passos, cast this willingness to speak as a form of heroism and resistance:

> It takes a brave man to stand up and speak his mind, when he knows that his opponents are taking down everything he says so as to twist it into the basis for an indictment, when he knows that his opponents have at their command all the force of the law, of the state, the money power, and hired gunmen besides to fight him with. The miners and the miners' wives who spoke at Straight Creek and at Wallins Creek were brave men and women; they knew what they were up against [294].

While the form of *Harlan Miners Speak* may indicate a certain recognition of—even dissatisfaction with—the limitations of sentimentalism as a strategy for effecting immediate political change on the part of Dreiser, Dos Passos, and the National Committee for the Defense of Political Prisoners, the book is certainly not a repudiation of *Labor Defender* or its preferred mode of representing its subjects. On the contrary, one idea that links Dreiser's chapter in *Harlan Miners Speak* to his essays about the miners for *Labor Defender* is the need for alternative media, such as *Labor Defender* itself, that bypass the profit-driven newspapers and magazines, which invariably sided with the mine owners. In *Harlan Miners Speak*, Dreiser complained that "a large portion of the press [...] appeared to be determined to either modify, limit or ignore such facts as were testified to, and, worse, to make light of and discredit the significance if not the ambitions of the Committee" (8). The same complaint appears in "I Go to Harlan," Dreiser's December 1931 contribution to *Labor Defender*, but the solution appears, too: "The newspaper men couldn't get [the truth]. They were shot when they got into the country. Even those who brought anything out with one or two exceptions didn't print the whole truth. They couldn't. Their bosses belong to the same crowd that runs the coal mines. *So we went in*" (233, emphasis added). By "we," Dreiser means the National Committee for the Defense of Political Prisoners, but the fact that the ILD had commissioned the committee to go and the fact that *Labor Defender* provided the first venue for disseminating some of the committee's findings call attention to *Labor Defender*'s role and reaffirm its significance. *Labor Defender* and the other Leftist periodicals provided just the sort of alternative media that the Harlan miners—and Tom Mooney, the Scottsboro Boys, and others—needed in order to raise awareness of their plight.

Its role in raising awareness of these injustices and in raising funds for combating them is, of course, *Labor Defender*'s greatest legacy. While it is ultimately impossible to determine the full extent of the magazine's impact upon the causes it championed, there can be little doubt that its efforts at engendering compassion made a material difference for the suffering subjects it represented. As late as July of 1937, the same month that the state of Alabama dropped all charges against her son, Mamie Williams was still receiving financial support from the ILD as a dependent of one of the Scottsboro Boys. In a letter to *Labor Defender* that was printed in the "Voices from Prison" department, Williams thanked the ILD for its latest gift of $43, the amount it apparently cost to bury one of her other children. "I did not know where I was going to get it from," she acknowledged. "I guess you all think every time I turn around I am worrying you all. But I can't help it if all these troubles come upon me. You are the only friends I can turn to" (19). While Williams's expression of grief here was certainly genuine and not in the least exploitative, her letter employs the same sentimental strategies that can be found in the contributions of Dreiser, Dos Passos, and other writers: she presents herself as being as "friendless" as her son or the other "Negro children" with whom the National Committee for the Defense of Political Prisoners invited Governor Miller to sympathize. Thus while the crucial fact here is that *Labor Defender* helped to alleviate the suffering of Williams and other people like her, it also provided them with a forum in which they could express themselves and their feelings without needing to appear as heroic as *Harlan Miners Speak* or *New Masses* might have demanded. That Williams, who clearly was not a professional writer, recognized and responded appropriately to that forum speaks to the degree to which *Labor Defender* was identified with sentimentalism. That she was publishing alongside such writers as Michael Gold, John Dos Passos, and Theodore Dreiser speaks to the success with which the magazine created a space for the American literary Left to engage that sentimentalism.

NOTES

1. The conflation of sentimentalism and bourgeois values is not as self-evident from a Marxist perspective as it might appear at first. It is worth remembering that, in their *Manifesto of the Communist Party* (1848), Marx and Engels indicate that bourgeois society is itself antithetical to sentimentalism, claiming that "the bourgeoisie has torn away from the family its sentimental veil, and has reduced the family relation to a mere money relation" (476). As Gregg Crane notes, with its commitment to domestic rather than economic values, sentimental fiction shares with Marxism a tendency to critique "free market capitalism as the antithesis of compassion and permanent values" (111).

2. Indeed, Poole's *The Harbor* invokes the nineteenth-century sentimental tradition in its first chapter, which opens with the narrator attending a sermon of Henry Ward Beecher, the real-life brother of the author of *Uncle Tom's Cabin* (1852).

3. Notably, Gold still refused to reject sentimentalism outright in the later essay. He continued to assert that there were "many living forms" within the "new world of proletarian literature" (5). Realism, with its "technical precision," was only one; sentimentalism presumably remained another.

4. For an overview of the history of—and the interconnections between—these Leftist American magazines, see Walter Goldwater's *Radical Periodicals in America, 1890-1950: A Bibliography with Brief Notes*.

5. The ILD eventually became the Civil Rights Congress in 1946.

6. Richard H. Frost provides a comprehensive overview of Mooney's trial and imprisonment and of the efforts to release him in *The Mooney Case*.

7. In its use of photojournalism, *Labor Defender* was clearly indebted to *Soviet Russia Pictorial*, which had merged with *The Liberator* and *Labor Herald* to form *Workers Monthly* in 1924. Like the picture of Mooney in the October 1928 issue, however, most of the photographs appearing in *Labor Defender* were reprints. (Mooney's imprisonment—and thus his farewell to his mother—predated the existence of *Labor Defender* by nearly a decade.)

8. Mooney finally received a pardon in 1939, a little over a year after *Labor Defender* ceased publication.

9. Both the Harlan County War and the Scottsboro Boys' trials are far too complicated to summarize adequately here. For general introductions to these two events, please see John W. Hevener's *Which Side Are You On? The Harlan County Coal Miners, 1931-39* and Dan T. Carter's *Scottsboro: A Tragedy of the American South*, rev. ed.

10. According to the 1930 U.S. Census, African Americans made up only about nine percent of Harlan County's population (Hevener 3-4).

Works Cited

Brissenden, Paul Frederick. *The I.W.W.: A Study of American Syndicalism*. New York: Columbia University Press, 1919. *Studies in History, Economics and Public Law* 83.193. Print.
Cannon, James P. "The *Labor Defender* and the I.L.D." *Labor Defender* (January 1926): 7. Print.
Carter, Dan T. *Scottsboro: A Tragedy of the American South*. Rev. ed. Baton Rouge: Louisiana State University Press, 2007. Print.
Crane, Gregg. *The Cambridge Introduction to the Nineteenth-Century American Novel*. Cambridge: Cambridge University Press, 2007. Print.
Dos Passos, John. "The American Standard in the Mines." *Labor Defender* (December 1931): 234. Print.
———. "Scottsboro's Testimony." *Labor Defender* (July 1931): 131. Print.
Dreiser, Theodore. "Dreiser on Scottsboro." *Labor Defender* (June 1931): 108. Print.
———. "I Go to Harlan." *Labor Defender* (December 1931): 233. Print.
Dreiser, Theodore, et al. (National Committee for the Defense of Political Prisoners). *Harlan Miners Speak: Report on Terrorism in the Kentucky Coal Fields Prepared by Members of the National Committee for the Defense of Political Prisoners*. New York: Harcourt, Brace, 1932. Print.
———. "An Open Letter to the Governor of Alabama." *Labor Defender* (June 1931): 109. Print.
Farrell, James T. *A Note on Literary Criticism*. 1936. New York: Columbia University Press, 1992. Print.
Fisher, Philip. *Hard Facts: Setting and Form in the American Novel*. Oxford: Oxford University Press, 1985. Print.
Foley, Barbara. *Radical Representations: Politics and Form in U.S. Proletarian Fiction, 1929–1941*. Durham, NC: Duke University Press, 1993. Print.
Frost, Richard H. *The Mooney Case*. Stanford: Stanford University Press, 1968. Print.
Gold, Michael. "Go Left, Young Writers!" *New Masses* (January 1929): 3–4. Print.
———. "Greetings on May Day." *Labor Defender* (May 1928): 108. Print.
———. "Notes of the Month." *New Masses* (September 1930): 3–5. Print.
Goldwater, Walter. *Radical Periodicals in America, 1890–1950: A Bibliography with Brief Notes*. New Haven, NJ: Yale University Press, 1964. Print.
Gordon, Eugene. "Harlan and the Negro." *Labor Defender* (November 1931): 208, 221. Print.
Hart, James D., and Phillip W. Leininger. "Realism." *The Oxford Companion to American Literature*. 6th ed. New York: Oxford University Press, 1995. 552. Print.
Hevener, John W. *Which Side Are You On? The Harlan County Coal Miners, 1931–39*. Champaign: University of Illinois Press, 2002. Print.
The International Labor Defense (ILD). *Its Constitution and Organization Resolution*. New York: ILD, 1929. Print.
Karsner, Rose. "The Conviction of Sam Bonita in the Anthracite Frame-up." *Labor Defender* (May 1928): 100–01. Print.
Latham, Sean, and Robert Scholes. "The Rise of Periodical Studies." *PMLA* 121.2 (2006): 517–31. Print.
Marx, Karl, and Friedrich Engels. *Manifesto of the Communist Party*. 1848. In *The Marx-Engels Reader*. 2nd ed. Ed. Robert C. Tucker. New York: W.W. Norton, 1978. 469–500. Print.
McKay, Claude. *A Long Way from Home*. 1937. Ed. Gene Andrew Jarrett. New Brunswick, NJ: Rutgers University Press, 2007. Print.
Mooney, Tom. "The Prison Hell-hole of California." *Labor Defender* (January 1929): 6, 16. Print.

Morrisson, Mark S. *The Public Face of Modernism: Little Magazines, Audiences, and Reception, 1905–1920.* Madison: University of Wisconsin Press, 2000. Print.

North, Joseph. "The Bended Knee or Clenched Fist? Mooney—Harlan—Scottsboro." *Labor Defender* (November 1931): 210–11, 221. Print.

Rabinowitz, Paula. *Labor and Desire: Women's Revolutionary Fiction in Depression America.* Chapel Hill: University of North Carolina Press, 1991. Print.

Rideout, Walter B. *The Radical Novel in the United States, 1900–1954.* Cambridge, MA: Harvard University Press, 1956. Print.

Sinclair, Upton. "California: Land of Orange Groves and the Frame-up." *Labor Defender* (October 1928): 203. Print.

Wanzo, Rebecca. *The Suffering Will Not Be Televised: African American Women and Sentimental Political Storytelling.* Albany: SUNY Press, 2009. Print.

Williams, Mamie. "Voices from Prison." *Labor Defender* (July 1937): 19. Print.

The research necessary for completing this essay was supported by a 2012 Wolfsonian Infusion Grant, which was made possible with funding provided by the Andrew W. Mellon Foundation. I wish to thank the staff of The Wolfsonian Museum in Miami Beach, Florida, for granting me access to many of the periodicals I discuss in this essay, including the issues of Labor Defender *from which the images in Figures 1, 3, 4, and 5 are taken. I am particularly grateful to Frank Luca, Nicolae Harsanyi, and Jon Mogul for their assistance.*

"You give a damn about so many things I don't"

Hemingway's Gendered Sentimentalism in "The Snows of Kilimanjaro" and "The Short, Happy Life of Francis Macomber"

Michael T. Wilson

From its inception, modernist fiction has been framed in opposition to the sentimental fiction which came before it and which formed a large part of popular reading tastes. Scholars have both affirmed this interpretation of the modernist paradigm and complicated and revised it. As Thomas Strychacz observes, the modernist aesthetic joined style to gender and

> depended on aligning narrative strategies of omission with what seemed to be typically masculine virtues of emotional restraint [...]. [E]motion might be thought of as being submerged, iceberg-like, beneath the surface of the text, invisible, potent, leaving on display only those actions that are, in Ezra Pound's assessment of the Modernist response to Victorian poetics, "austere, direct, free from emotional slither" [21].

Modernists, in Strychacz's estimation, worked "to curtail Victorian sentimentalism and to trim the rhetorical excess they saw as its aesthetic sign" (22). Greg Forter echoes this idea with particular emphasis on Ernest Hemingway as a modernist intensely bent upon conveying a given set of values through style, noting that "these modernists often honed their styles as weapons against the perceived effeminacy of affect and emotional effusiveness" (34).

As more recent scholarship has noticed, however, this oppositional stance presented modernist writers with a considerable challenge, particularly for writers like Hemingway who focused on the yoke between, as Hemingway himself phrased it in 1932's *Death in the Afternoon*, "what really happened in action" and "the real thing, the sequence of motion and fact which made the emotion" (Strychacz 15). As Hemingway's statement of artistic intent might suggest, the sentimentalists and Hemingway had, in fact, a great deal in common. Perhaps most fundamentally, they both sought to convey strong emotional states to their reader, but there were other parallels as well, notably in the way that both embedded within their fiction a code for life. As Janice Todd notes of sensibility and its later development into sentimentalism these movements "initially showed people how to behave, how to express themselves in friendship and how to respond decently to life's experiences [before coming to pride themselves] more on making their readers weep and in teaching them when and how much to weep" (4).

It might then be usefully argued that Hemingway renews the didactic root of sentimentalism. He does so by valorizing a code for life in which rigorous, masculinized self-control is the ideal. His male protagonists struggle to attain this ideal in a way that moves them away from sentimentalism's "affective bonds" toward the opposite sex because the men fear that those bonds represent possibly wounding liabilities. At the same time, his male characters are drawn to those bonds in a way that clearly reflects Hemingway's entanglements between his own anti-sentimental artistic intentions and the conventions and concerns of that older literary tradition. As Leonard Cassuto notes in his study of the "hard-boiled fiction" which largely took a flattened version of Hemingway's own aesthetics as its template, "Inside every [hard-boiled] story is a sentimental narrative that's trying to come out" (7). Scholarship has increasingly focused on the ways in which that stylistic element of submerged gender may reflect an androgynous trope within Hemingway's work and life; in Forter's estimation,

> we have learned that manhood was for him a fraught and always fragile aspiration rather than an accomplished fact. For many of us, this has meant that what seems most moving in Hemingway now is his persistent struggle, against enormous psychic odds, to resist his ossification into a man whose gynophobic self-loathing leads him to despise all feminine "softness"—both within and without him [22].

The complex models by which Hemingway responded to the entanglement of gender, modernism, anti-sentimentalism and the tropes, conventions, and concerns of sentimentalism will be the focus of the remainder of this essay.

Two of Hemingway's most famous short stories, 1935's "The Short Happy Life of Francis Macomber" and "The Snows of Kilimanjaro," offer clear but distinct examples of Hemingway's models of adaptation between sentimentalism and modernism. In "Short Happy Life," Francis Macomber is cast initially as the sentimental heroine, defined by suffering and a complete lack of agency and autonomy, but re-gendered as male. Readers are invited to respond sympathetically to his emotional transformation, only to have their emotional investment in his triumph rebuffed by his immediately subsequent violent death in what becomes an attack on the sentimental reader as much as the idea of the sentimental heroine herself. The other primary characters in the story, "white hunter" Wilson and Macomber's wife Margot, serve to delineate the contours of Hemingway's adaptation of the sentimental model to modernist paradigms. "The Snows of Kilimanjaro" offers perhaps an even more complex entanglement of sentimentalism and modernism, since the narrative encourages readers both to condemn its sentimental protagonist, the dying writer Harry, on the grounds of his brutal emotional outbursts and self-pity and to sympathize with him at the same time, in a way and to an extent that we are not encouraged to feel toward Francis Macomber in his "Short Happy Life."

Hemingway's negotiation between sentimentalism and modernism in "The Short Happy Life of Francis Macomber" quickly moves into focus as Macomber's wife Margot parodies the sentimental heroine. In the story, Francis Macomber, an American on a big game safari, panics in the face of a wounded lion he has shot ineptly. His wife scorns his apparent cowardice, and Francis himself persists in examining the moment aloud, breaking the masculine code of silence about failure and embarrassing their "white hunter," Wilson. Margot then goes a step further, cuckolding her husband in their camp by slipping out to Wilson's tent in the night, not even attempting to conceal her adultery from Francis when she returns. The next day, however, Macomber seems to recover his courage, and this new confidence deeply disturbs Margot, who attempts to shake it and return to her dominant place in their relationship. Macomber refuses to be subordinated again, however, and his water buffalo hunt goes forward, enlisting even Wilson's reluctant empathy for Macomber's newfound courage. When a wounded water buffalo charges, Macomber kills it but is killed himself by a possibly intentional shot from Margot, who then falls weeping to the ground only to be scorned by Wilson.

In an early flashback to a conversation with her husband, Margot delineates the anxiety that leads up to his moment of cowardice, presenting the modernist aesthetic of stoicism under the guise of sentimental spousal advice and encouragement:

"Hearing the thing roar gets on my nerves."
"Well then, as Wilson said, kill him and stop his roaring."
"Yes, darling," said Francis Macomber. "It sounds easy, doesn't it?" [12]

Margot then pushes her husband to reveal his innermost emotions, cloaking her antagonism toward him in a cloud of wifely concern and satirizing sentimentalism's persistent attraction toward strong emotion and transparency of character: "You're not afraid, are you?" "Of course not. But I'm nervous from hearing him roar all night" (12). Having forced Macomber to lie explicitly— to be insincere in expressing his own emotions rather than reveal his own fear—Margot responds with effusive false emotion and certainty herself: "You'll kill him marvelously," she said. "I know you will. I'm awfully anxious to see it" (12). When Francis has turned and fled from the charging lion that he has shamefully and incompetently gut-shot, though, Margot rubs his nose in his failure by kissing Wilson in front of him, leaning over the back edge of the front seat to do so (17).

As Frances Kerr observes of modernism and the politics of emotion, "to lose control of one's woman or one's inner emotions in the presence of others is to risk losing one's masculinity," and Margot clearly places Macomber in this position of risk (410). She swings between effusing sentimentally about her (ironically) emasculating modernist emotions and goading her husband about his own lack of emotional self-control. In doing so, she acts herself, just as Wilson does from different motives, as a modernist brake on Macomber's sentimentalist tendencies, couching her criticism within her own ironic use of affectionate and emasculating terms: "If you make a scene I'll leave you, darling [...]. [Y]ou'll behave yourself" (20).

Margot thus combines the story's critique of the traditionally emotional female characters of sentimentalism with an even harsher critique of the "Modern Woman" (circa 1935), who is "enameled in that American female cruelty" (9) and who acts to enforce modernism's "typically masculine virtues of emotional restraint," a role for which she is actually criticized within the story despite its general ethos in favor of that restraint (Strychacz 21). From the story's perspective of Margot as "castrating wife," she may even be seen as the story's strongest example of modernism itself, or at least the way that modernism flexed itself in response to its perceptions of modern life; as Forter notes, modernist "writers pay homage to a type of virility that they argue is at once the best version of manhood and something that can no longer be socially incarnated—that cannot withstand the onslaught of a destructive and emasculating modernity" (25). Within the story's framework of masculinity as the self-control of emotions, Macomber's own cowardice (or, to put it another way, his entirely reasonable fear of a large nearby predator that could kill him) and Margot's scorn act in concert to form that "destructive and emasculating" presence, but only Margot represents the collapse of older traditions in a way that signals modernity. In that context, Margot is the story's fiercest exponent of modernism, and the story's criticism of her seems to reflect Hemingway's own ambivalent feelings about the ways in which modernism might revise traditional gender roles, particularly the female.

While Margot expresses her modernism as waves of scorn, Macomber does not succumb to her critique. Even after his epiphany-in-action, after he discovers his own capacity for courage in the immediate excitement of chasing the water buffalo, Macomber does not suppress his sentimental effusion of emotion with the self-restraint of modernism, but merely replaces the emasculating emotion of uncontrollable fear with elation at his own courage and "pure excitement" from the chase (25). As Forter notes, "Hemingway's inability to relinquish either male sentiment or male power [was] intimately connected with the meaning of his modernism" (27). When Macomber begins to express his newfound courage at some length, Wilson responds with careful logical evaluation: "Wilson looked at him appraisingly. Damned if this isn't a strange one, he thought. Yesterday he's scared sick and today he's a ruddy fire eater" (25). Macomber's emotional volatility arouses Wilson's sympathy and his concern and censorship over his client's garrulous self-examination. Interestingly, Macomber's reaction both evokes and somewhat refutes other critics of Hemingway's modernist, masculinist code. J. Donald Adams, an exact contemporary of Hemingway's, argued in 1939 that modernist arguments against an open display of emotion constituted a weakness in the writer's fiction: "Hemingway's men and women are never deeply stirred, they are never moved, they are never touched by aspiration, except in so far as such emotions can be the product of physical desire or satisfaction" (90). Macomber's elation is clearly deep emotion, and seems prompted by physical satisfaction in the face of danger, but nonetheless reflects inner psychological accomplishment. He displays the complexity of Hemingway's models of entangled sentimentalism and modernism, where modernism's control is repeatedly broken by sentimentalist eruptions, a sequence which calls attention to the alleged virtues of the former but nonetheless attests to the lasting power and influence of the latter as a trope in his fiction.

Although Macomber's elation is based on the experience of violent action, it's also clearly grounded in Macomber's sense of his own self-worth as a man within Hemingway's "heroic code" of "grace under pressure." Indeed, Macomber's reaction to the sudden self-awareness of his capacity for physical courage—truly, his self-salvation—seems precisely like that of a sentimental protagonist reaching a climactic self-revelation:

> Perhaps more than any other single factor, sentimental novels are defined by their depiction of the conversion moment, the moment when a flood of emotion transforms the individual, revealing moral truths and human connections previously

ignored by or invisible to the convert [...]. This emotional rush reveals the existence of a better, more caring self, and offers direct access to the values that give life meaning [Crane 104].

Macomber's own revealed existence is intensely narcissistic but otherwise clearly parallels the sentimentalist conversion experience.

Macomber's epiphany is not solitary, as might be expected from modernism's emphasis on "a celebration of masculine detachment" (Forter 7). Instead, he first attempts to reconnect to his wife and then, when she rebuffs him, to express his conversion experience to a fellow man, Wilson, who he also views as the proper judge for such emotions:

> "You know I don't think I'd ever be afraid of anything again," Macomber said to Wilson. "Something happened in me after we first saw the buff and started after him. Like a dam bursting. It was pure excitement."
> "Cleans out your liver," said Wilson. "Damn funny things happen to people."
> Macomber's face was shining. "You know something did happen to me," he said. "I feel absolutely different" [25].

Macomber's "shining face" evokes Crane's argument that "the plot of the sentimental novel is organized around the main character's reversal of spiritual fortunes (a reversal which often has material and social aspects as well)" as well as his assertion that "the idealism of sentimental fiction, its belief in absolute and fixed values, is reflected in the unambiguous nature of its characters—their relative transparency and typicality" (112). Macomber's emotions here are clearly conveyed in such a transparent fashion, reinforcing the impression that he operates in the same rhetorical space as the classic heroine of sentimental fiction.

Macomber's transformation, gleaming transparently through his face as well as his words, provokes a similar emotional response in Wilson that the hunter struggles to control in order to sustain the modernist, masculinist code. His struggle is reflected in the staccato language with which he recounts his emotion:

> "That's it," said Wilson. "Worst one can do is kill you. How does it go? Shakespeare. Damned good. See if I can remember. Oh, damned good. Used to quote it to myself at one time. Let's see. 'By my troth, I care not; a man can die but once; we owe God a death and let it go which way it will, he that dies this year is quit for the next.' Damned fine, eh?"
> He was very embarrassed, having brought out this thing he lived by, but he had seen men come of age before and it always moved him. It was not a matter of their twenty-first birthday [25].

Wilson seems embarrassed, not by his own emotional response, but rather by his public expression of it. Yet, why did men coming of age "always" move him emotionally, and at the risk of sentimentality? As Forter observes, Hemingway was unwilling to sever male characters from their emotional responses entirely, even while his modernist tendencies, as expressed in the masculine taciturnity that Susan F. Beegel terms "the soul of the Hemingway style" (537), were to constrain them: "Hemingway also felt this cauterization [a 'modernist cauterization of affect'] as a devastating loss to the capacity for creative living and self-making" (27–8). As the only truly "peer" male witness (with the African "boys" disqualified on the story's own racial grounds), Wilson's suppressed emotions are clearly intended to evoke something like those same feelings in audineces, recalling sentimentalism's "emphasis [...] on the communication of common feeling from sufferer or watcher to reader or audience" (Todd 4).

As the entanglement of sentimentalism and modernism continues to grow stronger in the story, it does so in a way that subtly favors modernism's tropes, but nonetheless fails to contain the former. Wilson observes of Macomber that the "Beggar had probably been afraid all his life. Don't know what started it. But over now. Hadn't had time to be afraid with the buff. That and being angry too. Motor car too. Motor cars made it familiar" (26). Wilson cannily observes that courage, like cowardice, is partially inherent and partially situational and that reactions in either direction depend to some extent on factors beyond one's control. The story thus seems to modernize sentimentalism's insistence on internal truth and character. As Crane argues, for the sentimental heroine, "the key to these young women's triumphs lies in their achievement of self-mastery" (113).

In Wilson's estimation, this mastery proves that Macomber will "Be a damn fire eater now. He'd seen it in the war work the same way. More of a change than any loss of virginity" (26). The true emotional transformation of a man is thus not a sexual one and thus (in the dominant heterosexual paradigm of the male modernists) is entirely out of the controlling sphere of a woman. Instead, violence and the male reaction to it determine the largest emotional change that is possible for a man, a stark revision of the core of the sentimental transformation. This equation directly contradicts the sentimental protagonist's key transformative experience; as Cindy Weinstein notes, "Marriage is the only acceptable conclusion for sentimental novels," yet, the destruction of the Macombers' marriage evokes modernism's emphasis on the fragmentation of tradition (216).

The narrative positions Wilson, the code-speaker, to bring Macomber back from his epiphanic euphoria: "'You're not supposed to mention it,' Wilson said, looking in the other's face. 'Much more fashionable to say you're scared. Mind you, you'll be scared too, plenty of times'" (26). Sincere emotional expression is *fashionable*, not authentic. Wilson here attempts to steer

Macomber back to external stoicism, lest he become effusively emotional about his new feelings; indeed, if the story is to remain somewhat contained within Hemingway's coded version of modernism and to resist sentimentalism, Wilson's tutelage is necessary, given the intensely melodramatic (hence sentimentalized) nature of Macomber's remasculinization: discovering courage in the face of a giant animal that can kill you is surely an archaic and exceptional event in modern life.

Despite Wilson's instruction, Macomber persists, as intent on exploring his emotions and expressing them freely as a brave man as he was when a coward: "But you have a feeling of happiness about action to come?" (26). Macomber seems to want to force Wilson into a revelation of the hunter's own feelings, to force Wilson into a sentimental posture as well, pushing "the parallel between his or her experience and that of another" or, as Braudy notes, embracing "an emotional and philosophical ethos that celebrates human connection, both personal and communal" (5).

Macomber's triumph is personal, but he attempts to understand its contours and celebrate it communally with the only other relevant (i.e., white) man present. Wilson answers: "Yes [...] There's that. Doesn't do to talk too much about all this. Talk the whole thing away. No pleasure in anything if you mouth it up too much" (26). Wilson places genuine emotional transformation in sharp opposition to *talking* about the transformation; the moment remains authentic only because it is contained by self-control—the flood of effusive emotion that Macomber is feeling must be controlled in the same fashion as his earlier fear. Like Hemingway's valuation of male courage as an unchanging ideal, "the religious and emotional ideals of the sentimental novel are static and unchanging, and the typical sentimental novel's protagonist seeks a kind of spiritual and emotional calm by faithfully adhering to these moral absolutes" (Crane 110). Unlike Wilson's sympathetic response, Margot's last words to her husband are still scornful, rejecting any possibility of communal inclusion in his emotion or his transformation and, significantly, rejecting even Wilson's moral instruction as itself emotionally self-indulgent and effusive:

> "You're both talking rot," said Margot. "Just because you've chased some helpless animals in a motor car you talk like heroes."
> "Sorry," said Wilson. "I have been gassing too much." She's worried about it already, he thought [26].

Wilson speculates that Margaret Macomber fears losing her dominant position in her marriage if her husband becomes courageous and self-controlled; exercising that power is her only happiness, although "the way they were together now was no one person's fault" (26). Earlier, Wilson had said to Macomber, "Why not order her to stay in camp?" and Macomber replied, "You order her"

(19), but now Macomber moves immediately to extend control over her as well, or at least to enforce the boundaries of his own new self-respect: "If you don't know what we're talking about why not keep out of it?" (26). Macomber seems to assume here that his wife can't understand the nature of his transformation from a coward into a "hero," removing that experience further from the world of women.

Margot plays a key role in the famous shooting which ends the story and also leaves its entanglement with sentimentalism strongly foregrounded. As Hemingway phrases it, the shooting is clearly an accident, since "Mrs. Macomber, in the car, had shot at the buffalo" (28). Wilson, however, is coldly furious; his emotional investment in Macomber's transformation has been violently and abruptly cut short: "I was a little angry. I'd begun to like your husband" (28). His response to Macomber's death, and to his truncated feelings, is scornful anger that closely echoes the way Margot had excoriated her husband's cowardice earlier: "That was a pretty thing to do [...]. He would have left you too [...]. Why didn't you poison him? That's what they do in England" (28). In the face of what the narrative seems to depict as either female incompetence or malice, and within the context of her previous reaction to her husband's suffering—a reaction that had fully embraced the most stringent version of the modernist reaction against the sentimental—Margot is finally pushed into her final, seemingly "normal" sentimental response to her accidental homicide, that of "crying hysterically" (28). Wilson, who has begun to forge modernism's male-to-male adaptation of the traditional sentimental bond, not with Margot, his casual sexual partner, but with her cuckolded husband, forces her to beg him before he will stop his own angry, emotional outbursts: "Stop it. Stop it. Stop it," she cries out (28). Margot, earlier critiqued by the story as a castrating modern woman, is finally judged as a failure on the grounds that her sentimental emotion is itself insincere. Only then does Wilson return to his own position within modernism's taciturnity: "Please is much better. Now I'll stop" (28). Emotion has thus coursed between arcs of modernist control and sentimentally free expression in the story but closes on what seems intended as a reification of the modernist ethos as the story finally works to contain the elements of sentimentalism that it has extensively used to engage and position readers.

In the end, the strongest emotional camaraderie has been between the two men as they struggle together to express and then ultimately to contain the sentimentalist effusion accompanying Macomber's transformation from cowardice to bravery. This structure first echoes sentimentalism's traditional desire to create sympathy through "an overwhelming emotional reaction" and then moves decisively against the expression of that reaction as a gender transgression (Crane 104). In much the same fashion, the story first encourages the reader to invest emotionally in Macomber's changes in a way that mirrors Wilson's own investment and then destroys him in a melodramatic moment that both invites the reader to an emotional catharsis and tamps it down at the same time, with even the flattened language of the moment echoing the lines of Wilson's own guidelines about the dangers of emotional speech: "he felt a sudden white-hot, blinding flash explode inside his head and that was all he ever felt" (27). Hemingway's narrative thus engages with—and rather fully implements—several of the core elements of sentimental fiction. It even links sentimentalism's "idealistic conception of absolute and fixed values" with a romantic attachment to the idea of male courage before the story's paradoxical conclusion. The conclusion wraps the story's sentimentalist core within a modernist framework that this core repeatedly threatens to escape, and it does so by both taking advantage of Macomber's death as emotional catharsis and by simultaneously moving away from that catharsis in an attempt to sever any ties to the sentimental implications of the emotions in the story. Elizabeth Maddock Dillon's definition of sentimentalism as affirming "one's own self-definition of a personhood grounded in integrity and personal convictions" and producing "a strong sense of subjective identity" is quite clearly present in Macomber's still-progressing attempt to contain his sentimental transformation within the coded boundaries of modernism in much the same sense that the story itself attempts to contain the sentimental aspects of Macomber himself (16).

"The Snows of Kilimanjaro," by contrast, collapses Macomber, the sentimental hero in transformation, and Wilson, the teacher of modernism's code of self-restraint, into the single figure of the semi-autobiographical protagonist, Harry, alternately prone to emotional outbursts and attempts to control those eruptions. His strongest emotions are reserved for himself. Just as Margot judges Macomber's lack of self-control as unmanly, Harry's wife Helen also objects to his emotional outpourings but does so largely within the context of craving a different sort of sentiment instead—one that reaffirms rather than damages or destroys their supposedly happy marriage. Both women, accordingly, voice elements of the codes of modernism but are firmly placed in a sentimental version of traditional gender roles by the end of their stories. Harry himself, sentimentally attached to the stories he will never now be able to tell and to the memories that lie behind them rather than to his wife, calls to mind Suzanne Clark's observation that in modernism "the adoration of the angel in the house became the adoration of [...] texts" (7).

Just as "The Short Happy Life of Francis Macomber" begins with the characters "pretending that nothing had happened" (5), "The Snows of

Kilimanjaro" starts with a note of deeply suppressed emotion channeled as a self-restrained masculine performance of modernism's stoicism. As the story begins, Harry, an American writer who has taken his rich wife on safari in Africa in an attempt to recover his writing prowess, is dying of a gangrenous thorn scratch. Attended by his wife and the safari staff, he will be unable to return to civilization for treatment unless a plane arrives in time. Forced into painful introspection about his past willingness to trade his commitment to authentic writing for the luxurious life made possible by a succession of ever-wealthier wives, Harry alternately lashes out at his long-suffering wife for his failures and recalls his past in a series of evocative passages meant to convey his true potential as a writer. In the story's famous final passage, Harry dreams that the plane has arrived, but the flight turns toward the snowy peak of Mt. Kilimanjaro as Harry's wife awakes to find him dead.

Seemingly dispassionate at the beginning, Harry observes of his impending death by blood-poisoning: "The marvelous thing is that it's painless [...]. That's how you know when it starts." Harry's wife responds with a note of self-restraint that matches his tone: "Is it really?" (39). The story's opening is thus fully embedded within modernism's entrenchment against sentimentalism. This resistance to emotion is quickly complicated, however, by Harry's attempts to provoke his wife into an emotional response. When his wife offers to read to him to help pass the time, Harry answers, "I can't listen to it [...] Talking is the easiest. We quarrel and that makes the time pass" (40). His wife, in every way the direct opposite of Margot Macomber in appeasing rather than attacking her husband, attempts to conciliate him: "I don't quarrel. I never want to quarrel. Let's not quarrel any more. No matter how nervous we get. Maybe they will be back with another truck today. Maybe the plane will come" (40).

With these placating comments, Helen goes directly to the depths of her husband's emotional outbursts and irritability, his fear of death, and strips him of his attempt to recast sentimental self-pity as righteous accusation. When she suggests moving him for the sake of his leg, Harry says, "I don't want to move [...]. There is no sense in moving now except to make it easier for you" (40). Despite the story grounding her largely in traditional wifely emotions, Helen responds to her husband's petulant outburst with a statement that echoes the persistent threat that Margot represents: "That's cowardly" (40). Again Harry evades the direct attack as best he can: "Can't you let a man die as comfortably as he can without calling him names? What's the use of slanging me?" (40). Harry's attempt to redefine his anxieties as a concern with "dying comfortably," removing them from any taint of sentimentalism, is echoed by the very non-melodramatic cause of his impending death: he is dying as the result of an infected scratch from a thorn bush, rather than being trampled by a charging buffalo, torn apart by a wounded lion, or shot in the head by his wife.

The story's complexity of tone regarding Harry, particularly his own sense of wasted potential, complicates a reading of this initial scene. As an artist, his italicized "writing sample" passages of memory convey a sense that he is a powerful writer, and so readers are encouraged to temper their reactions against his self-pity with sympathy for what might have been a great talent. The audience is essentially being edged, albeit with a sense of narrative ambivalence, into the sort of intimate reader-to-character emotional relationship that sentimentalism took among its highest goals. On one level, Harry seems a sentimental protagonist because he vents his emotions so freely. Unlike Macomber at the beginning of his story, Harry's suffering, more physical than emotional, does not serve to define and transgender him within that sentimental context since he insists from his opening words on claiming agency for himself.

Harry also models the sentimental hero in the process of redeeming himself, although with an emphasis on modernism's (and Hemingway's modernism in particular) idea of authenticity. This entanglement is visible even in his savage attempts to force Helen toward "honesty" in admitting their marriage is a sham. He thus prioritizes emotional truth as the highest virtue, particularly above compassion. At the same time, Harry's sentimentalism ultimately serves to indulge his deep self-pity. He laments that "Now he would never write the things he had saved to write until he knew enough to write them well. Well, he would not have to fail at trying to write them, either" (41). Harry repeatedly loops through sentimentalizing his past and then forcing it into a semblance of stoicism.

One strong example of this recursive loop of sentimental eruption and modernist suppression occurs in Harry's first italicized "memory." When "Barker" comes back from machine-gunning a trainload of Austrian officers on leave to tell how they fled before him, the mess hall grows quiet and someone curses him with "You bloody murderous bastard," shutting down both Barker's sadistic boasting and any other emotional response to that boasting (42). Half a page later, though, Harry simply—and with no sense of self-awareness—recapitulates Barker's sadism with his own, telling Helen, "All right then. I'll go on hurting you. It's more amusing. The only thing I ever really liked to do with you I can't do now" (43). Harry's desire not only to mourn his own death but also to strip it of any emotional connection with or resonance for his wife results in of the story's most famous lines: "Love is a dunghill [...]. And I'm the cock that gets on it to crow" (43). In a swift double-reversal that illustrates either his conscious cruelty or emotional volatility, or possibly both, he then "slip[s] into the familiar lie he made his bread and butter by" as he tells her that he's "crazy as a coot" and that "I love you, really." He calls her a "rich bitch," ironically aggrandizing his oratorical spite and self-disgust as art because he's "full of poetry now. Rot and poetry. Rotten poetry" (43). Harry veers between trying to force Helen to respond to and acknowledge his emotional revelations in a cruel parody of sentimentalism and defusing them with a false effusion of emotion in order to protect his own narcissistic (and modernist) emotional boundaries.

Harry repeatedly combines sentimentalism about his own death with attempts to deny that sentimentalism and its ethos. After he naps into the evening, Harry thinks to himself, in a passage illustrating both his self-pity and premature willingness to be dead, "It was not her fault that when he went to her he was already over. How could a woman know that you meant nothing that you said; that you spoke only from habit and to be comfortable?" (44). Harry thus strikes at the heart of sentimentalism—verbal expression as emotional sincerity—and yet the narrative around him operates in a more complicated way, given its own apparent judgment on Harry as a failed writer who has bargained his sincerity for comfort and leisure.

Harry then goes one step further, indicting the failure of women, the traditional producers and consumers of sentimentalism, to detect insincere emotion; even more damning, they seem to exhibit a preference for it: "After he no longer meant what he said, his lies were more successful with women than when he had told them the truth" (44). Harry is certain that his current wife is a perfect example of this fundamental female failure: "It was strange that when he did not love her at all and was lying, that he should be able to give her more for her money than when he had really loved" (45). Throughout the story, it is made repeatedly clear that Helen prefers an insincere but palatable expression of emotion to the spiteful truths that Harry keeps insisting on expressing as moral beacons testifying to his impending death. Hemingway thus stages a directly inverted depiction of the sentimental death scene as an affirmation of conventional Christian morality and a celebration of familial devotion.

Harry's plan to "work the fat off his soul" and return to writing authentically, which has led him to his doom in Africa, also begs the question of whether such a plan could ever have succeeded while he remained in a compromised and insincere relationship with his wealthy wife. Their marriage is insincere because of his emotional compromises and, as he views it, because of the "steps by which she acquired him and the way in which she had finally fallen in love with him," a procedural rather than romanticized notion of love (44). The narrative thus seems to join the idea of Harry's goal, writing authentically, with the sincere expression of emotion rather than with Harry's past deceptions or his wife's self-machinations; yet, it also repeatedly attempts to strip them of their sentimental implications. Harry is clearly torn between the urge to freely express his emotion about his impending death and his sense that he has wasted his talent and the modernist code that urges him to practice masculinity through emotional self-restraint. Hemingway's narrative compromises accordingly in a way that attempts to favor modernism's ethos over sentimentalism's by limiting Harry's positive emotional bonds to his own memories rather than to Helen or any other person and watching him release the psychological pressure created by revisiting those memories at the point of death by savaging his hapless wife. The final effect is to displace sentimentalism's emphasis on love and compassion with modernism's self-created sense of male autonomy, but the very act of doing so serves to emphasize precisely those emotions which are being displaced, reinforcing the entanglement of modernism and sentimentalism.

Even Harry's attempts to salve and suppress Helen's reactions to his words reflect an attempt to reorder sentimental emotions within modernist boundaries. Harry repeatedly expresses a constrained sort of praise for his wife in his words to her: "You shoot marvelously" (46) he admits, and tells her that he would "like to destroy [her] a few times in bed," following her choice of "destruction" as a term for his earlier verbal attacks (47). "You're a fine woman," he tells her, "Don't pay any attention to me" (49). Harry, in short, pays lip service to an idea of sentimentalized love that centers around the idea of communal emotions and compassion, but solely in order to give himself a space of relative peace for self-reflection. He never, however, tells her again that he loves her, leaving that idea buried under the curse, "you rich bitch" (43). In a sense, this decisive movement against love is an intensely modernist idea, anchoring Harry firmly within self-autonomy, modernism's attempt to avoid "the 'sloppy sentimentality' of direct emotional expression" (Forter 34) and within its "reversal of values which emphasized erotic desire, not love" (Clark 1).

Harry's meager emotional connections to his wife are similarly qualified and compromised by his external stoicism and internal emphasis on his own emotional drama, itself conflicted by loops of sentimentalism and self-control. The praise for his wife that Harry seems almost enthusiastically detailed about is that she is good in bed, although not, alas, terribly good looking; but she is still a "good-looking woman" with a "pleasant body" who "had a great talent and appreciation for the bed," "not pretty, but he liked her face" (45). Even on this score, he is equivocal: "he would as soon be in bed with her as any one" (45). His deathbed decision to dampen his criticism of her many failures at enabling him to become a more authentic writer seems to derive from his praise of her negative virtue: "she never made scenes" (46). Even his apparent compassion seems linked to his own self-pity over his impending death: "he would rather be in better company" (53), but "the one experience that he had never had he was not going to spoil now [although] he probably would" (50). Within a single sentence, Harry expresses a sentimental hope for potential transformation, only to immediately quash that hope with his own deep cynicism.

Perhaps the story's strongest expression of the code of modernism is Harry's utter unwillingness to express an inauthentic emotion by claiming he loves his wife when he does not or, less charitably, his unwillingness to continue any affective bonds with others in the approach of his own death. In all these ways, Harry's refusal to allow his wife "into" his emotional state about his death constitutes a rebuff of sentimentalism's "emotional and philosophical ethos that celebrates human connection, both personal and communal, and acknowledges the shared devastation of affectional loss" (Braudy 5). For Harry, the loss is intensely and completely personal; he never once considers the after effects of his death on his wife. His last words directly to his wife are "Christ [...]. How little a woman knows. What is that? Your intuition?" (54).

Harry's wife, on the other hand, although serving as a voice for modernism's code by repeatedly denying his impending death and thus pushing him to suppress his own emotions about dying, seems the very epitome of the long-suffering sentimental "type." Harry interprets her emotions as being "relatively transparent" in just the way that Crane describes those of sentimental characters (110), and she seems very much that classic sentimental character: the defenseless, long-suffering woman who can only make emotional appeals for sympathy from the midst of her suffering and who has already been "destroyed two or three times" by deaths. She laments, "You wouldn't want to destroy me again, would you?" (47). As Crane notes of sentimentalism's heroines, Harry's wife can only resort to "entreaty and moral suasion" (116). As such, Harry's scorn of her emotionalism conveys the narrative's rebuke of sentimentalism. At the same time, however, to the extent that the narrative embodies an ironic skepticism toward Harry himself and toward what seem clearly presented as his cruel comments to a woman who loves him, the reader is invited to reconsider that rebuke of sentimentalism in the light of his or her own sympathy for Harry's wife and engagement with her feelings.

In the end, then, if Harry constitutes to some degree Hemingway's critique of himself, as is frequently suggested—a reading strengthened by Hemingway's own claim that he "never wrote so directly about myself as in that story"—then the nature of Harry's death surely reflects Hemingway's own complex feelings about sentimentalism (Hotchner 162). In "Snows," as in "Short Happy Life," Hemingway either cannot separate his model of modernism from its sentimental implications or chooses not to do so, perhaps in order to take advantage of the range of reader response that sentimentalism was widely, if pejoratively, viewed as making available to an author. Consciously or unconsciously, combining the two models allowed him to espouse his code of modernism while at the same time drawing upon the emotional power of sentimentalism's older traditions and enlisting them in support of his male characters.

Hemingway scholars through the early 1970s largely judged such entanglements with sentimentalism on Hemingway's part as aesthetic failures by the terms of his own (and modernism's) standards. Regarding a story like the potentially very sentimental "A Day's Wait," in which a boy waits stoically for his own death, Grebstein argues that "Hemingway handles a potentially sentimental situation without expressing feeling in overt terms and without calling directly upon the reader's sense of pathos" (qtd. in Beegel 537). Wilson's bursts of emotion in "Short Happy Life" would seem to place that story in a more sentimental category, since Wilson clearly stands in for the reader in his sympathy for Macomber, while at the same time serving to school both Macomber and the reader in the ways in which that sympathy can legitimately be expressed.

Instead, it can be suggested that "Short Happy Life" presents a remarkably effective model of the ways in which the entanglement of sentimentalism with Hemingway's own codified modernist reaction to it could create their own sort of energy, precisely by first engaging and then frustrating the reader's emotions in the same way that sentimentalism frequently, as Herbert Ross Brown observes, presented characters and readers with "the almost consummation of their wishes" after "a pitiless succession of exquisite 'might-have-beens'" (173). In contrast, fiction that perfectly expressed modernism's ethos of emotional suppression—as encapsulated in Hemingway's "iceberg theory" in which "an economy of narrative information allows the reader to infer [...] emotional complexities" (Strychaz 15)—would ultimately founder on the shores of pure experimentalism in what Forter terms "Hemingway's proclivity toward the coldly dehumanized and austere" (30). Both "The Short Happy Life of Francis Macomber" and "The Snows of Kilimanjaro," then, serve as examples of the ways in which popular modernism "failed," ultimately, to disentangle itself from sentimentalism.

At the same time, however, both stories succeeded far more significantly in terms of their continued appeal to readers less concerned with the purity of literary technique than with their own response to what Hemingway's ongoing dialectic between the two schools of literary thought produced in his own fiction. If his fiction blurred the lines of his own often-pronounced standards of writing—standards paralleling modernism's focus on those "typically masculine virtues of emotional restraint"—it often did so in ways that actually heightened its emotional appeal, or at any rate its emotional effect, on his reading audience—then and now. Where both relentless stoicism and constant outbursts of emotional expression surely pall as a reading experience, the conflict between those two extremes in Hemingway's fiction has continued to interest readers as his work moves into a new century.

WORKS CITED

Adams, J. Donald. "Ernest Hemingway." *The English Journal* 28.2 (February 1939): 87–94. Print.
Beegel, Susan F. "Howard Pyle's Book of Pirates and Male Taciturnity in Hemingway's 'A Day's Wait.'" *Studies in Short Fiction* 30.4 (Fall 1993): 535–541. Print.
Braudy, Leo. "The Form of the Sentimental Novel." *NOVEL: A Forum on Fiction* 7.1 (Autumn 1973): 5–13. Print.
Brown, Herbert Ross. *The Sentimental Novel in America, 1789–1860*. Durham, NC: Duke University Press, 1940. Print.
Cassuto, Leonard. *Hard-boiled Sentimentality: The Secret History of American Crime Stories*. New York: Columbia University Press, 2009. Print.
Clark, Suzanne. *Sentimental Modernism: Women Writers and the Revolution of the Word*. Bloomington: Indiana University Press, 1991. Print.
Crane, Gregg. *The Cambridge Introduction to the Nineteenth-Century American Novel*. New York: Cambridge University Press, 2007. Print.
Forter, Greg. *Gender, Race, and Mourning in American Modernism*. New York: Cambridge University Press, 2011. Print.
Hemingway, Ernest. "The Short Happy Life of Francis Macomber." *The Complete Short Stories of Ernest Hemingway: The Finca Vigia Edition*. New York: Charles Scribner's Sons, 1987. 5–28. Print.
———. "The Snows of Kilimanjaro." *The Complete Short Stories of Ernest Hemingway: The Finca Vigia Edition*. New York: Charles Scribner's Sons, 1987. 39–56. Print.
Hotchner, A. E. *Papa Hemingway*. New York: Random House, 1966. Print.
Kerr, Frances. "Feeling 'Half Feminine': Modernism and the Politics of Emotion in *The Great Gatsby*." *American Literature* 68.2 (June 1996): 405–431. Print.
Maddock Dillon, Elizabeth. *The Gender of Freedom: Fictions of Liberalism and the Literary Public Sphere*. Stanford, CA: Stanford University Press, 2004. Print.
Strychacz, Thomas. *Hemingway's Theaters of Masculinity*. Baton Rouge: Louisiana State University Press, 2003. Print.
Todd, Janice. *Sensibility: An Introduction*. London: Routledge, 1986. Print.
Weinstein, Cindy. "Sentimentalism." *The Cambridge History of the American Novel*. Ed. Leonard Cassuto, Clare Virginia Eby, and Benjamin Reiss. New York: Cambridge University Press, 2011. 209–220. Print.

Sentimentalism and Celebrity Culture

Mae West as Novelist

Anne-Marie Evans

In 1934, Mae West was such an icon of American popular culture that she inspired one of Salvador Dalí's most famous artworks, *Face of Mae West Which Mae Be Used as an Apartment*. The very title of Dalí's picture and his pun on "Mae" reveals a clear understanding of West's dual status as both actress and celebrity product. The picture is remarkable, as Dalí translates West's famous features into a domestic space and deconstructs the artificiality of "Mae West"; her lips are revealed as a sofa, and her nose is transformed into a mantelpiece for a clock. As Emily Wortis Leider has noted, "Mae West's image is literally where she lives" (346). Dalí's implication is that West's image is not just where she lives, but where everyone lives, demonstrating the sheer profundity of her public persona in the 1930s. Dalí's interest in West as a metaphor for celebrity and the production of public image quite literally illustrates her prominent role as both an actress and a carefully constructed cultural product.

West is remembered primarily today as a curvaceous blonde with a highly provocative sense of humor. The dominant female sex symbol of America in the late 1920s and throughout the 1930s, West's status as a cultural icon has long since eclipsed her accomplishments as an author. As well as being a successful actress, she was also a playwright, novelist, screenwriter, and comedienne who insisted on maintaining absolute creative control over her work. This essay places West's fiction, specifically her 1932 novel *She Done Him Wrong*, within a framework of sentimental literature. It explores how sentimental writing actually informs the structure of West's novel and suggests that this is a new way of reading and re-evaluating her work. West's manipulation of her public image also informs part of this discussion as the "Mae West" brand was painstakingly assembled and her writing played an instrumental part in her creation of a public self. West writes about criminals, prostitutes, drug addicts, and hard-bitten policemen, a world away from the classic sentimental literature of the nineteenth century that traditionally explored the politics of feeling as a potential way of gaining female autonomy. West's fiction presents the reader with decidedly unsentimental heroines who nevertheless exist in worlds where sentimental ethics still seem to have a role to play.

The determination with which West developed from a performer to a successful author highlights her tenacity in a patriarchal environment. Mae West was born Mary Jane West in Brooklyn in 1893 and left school at the age of seven (Hamilton 6). She was routinely vague about her age and family background, even denying the existence of her early 1911 marriage to fellow vaudevillian Frank Wallace until the story broke in 1935 (Hamilton 14). West enjoyed a steady career in vaudeville throughout her teens that allowed her to tour the United States extensively and gain valuable stage experience as a singer and comedienne. Influenced by the new sounds of jazz, West introduced her famous "shimmy" dance into her act around 1917 before breaking onto Broadway and from there into the film industry (Louvish 73). Once she became an established presence on the Broadway scene West swiftly recognized the value of producing her own material and writing became a crucial part of her career management.

The evolution of West's *Diamond Lil* production showcases West's skills as a writer, producer, and entrepreneur. Her play, partly based on an earlier work by Mark Linder, premiered on April 9, 1928, and was West's fourth playwriting credit after her earlier works *Sex* (1926), *The Drag* (1927), and *The Wicked Age* (1927). In 1932 she turned *Diamond Lil* into a novel; the film version, starring West and a rising young actor named Cary Grant, was released in 1933. On screen, *Diamond Lil* was given the grittier title of *She Done Him Wrong* and "Lil" was renamed "Lou." By writing, re-writing and adapting her own material for the stage and page, West remained in artistic control. As Faye Hammill suggests, West "repeatedly identified writing as central to all her activity" (79).

West was writing to further her own acting career; she was not a screenwriter like other women in Hollywood such as Anita Loos, who penned the novel and screen versions of *Gentlemen Prefer Blondes* (1925 and 1953, respectively) without starring in either. West was writing specifically for Mae West, searching for scripts or ideas that would allow her to play the kinds of roles in which she knew the public wanted to see her. In her 1959 autobiography, *Goodness Had Nothing to Do with It*, West claims, "I became a writer by the accident of needing material and having no place to get it" (*Goodness* 72). By producing her own material that she could also star in, West found a sure-fire way to evade becoming a pawn of the all-powerful Hollywood studios.[1] By playing the sexy blonde on stage and screen and embracing the role of writer and creator off-screen she managed her career with remarkable success. Never one to underestimate the importance of appearance, and knowing that many would value her looks over her brains, West was adept at manipulating her public image: "West deliberately played on the discrepancy between her feminine, sexy appearance and her intellectual abilities" (Hammill 79). The role of "writer" therefore became yet another career position that she was able to carve out for herself with demonstrable success.[2]

West's novels, of which she wrote several, are not usually considered in conjunction with the sentimental novel. Sentimental fiction is a complex genre, and the stalwarts of the tradition—female suffering, friendship and sacrifice—are merely the hallmarks of a rich and nuanced engagement with a range of social issues. Cindy Weinstein defines some of the key features of the genre as including "a focus on day-to-day activities in the domestic sphere, a concentration on relationships, and a profound interest in the emotional lives of women" (Weinstein 209). Broadly speaking, all of these features are displayed and explored in *She Done Him Wrong*, and West essentially utilizes the structure of the sentimental novel and usurps it to promote her own purposes and self-image. This essay considers West's text in terms of three of the central concerns of the sentimental novel: relationships between women; the exploration of female sexuality; and the Christian framework that informed so many popular works of sentimental literature such as Susan Warner's bestselling *The Wide, Wide World* (1850). By using these concepts as a template, this essay explores how West engages (and disengages) with sentimentalism.

She Done Him Wrong allowed West to rewrite her earlier Broadway triumph *Diamond Lil* for a public that was always ready to read material by and about Mae West. Set in the rough and tawdry Bowery area of New York during the 1890s, the novel tells the story of Lil, a former prostitute who is now the mistress of the small-time criminal and dance hall owner Gus Jordan. As her name implies, Lil's love of diamonds inspires her far more than her desire for any particular man. As the text progresses, Lil's interaction with the handsome Captain Cummings of the Salvation Army prompts her to reflect on her obsession with material goods and leads to a gradual moral and spiritual awakening. Cummings, meanwhile, turns out to be an undercover policeman known only as "the Hawk," intent on fighting corruption in the New York underworld.

Lil's growing attraction to the handsome Captain, and her growing interest in saving her soul, propels the second half of the novel, and Diamond Lil eventually gets her man (indeed, it is hard to imagine a West heroine *not* getting her man at the end of the story), although the revelation of Cummings's true identity compromises Lil's developing sense of an ethical self.

As the title suggests, *She Done Him Wrong* is primarily a novel about Diamond Lil's relationships with various men, but thinking about the relationships between women in the novel offers a useful way of exploring West's work in the light of sentimentalism. Sally Glynn, the young pregnant girl who makes the mistake of wandering into Jordan's dance hall, known locally as "Suicide Hall," is clearly in need of a friend. As a character she is the stock type of the "fallen woman" figure that appeared in sentimental literature throughout the twenties and thirties. Seduced by a married man, she is soon identified to the reader as an innocent abroad: "Her eyes were dark pools of ineffable tragedy. On her cheeks were the traces of tears that had dried" (West 22). West's language here echoes the occasional melodrama of sentimental fiction, and Sally is constructed as a classic sentimental heroine struggling for self-control (Tompkins 172). Instead of being rescued, however, as might be expected from a sentimental novel, and discovering and retaining a sense of self, Sally is dealt with in a surprisingly unsentimental manner.

A major sub-plot in the novel is Jordan's links to the white slave trade: he tricks young women into sailing to South America, promising them careers as showgirls before selling them into brothels. West is typically forthright in describing the horrors of this practice. Jordan is aware that the women he helps to deceive are being sent to their deaths: "A good girl could earn up to fifty thousand dollars for her house before she was ready for the ash-bin or a mosquito swamp" (West 33). Although he is at first a reluctant conspirator, he soon "discover[s] that dirty money ha[s] the same power as clean" (West 32). Like Harriet Beecher Stowe's *Uncle Tom's Cabin* (1850), one of the founding texts of the sentimental genre, West's work is intent on exposing the horrors of the slave trade. But unlike Stowe, West avoids dealing with these horrors on any ethical or moral level.[3] West has no interest in making a political statement. What was for Stowe the driving force behind the novel is for West merely a useful plot device that allows her protagonist to have some flickers of conscience, although West is particular in her description of the victimization of women. All the doomed young women are named—Violet, Bessie, Polly and Adelaide—and thus the poignancy of their predicament is heightened.

What is particularly interesting about West's portrayal of this echelon of society is her critique of female culpability. Rita Christinia—the "dark, vivacious" (West 32)—is a Latin American madam who travels to America four times a year to collect shipments of girls to sell to South American brothels. The danger of the "flesh marts" (West 31) is taken seriously by West, and Rita's sadism (and her jealousy of Lil) is repeatedly highlighted throughout the text: "How she [Rita] would have liked to lash Lil's white flesh with a cat-o'nine-tails, as she had lashed so many of her charges who had proved the least bit recalcitrant" (West 32). Writing in prose rather than for the stage allows West to develop her characters in far more graphic detail, as her description of female sadism illustrates. As Hammill notes, "[t]he increased freedom offered by print publication is likely the reason why West's fiction is more detailed and explicit with regard to taboo subjects than is her work in other media" (94). In addition to the obvious contrast West establishes between Lil's whiteness and Rita's darker coloring, Rita's role as chief danger to female virtue is established. Instead of the plot revolving around whether or not poor Sally and the other young women can be saved from the slave trade, West is entirely focused on Lil and her attempts to seduce Captain Cummings. Sally, the text later informs the reader, has indeed been shipped to South America, and thus becomes the main casualty of the narrative. At no point does Lil display any shock at Sally's fate; female solidarity is always second to Lil's relationship with men. Contemporary feminist readings of the text would rightly take issue with Lil's casual attitude to the source of her lover's money, as West continuously mistakes female self-obsession for female independence.

Rather than considering Lil's position as part of a community of women, West always characterizes Lil as being different and separate from other females. Lil's understanding of what is actually going on at Suicide Hall, and what is happening to other women in her neighborhood, is carefully circumscribed in the text, and West makes it clear that Lil does not fully comprehend what her lover is involved in:

> She was perfectly indifferent as to how Jordan made his money, as long as he did make it, but she would have drawn the line at white slavery had she known that that traffic was his chief source of revenue. Lil was funny that way. Certainly sex held no mysteries for her. But if she knew that most of the money that Gus spent to buy her diamonds came from the marketing of women's bodies she would have resented it strongly. True enough, she had sold her own body, but she had always been a complete mistress of herself and her emotions; she had never been a pawn in a man's game. These girls who were rustled down to Rio were no better than sheep led to the slaughter. They had not her strength of mind, her ability to make cool decisions, nor her all-alluring voluptuousness that bent men to her will. She felt an instinctive sorrow for women who lacked her capacity to keep the predatory male under control [West 75].

Once placed within the framework of sentimental literature, this is a remarkable piece of writing. Ostensibly seeking to establish Lil's sympathy for female victims, the passage actually confirms Lil's status as different from other women: she perceives herself as more of a sexual predator than a victim, whereas sentimental heroines (such as Warner's Ellen Montgomery, or Gertrude Flint from Maria Susanna Cummins's *The Lamplighter* [1854]) must usually suffer some form of emotional abuse before attaining self-mastery.

Lil seems to sense at least some of the irony inherent in seeing herself as belonging to a different class of womanhood, admitting that "she had sold her own body," but the passage situates money, rather than sentimental feeling, at the heart of West's narrative. Lil is "perfectly indifferent" to the source of Jordan's money but the reader is assured she would admit to a qualm if she knew it came from the "marketing of women's bodies." Paradoxically, the text emphasizes from the start that "Diamond Lil" is only able to function through the marketing of her own body and image. At the back of the Suicide Hall's bar, a large painting depicts an "alabaster and gold Lil reclining in all her voluptuous nudity upon a background of purple velvet" (West 14). Lil does not recognize that there is a parallel between the marketing and exploitation of her own body—even though hers is consensual—and the "marketing" of the women destined for South American brothels. She perceives that these women are "no better than sheep led to the slaughter" but does not examine the source of her blood diamonds too closely.

In addition to considering, and problematizing, relationships between women, West explores the concept of female sexuality, a topic that several of her previous works had also interrogated. In 1926 West was arrested for obscenity for performing in her play *Sex*. The play was one of Broadway's biggest hits of the year (Hamilton 38), an achievement no doubt helped by the notoriety surrounding the production, in which West played a prostitute and brothel owner named Margy Lamont. In West's texts sex often has the power to liberate the female instead of simply oppressing her, and this belief clearly influenced West's management of her own public image. If sentimental fiction can be interpreted as a form of cultural and social critique, then West's creation of the self-aware "loose woman," as opposed to the traditionally virtuous sentimental heroine, marks part of her complex engagement with sentimental literature.

The American and English traditions of sentimental literature often centered on the seduction narrative (as in Susanna Rowson's *Charlotte Temple* [1791] and Samuel Richardson's *Pamela* [1740]), but in *She Done Him Wrong* sex is primarily initiated by Lil. When Lil meets Pablo Juarez, one of Rita's associates whom she will later sleep with, she surveys his handsome figure and "ma[kes] a mental note to give him closer inspection at her leisure" (West 42). Displaying a sexual freedom unavailable to many women in the 1930s, Lil never attempts to ignore her desires, and certainly never regards them as something other than normal and healthy.

Much of the plot of the novel focuses on Lil's attempts to seduce the righteous Captain Cummings, and she is far more interested in Cummings's body than his mind. Discussing sentimental fiction of the nineteenth century, Weinstein explores how women authors engaged with the complexities of the marriage question: "If the heroine's *Bildungsroman* represents a journey toward self-possession, which culminates in the decision to marry the man of her choice, what then happens to that story of self-possession when she becomes legally possessed by another? When she becomes, analogically speaking, like a slave?" (Weinstein 212). Weinstein's question is a crucial one, and one that West seems—partly, at least—to attempt to answer in the ending of her text. Lil, a self-possessed heroine if ever there was one, does end the novel with the man of her choice, but not necessarily on her terms. There is no guarantee that she will not be arrested later, after all, and even in the final lines Lil tries to convince herself that this is a love match rather than a match of necessity. West thus rewrites the sentimental ending: Lil, it seems, will continue as a mistress, a sex symbol, a possession, and an emblem of male success. Hamilton suggests a correlation between West's own jail sentence for obscenity and Lil's willingness to be arrested at the end of *She Done Him Wrong* (116). Unlike her creator, Lil will presumably be able to bargain (her body) out of this predicament.

Weinstein also suggests that "one of the most complex issues taken up by sentimental fiction is the marriage relation, because sentimentalism demands that its novels conclude in marriage" (212). West's novel famously concludes with the threat of handcuffs for Lil rather than with any account of marriage (although Cummings seems curiously reluctant to actually arrest her). Cummings—now revealed as the "Hawk," scourge of the Bowery and pride of the New York police department—at no time professes his love for Lil, nor she for him. The emphasis is placed instead on sexual desire, and the novel ends with Lil celebrating the fact that Cummings has become one in a long line of men that she has been able, at last, to seduce. Cummings sweeps Lil into his arms and declares: "I tell you that I'm mad about you. I want you!" (West 187). West's hero does not confess his love for Lil, only his desire to sexually possess her, and he does not propose marriage.

West is unashamedly romantic and ends the text with a kiss between hero and heroine because she knows it sells, and the ending can be interpreted as a happy one in the sense that Lil finally gets the man she has wanted for the last hundred and fifty pages. Cummings perceives Lil as redeemable: "I know that giving Jacobsens's Hall to the Salvation Army isn't the only good thing you've done" (West 187). Cummings knows that Lil is a gangster's mistress and that this is a role she has played before with other men, but in the final scenes of the novel he is compelled to translate her into a Jezebel with a heart of gold. Lil must play another role for another type of man: "Diamond Lil" must now become "Lil the good Samaritan." She is allowed her version of a happy ending, despite the fact that by the end of the narrative she has murdered Rita, engineered the arrest of her former lover Chick Clark, and arranged the shooting of small time criminal Dan Flynn for trying to encroach on Jordan's business interests. Lil may end the novel by kissing the man of her choice, but even in the final lines there is a sense of performativity and insincerity:

> A wild gladness surged up within her at the words which told her that the man she had wanted for so long was hers; yet, she asked herself, "Is this love? Really love? Or something just for the winter season?"
> But her self-confidence had returned to her completely, and it was sweet triumph. As her lips were crushed hotly to his she murmured: "I always *knew* you could be *had*!" [West 187]

The sense of any kind of a moral or spiritual awakening is completely lacking in this ending.

Even as Cummings is finally professing his attraction to her, Lil is congratulating herself. The "wild gladness" is ambiguous as it also signifies her relief that she (probably) will not have to go to jail if the arresting officer is infatuated with her. The fact that Lil questions whether she might (or might not) be in love suggests some authenticity, for though several male characters in the story (Chick Clark, Pablo Juarez, Gus Jordan) profess strong feelings for Lil, her reciprocation on anything other than a sexual level is never implied. She is clearly still questioning whether a relationship with Cummings could be yet another temporary measure, just "something for the winter season." Although the ending is framed as Lil's great triumph over another man apparently rendered helpless by her blatant sexuality, West allows her heroine one final pun. Lil's self-congratulatory comment that Cummings could be "*had*" functions on two levels: she can now enjoy him sexually, as she always suspected she would, but he has also been "had" in the sense that he has been tricked. He has fallen for her charms like so many before him. Lil does not question his new identity—indeed, his actual name is never revealed—so the final irony of the text is that Diamond Lil, that great image of Bowery sexuality, has herself fallen for a fabricated persona.

In addition to the attention paid to relationships between women and West's consideration of female sexuality, the text is also placed within a framework of Christian belief. West, who was herself raised Roman Catholic, not only problematizes the concept of organized religion but also uses it as a device to explore Lil's potential for spiritual awakening. It is no coincidence that Cummings poses as a captain in the Salvation Army, a Christian group focused on outreach and with an emphasis—as its name suggests—on salvation and redemption; surely there are multiple identities he could have assumed in the Bowery. West's decision to affiliate her hero with Christianity offers a way for her to explore Lil's sense of her own morality, and thus parallels many nineteenth-century sentimental texts in which religion and religious awakening inform the plot.

West continually places the spiritual at odds with the material, represented in the text by Lil's love for diamonds. When the play opened in 1928 it had been only three years since another blonde bombshell, Lorelei Lee, had famously declared in *Gentleman Prefer Blondes* that "Kissing your hand may make you feel very very good but a diamond and sapphire bracelet lasts forever" (Loos 55). Curiously, West does not reference Loos's hit, except perhaps in her attempt to associate her heroine even more closely with diamonds by making the gemstone a part of Lil's name. Just as in Loos's comic masterpiece, diamonds are a central motif in West's text. In real life, West was a prolific collector herself, claiming in her autobiography that, like her fictional creation, all her diamonds came from appreciative gentlemen admirers. "I hadn't started out to collect diamonds," she claimed, "but somehow they piled up on me and in self-protection I became a gem expert" (West, *Goodness* 107). She actually pawned her diamond collection to help finance the original production of *Diamond Lil* (West, *Goodness* 124), so *Diamond Lil* was literally constructed by the diamond trade.

Diamond Lil was first performed before the Wall Street crash of 1929, although West did not convert the play into a novel until 1932, when America was in the fierce grip of the Depression. Even though the action is set in the 1890s, at no point does West reveal any concern about the discrepancy between Lil's appreciation for material goods and the dire economic circumstances of most Americans. Lauren Berlant suggests that "the turn to sentimental rhetoric at moments of social anxiety constitutes a generic wish for an unconflicted world" (21). Applied to West's work, this assertion suggests that *She Done Him Wrong* can be categorized as escapist fiction, offering a nostalgic view of an America in which diamonds were plentiful and the threat of unemployment and homelessness were as yet unknown.

As Lil lies in bed with Juarez (she eventually does take that moment to "give him closer inspection") and they discuss her affinity for jewelry, she declares that "Diamonds is my career!" (West 89). Indeed, diamonds are the markers of Lil's career as a singer and a high-class prostitute; they demonstrate her worth and operate as an example of Thorstein Veblen's theory of "conspicuous consumption." Lil believes in showcasing her worth and, by extension, her skill as a mistress: "On her fingers and wrists was a profusion of other diamonds all calculated to blind the percipient male" (West 10). Diamonds are Lil's armor, her weapon, and her main choice of payment, and West continually details Lil's fondness for them. On Lil's dressing table, "her diamonds lay heaped from the night before. Bracelets, rings, pendants, necklaces, dog-collars, she let them ripple through her fingers with a feeling of exultation. They represented progress and conquest" (West 6). Lil knows that she is an expensive commodity, and as the text progresses, there is the promise that she may begin to measure her self-worth in other, less material ways. Her relationship with Cummings is therefore the catalyst for her moral interrogation of herself.

Lil's main problem with religion concerns hypocrisy (there is never any reason or backstory given for this in the text); she describes the singing of the Salvation Army as "holy howling" (West 10). When Lil first sees Cummings from her bedroom window she concedes, "He's the best looking thing I've seen in a long time" (West 11), but her attraction to him is immediately problematized by the realization that the Captain is a religious man: "Lil had no illusions concerning men. She knew them too well. If this young preacher yielded to his fleshly desires, how then did he square that up with denouncing those desires in others?" (West 11). Lil cannot separate the man from the moral, although she has little problem separating the man from the crime—as evidenced by her association with men such as Clark, Jordan, and Juarez. Cummings's religious leanings upset her far more than the well-documented criminality of all of her former and present lovers. This is clearly because Cummings's faith prompts Lil to explore her own sense of self in more detail than she is accustomed to.

Prior to meeting Cummings, Lil has attempted to model her character on the hard beauty of the diamond. She "[does] not like to think herself soft in any respect" (West 49) and never sheds a tear in the text—an interesting trait considering the importance of weeping in the sentimental novel (Weinstein 213). Lil's attachment to diamonds comes when she is at her most emotional, and when the sentimental language of feeling plays its main role in the text—when she thinks she is about to die—she thinks not of Cummings but of her gem collection: "She couldn't die and leave her diamonds. That couldn't be!" (West 150). Unlike the sentimental heroines of the previous century, Lil searches not for self-possession but for material possessions; accruing and safeguarding her considerable stockpile of movable wealth is her primary motivation throughout the novel.

It is only her conversations with Cummings that begin to dent Lil's tough exterior. When Cummings first comes to visit Lil she compares herself to Mary Magdalene, but the Captain swiftly reveals that he has come to thank her for various donations to the Salvation Army (West 111). Lil is quick to silence him, but the exchange reveals a softer side of her character: the hard-as-nails showgirl apparently has a history of charitable donations. During their debate about religion Lil continues to align herself with the fallen women of the Bible: "I'm the scarlet woman. When I die, I'm going to burn in hell" (West 116). Lil is able to demonstrate that her lack of interest in religion does not stem from ignorance; she has read the Bible and admits that "Samson intrigued her" and "she adored Solomon" but the "pale Nazarene and his doctrine of self-abnegation were too meek and mild for her" (West 101). Lil perceives the Bible only in the form of a spectacle, as entertainment. She is interested in Biblical figures as characters rather than metaphors, focusing on the surface image as opposed to the underlying message. Lil may not believe in the teachings of the "pale Nazarene," but she clearly believes in divine retribution. Casting Lil's character within the framework of religious debate helps to humanize her; she may scoff at religion but she clearly fears for her soul. When Cummings tells her that "the good will come to the top, if you'll only give it half a chance," the comment can be read on two levels: in his guise as Captain Cummings he is warning her to repent, but as the "Hawk" he is also warning her to change her lifestyle (West 116). The quest to "save" Lil functions on both physical and metaphysical levels.

West is aware that for Lil to have a moment of spiritual epiphany would be entirely out of character, but she is also aware that some kind of religious awakening is needed to validate Lil's attraction to Cummings. Slowly, the path to Lil's potential salvation is made apparent. She feels "certain qualms of conscience" after sleeping with Juarez even though she "could be bothered with a conscience only just so long" (West 100). It is obvious that it is only the handsome presence of Cummings that has attracted Lil; the beginnings of her moral awakening are not linked to Sally's plight, as they would be in the nineteenth-century novel, for example. Religion has to be appealing and attractive in Lil's eyes; she remarks that it "[j]ust goes to show that religion'd be more of a success if they had better-lookin' people sellin' it" (West 106). Religion, like everything else in Lil's world, is framed in purely economic and material terms. It is a product to be sold, and therefore the salesperson needs to be attractive.

Lil's desire for Cummings becomes inextricably bound to her self-reflection, "her reaction and subsequent high-handed treatment of the captain" acting as "an instinctive protest growing out of the feeling that she was inferior, at least morally, to this man who professed Jesus and did the work of God"

(West 127). Lil has no wish to become a project for the Captain—"He would be interested in her only from the angle of redemption. And that was not at all the way in which Lil wanted him to be interested in her" (West 127)—but against all the odds, one conversation with Cummings serves as a catalyst for Lil's spiritual awakening: "down in her heart she felt an impulse, a desire to be raised up to this level" (West 129). This line might have come directly from a nineteenth-century sentimental novel by Warner or Sedgwick.

Finally, West places the emphasis on feeling rather than acquiring. Even finding out that Cummings has no money does not dull Lil's ardor, as it would have for the Diamond Lil of old (West 134). Instead, she spends her money buying the Salvation Army meeting place, Jacobsens's Hall, so that the organization can continue its work. Cummings makes clear the difference between the image of Diamond Lil and the woman that she has the potential to become: "Diamonds always seem so cold to me. They have no warmth. No soul" (West 143). Lil sees diamonds only for the financial value; Cummings perceives the materialism that they represent.

The irony that the Captain is interested in Lil's redemption purely in a legal sense is not made apparent until the final few pages of the novel. And of course, Lil is eventually proven right: the captain is sexually interested, but the debates between them allow West to explore the relationship between the physical and the metaphysical in some detail. In a traditional sentimental novel, the handsome Captain would redeem Lil, and the text would chart her journey back to God through the love of a good man. In this text, Lil's awakening is rendered null and void by the revelation of the captain's true identity. And yet, the Captain's inherent goodness—he is "so utterly clean," Lil believes—forms a significant part of his attraction (West 128). She even debates whether she would be "willing to make an effort to tread the straight and narrow for him" (West 128). If part of Cummings's attraction is his moral candor as a Captain of the Salvation Army, his allegiance to another type of institution, the police force, does not give Lil much pause. The final joke, it is implied, could actually be on her.

Lil, never one to miss a trick, is quick to capitalize on her new status as the deceived party; she "ha[s] by no means exhausted her bag of tricks" and protests Cummings's embrace with "calculating weakness" (West 186). The chances are good that Lil will escape jail, but her awakening was for nothing. She may not need to be Diamond Lil in quite the same capacity as before but she is still being forced to play a role. She is very clearly in command of the situation again by the end of the novel, and has already perceived the potential benefits of being involved with a policeman. As Gregory D. Black explains, this was very much part of the typical Mae West character: "The role West carved out for herself was that of a woman who enjoys sex, who controls men not by her body but by her brain: She simply outsmarts them" (73).

In conclusion, *She Done Him Wrong* is not a sentimental novel in the traditional sense, but West's novel clearly engages certain elements of the sentimental tradition. Like her most famous creation, West managed her career by using her image as a superb tool for self-promotion. As the years went on, the line between "Mae West" and "Diamond Lil" grew increasingly blurry, and in 1963, a Los Angeles court decreed that the "Diamond Lil" brand and identity legally belonged to West (Leider 202). Four years before the court ruling, West revealed her role as the author of her own image and brand: "I first had to create myself, and to create the fully mature image I had to write it out to begin with" (West, *Goodness* 72). However, it is hard to imagine that West was offering anything other than a self-description when she described Lil in lushly glamorous terms: "There was nothing tough about her; she was young, her waist was like the stem of a wine-glass and her breasts were full and firm. Her eyes were large cool blue ponds, her hair was yellow as maize and she wore it in an astonishingly lovely style of her own" (West 2).

This is ostensibly Clark's recollection of the first time he saw Lil, but taken out of context, it could describe almost any publicity photograph of West from the mid–1920s onwards. West's decision to deliberately market herself as a modern and highly sexualized woman reveals a savvy understanding of the entertainment industry, as she emphasized her femininity to survive in a patriarchal environment. She fully understood the power of the Mae West brand, and her image was widely used on fans, soap advertisements, and perfume bottles (Hammill 87). When discussing Lil, a role she would continue to inhabit until the 1960s, West finally admitted that the line between creator and creation was increasingly blurred: "Lil in her various incarnations—play, novel, motion picture—and I have been one" (West, *Goodness* 115).

In creating Lil on stage and translating her to the page in *She Done Him Wrong*, West uses key components of the sentimental tradition—relationships between women, the concept of female sexuality, and an engagement with religion—and updates them for a specific context and audience. If questioned, West likely would have argued strenuously against any type of sentimentality because, like Lil, West wanted to be seen as a businesswoman. Yet, her writing reveals an acute awareness of one of the major trends in American literature. Diamond Lil is not a sentimental heroine in the traditional sense, but she is part of a text that operates within the sentimental tradition. By re-imaging the main components of the sentimental novel, West used a well-established and popular genre to help launch her writing career, creating the "Diamond Lil" brand for the twentieth century.

Notes

1. Although West was proud of her literary achievements, the novelization of *Diamond Lil* in 1932 warrants only a footnote in her autobiography (West, *Goodness* 115).
2. West was not keen to share the credit or the limelight. *Diamond Lil* is partly based on a 1915 play called *Chatham Square* written by Mark Linder, the brother of vaudeville agent Jack Linder (Leider 188). West rewrote the play extensively and Linder was given a fifty percent financial share in the original stage production. Linder sued, claiming he deserved more of a share of the considerable profits, but the case was later thrown out of court (Leider 194).
3. West actually references the book directly when Chick Clark, Lil's incarcerated former lover, hears that Lil now has enough diamonds to mount a production of *Uncle Tom's Cabin*.

Works Cited

Berlant, Lauren. *The Female Complaint: The Unfinished Business of Sentimentality in American Culture*. Durham, NC: Duke University Press, 2008. Print.
Black, Gregory D. *Hollywood Censored: Morality Codes, Catholics and the Movies*. Cambridge: Cambridge University Press, 1994. Print.
Hamilton, Marybeth. *The Queen of Camp: Mae West, Sex and Popular Culture*. London: HarperCollins, 1995. Print.
Hammill, Faye. *Women, Celebrity, and Literary Culture Between the Wars*. Austin: University of Texas Press, 2007. Print.
Leider, Emily Wortis. *Becoming Mae West*. New York: Farrar, Straus and Giroux, 1997. Print.
Loos, Anita. *Gentlemen Prefer Blondes*. London: Penguin, 1998. Print.
Louvish, Simon. *Mae West, It Ain't No Sin*. London: Faber, 2006. Print.
Tompkins, Jane. *Sensational Designs: The Cultural Work of American Fiction 1790–1860*. New York: Oxford University Press, 1986. Print.
Watts, Jill. *Mae West: An Icon in Black and White*. Oxford: Oxford University Press, 2001. Print.
Weinstein, Cindy. "Sentimentalism." *The Cambridge History of the American Novel*. Ed. Leonard Cassuto. Cambridge: Cambridge University Press, 2011. 209–220. Print.
West, Mae. *The Constant Sinner*. London: Virago, 1995. Print.
_____. *Goodness Had Nothing to Do with It*. New Jersey: Prentice-Hall, 1959. Print.
_____. *She Done Him Wrong*. London: Virago, 1995. Print.

Swedenborgian Sentimentalism in John Rechy's *City of Night*

María DeGuzmán

This essay focuses on the sentimentalism of El Paso–born, Los Angeles–adopting Chicano writer John Rechy's 1963 "underground" classic American novel *City of Night*. Many reviewers of this novel claim that it is the opposite of sentimentalism—without sentimentality or sentimentalism. Reviewers seem to have based that claim on a face-value appraisal of the novel's most obvious subject matter—pre-Stonewall homosexual hustling—and on the public image of the novel's author: a worldly-wise, muscle-bound gay man who also worked for years on the streets as a hustler himself until he settled down in the late 1970s with his partner Michael Snyder (Casillo 260–280). Subject matter and pre-conceived stereotypes about gender and occupation (male hustlers must be tough, streetwise, and too jaded for sentimentality) seem to have produced the evaluation concerning anti-sentimentality. I disagree with such claims and seek to complicate facile notions. All of John (Juan Francisco) Rechy's works attest to an extremely well read writer who produces texts richly layered in terms of cultural references and emotional registers. Rechy's *City of Night* manipulates numerous strains of sentimentalism on many levels. The one on which I focus—Swedenborgianism—leads this essay to consider the novel's philosophically and theologically "heretical" ambitions in relation to the cultural critique it unfolds via its representations.

The novel's adaptation of Swedenborgianism is starkly evident in the fifth chapter of Part I: THE PROFESSOR: The Flight of Angels. This chapter presents readers with one of the most seemingly bizarre characters in the whole novel: the Professor, a sort of physically paralyzed Liberace figure from whose mouth pours Swedenborgian rhetoric. This character and his cosmology, conveyed through his dramatic monologue, lie at the very "heart" of Rechy's critique of U.S. culture and its values. I argue that the Professor and the contents of his monologue are modeled on the persona and ideas of the 18th century Swedish scientist, inventor, philosopher, mystic, and theologian Emanuel Swedenborg (1688–1772) who wrote a treatise entitled *Heaven and Hell* (1758) as well as many other works such as *Arcana Coelestia* (Heavenly Secrets) and *True Christian Religion* that relatively recently have been excerpted, compiled, and translated as *Conversations with Angels* and *Debates with Devils*. I draw out the larger implications of this modeling of the professor on Swedenborg, particularly as it pertains to an ingenious and surprising adaptation of sentimentalism to this rebellious novel, a novel by a Chicano gay man about the homosexual underworld of the 1960s seen through the eyes of a partly Latino "Youngman" from El Paso, Texas, turned prodigal son of his parents and of "American" culture at large.

The sentimentalism I am discussing can be traced back to the 18th century, but it emerged strongly in 19th century U.S. culture. Swedenborgian sentimentalism had enormous influence on Emerson and Whitman and many American 19th century writers, artists, and reformers. I name a few here, and the list is rather staggering: in addition to Emerson and Whitman, the preacher and abolitionist Henry Ward Beecher, painters Thomas Cole, Frederick Church, and George Inness (Hudson River School), architects Daniel Burnham and Louis Sullivan, more champions of the anti-slavery movement such as Lydia Maria Child and, to some extent, Abraham Lincoln, and early feminists such as Margaret Fuller (per *Emanuel Swedenborg: A Continuing Vision*, edited by Robin Larsen). Also, in that list belong reformer Andrew Jackson Davis; journalist and creative writer Edgar Allan Poe; curator of apple nurseries John Chapman otherwise known as Johnny Appleseed; homeopathic physician William Henry Holcombe (Horowitz 35–41 and 86); and Henry and William James. According to Sydney E. Ahlstrom's *Religious History of the American People*, Swedenborgianism heavily informed Transcendentalism, communitarian experiments such as Brook Farm, mesmerism, spiritualism, faith healing, and the free love movement. In short, Swedenborgian sentimentalism was a major theological-philosophical phenomenon of the long 19th century in the United States, and it had vast artistic and social impact. The 1998 Hollywood film *What Dreams May Come* starring Robin Williams and Cuba Gooding, Jr. attempts to convey the visual impact of Swedenborgianism especially on early-nineteenth-century U.S. painters such as Thomas Cole.

What will be surprising to many Rechy fans and other readers of Rechy is how *City of Night* picks up on Swedenborgian strains and manipulates them to its own ends, ends that exceed mere parody—even though it might be argued that they are parodic—thereby reinforcing the thesis that the book is anti-sentimentalist. However, the parody of the replication of Swedenborg's cosmology in darker and more desperate strains is framed by a deep anguish that serves as both motive and continually burning question, arising from a memory of loss, death, and rot for the partly Latino "Youngman" narrator, from "the incident of [his] early childhood that [he] remembers most often" (12), the slow and painful death of his dog Winnie and his Catholic mother's statement that dogs cannot go to heaven because, supposedly, they do not have souls (11). The question and its myriad implications haunt the narrator—and through the narrator, the reader—for the entirety of the novel, the last line of which is: It isn't fair! *Why cant dogs go to heaven*? (380).

The question about the relation of bodies to souls and vice versa haunts all of Rechy's work. It does so from the perspective of an erudite hustler with not only a vast storehouse of knowledge about world literature and philosophy (as a voracious and largely self-educated reader) but also experience as a career sex worker—one who is an observer of and a participant in people's fantasies (many of them kept off-limits or highly censored in normative society). I point this out not to recommend a second or third job in sex work; far too many people are already compelled to subsidize their very existence—and, if they have them, additional projects—in this manner. I underscore Rechy's hustler life to emphasize the social depths to which Rechy has plumbed this question of bodies and souls, as he certainly has not examined the question from a rarefied or "protected" position, a fact that has repeatedly earned his work the adjectives "gritty" and "raw," thereby reinforcing perceptions that his approach is anti-sentimentalist. But, such is not the case, and I would point to the continual preoccupation with "souls" as evidence.

Such a preoccupation accords with—and, frankly, stems from—concerns about moral philosophy undergirded by a metaphysical and/or religious postulate: the existence of a soul, a sentient entity capable of thought and feeling (if not thought, then most certainly *feeling*) that cannot be reduced to mere matter or contained and explained away by a materialist philosophy. The question makes an explicit appearance in his 1983 novel *Bodies and Souls*. This text is about what reviewers have inevitably referred to as the "seamy underside" of modern Los Angeles, which, in the novel, Rechy dubs "Lost Angeles" as in City of Lost Angels. In his 2001 introduction to the work, he suggests that readers "view the City as the place of exile chosen by banished angels after expulsion from Heaven for disobedience, angels still restive" (ix). The novel repeatedly mixes and juxtaposes the erotic with the pornographic and uses sometimes subtle differences between the two (with regards to liberation and oppression) to expose the spiritual struggles of the protagonists engaged in these scenarios—their longings, their sense of betrayal, and their confused desire for redemption. The intricacies are well summed up in the image of a Mexican American juvenile delinquent who wants "a naked Christ tattooed on his chest" (56). Rather than an *either/or* logic severing body from soul or sinner from saint, readers are confronted with a *both/and* logic—and, not surprisingly, this too is very much in keeping with Swedenborgianism.

In the earlier novel *City of Night* (1963) the question of bodies and souls takes many forms, but it is very significantly encapsulated in the question "Why can't dogs go to heaven?"; I say "very significantly" because the question is formulated in relation not just to humans per se, but also in relation to animals, too often deemed sub-human or inferior to the human particularly in mainstream Christianity. Gauri Viswanathan discusses this classification in an article on alternative religious movements such as Theosophy (partly indebted to Swedenborgianism and greatly indebted to Hinduism, Sufism, and Kabbalism) that presented a challenge to this view (Viswanathan 445). And not only is the question formulated in relation to animals but in relation to an animal—the dog—that, despite its long history of fidelity to humans as "man's best friend," has been made to stand in for the very inferiority of all (other) animals to humans. This abjection of "dogs" as both inferior and unclean animals has a long history. Among many other places, traces of the view may be found in the Bible, as this verse from the last chapter of *The Book of Revelation* illustrates: "Outside are the dogs, those who practice magic arts, the sexually immoral, the murderers, the idolaters and everyone who loves and practices falsehood" (Chapter 22, verse 15). This verse designates those who will be barred from entering the Kingdom of Heaven and partaking of the tree of life. It does so by deploying "dogs" to designate all cases of moral abjection and/or impurity on the part of humans. "Dogs" here clearly signify the unclean and everything that is not sufficiently pure or of God, including actual dogs themselves who, according to Levitical law, were considered "unclean" animals along with cloven-hoofed ones that do not ruminate (or chew their cud). Dogs are considered unclean because they walk upon their hands or paws without the protection of a hoof, and cloven-hoofed animals that do not ruminate are considered unclean because they are seen as *mixtures* between two distinct categories: those animals who are cloven-hoofed and chew their cud and those who do not.

So, what does this question—"Why can't dogs go to heaven?"—have to do with Rechy's adaptation and manipulation of Swedenborgian sentimentalism in the fifth chapter of Part I: THE PROFESSOR: The Flight of Angels? Everything, I argue. However, some background connections must be explored first to enable a full appreciation of how this is so. In tension with *The Book of Revelation*, *City of Night*—a title that echoes that of St. Augustine's *City of God* as well as Scottish Victorian poet and essayist James Thomson's *The City of Dreadful Night*—early on presents readers with a literal, not a metaphoric, dog: the narrator's pet Winnie. Winnie dies while the narrator is still a very young boy living in a dysfunctional household with a violently temperamental father who molests him and a mother whose love smothers him. The boy bonds with his dog as a benign love object, but then the dog sickens and dies. In answer to his question about what will happen to Winnie after death, his Catholic mother answers: "Shes dead, thats all [...] the body just disappears, becomes dirt" (11). The narrator and his brother bury their dog and hold a funeral at which the narrator prays that she be let into heaven. Later, the boys exhume the body only to encounter the stench of decay. Caught between his father's selfishness and hatred toward him and his mother's "crushing tenderness" and doctrinal inflexibility (as a traditional Catholic) and faced with the sickening loss of his beloved pet who never harmed him, he begins to lose his trust in God and God's love, at first gradually and then more intensely as he grows into a teenager, a young man:

> Soon, I stopped going to Mass. I stopped praying. The God that would allow this vast unhappiness was a God I would rebel against. The seeds of that rebellion—planted that ugly afternoon when I saw my dog's body beginning to decay, the soul shut out by Heaven—were beginning to germinate [17].

Without sufficient parental support, socially isolated in South Texas not only on account of family dysfunction but as a part–Mexican, part–Scottish boy who fits in nowhere comfortably (this part readers are not told directly but it can be deduced by putting all of the novel's ethno-racial and socio-economic clues together), subjected to the humiliations of increasing family poverty ("house ... in the government projects ... with winged cockroaches," 19), and exploited in "a series of after-school jobs" (18), the narrator claims that he rebelled against God and, in turning away from God, turned inward toward himself:

> And, it was somewhere about that time that the narcissistic pattern of my life began. From my father's inexplicable hatred of me and my mother's blind carnivorous love, I fled to the Mirror. I would stand before it, thinking: I have only Me! [18]

In the wake of these thoughts and of his father's death (among his other losses as a child and young adult), the narrator leaves El Paso for New York City to embark on the odyssey of a prodigal son. He describes this odyssey as "that journey through nightcities and nightlives—looking for I don't know what— perhaps some substitute for salvation" (19).

The novel's second chapter clarifies that the narrator becomes a male hustler working in and around Times Square and eventually in many other U.S. cities. He describes this decision to become a male hustler as a compulsion for which he did not "have clear-cut reasons": "Perhaps in part it was because of the obsessive ravenous narcissism craving attention" (21). His speculative explanation is couched in the language and paradigms of psychoanalysis—both Freudian (narcissism) and Lacanian (the Mirror, if the reader considers the Mirror stage and its repetitions as delivering a false sense of integration: "Me!"). Rechy's familiarity with both Freudian and Lacanian theories of subject formation and subjectivity is evident in the chapter "The Lecturer: 'On Nothing'" from his novel *Bodies and Souls*. In this chapter, he refers to Freud, Foucault, and Lacan in one knowing sentence (212). But, more to the point for this essay with regards to the uses of Swedenborgian sentimentalism, Rechy's narrator is ostensibly rebelling against religion (presumably Catholicism) and God, but his descriptions of this rebellion are not being generated merely through a secular and/or 20th century psychoanalytic lens. Rather, the account of turning away from God and toward himself—and seeking no less than "some substitute for salvation"—perfectly dovetails with many traditional and alternative, esoteric "Christian" accounts, as in Swedenborg's, of spiritual rebellion. Swedenborg's versions of these accounts are notably *sentimental* to the extent that they assign a crucial role to the affections (emotions, passions directed toward an object) in relation to decisive choices/actions. Swedenborg's gloss on the notion of the fall in the Book of Genesis in his own work *Conjugal Love* (or *Marriage Love*) casts this fall in terms of love that no longer flows back toward God but rather toward self:

> And then, because they turned away from God, and turned to themselves as though to a god, they created in themselves the origin of evil. Eating of that tree symbolized their believing that a person knows good and evil and is wise on his own, and not from God.
> [...]
> God did not create evil, but evil was introduced by man himself, since man turns the good which is continually flowing in from God into evil, whereby he turns himself away from God and toward himself [As quoted in *Debates with Devils*, xxxiii, xxxv].

By the end of the first chapter of *City of Night*, the narrator has ceased to trust God because, it would seem, he has ceased to believe in God's love and has decided that he has only himself on whom to rely. As for heaven, in his mind not only do dogs not get to go there, but its gates have been closed to him as well. He begins his life of exile and wandering haunted by the question: "Why can't dogs go to heaven?" As the novel unfolds, the word "dogs" accrues meaning.

Not only does the word reference "Winnie" but also all the socially marginalized—including the gay male hustlers, the lonely johns, the transvestites, former beauty "queens" of both sexes who have aged and are losing the beauty that gave them a modicum of social status and distinction. The term also applies to the narrator himself as a young, evidently gay, half–Mexican man who will not readily admit to either "fact" about himself. He prides himself above all else on being desirable to his clients, but never desiring, much less loving, anyone in return since "love" betrayed him at a tender age.

When the social and metaphysical problem of "love" and the question of "Why can't dogs go to heaven?" meet in the episode "THE PROFESSOR: The Flight of Angels," the novel's adaptation and manipulation of Swedenborgian sentimentalism becomes evident. The professor is one of the narrator-hustler's clients in New York City. The narrator is called to a man's apartment and there finds an enormous, 60-plus man with head shaved and huge dark bulging eyes behind thick glasses lying in bed attended by a "young malenurse" (58). The man appears to be the opposite of every social convention of desirability: he is fat, disabled from having been hit by a car, and eccentric. His apartment is "well-furnished" but his bedroom is unkempt and clogged with remnants of the past: "Scattered about the floor are manuscripts, books, magazines. The room is cluttered with statues, unhung paintings, vases with withered flowers" (58). The man greets the narrator with the statement: "My dear youngman [...] you are about to join the ranks of: My Angels!" (59). He launches into an extensive dramatic monologue about himself, his past, the other young men whose company he has bought over the years (some of whom stayed with him and others who eventually left or disappeared from his life), and his views on God, good and evil, human motivations and sufferings, the cruelty and coldness of the world, and foiled ambitions/desires (his own, those of the young men, "his angels," and those of a handful of other people). Summary of his disquisitions does not do them justice because their overall effect is conveyed just as much by the style in which he explains them as by their ostensible content. This style is at once epic, declamatory, hyperbolic, and overwrought—as if Oscar Wilde's "prose" (hardly prosaic) at its most "purple" were mixed with Swedenborgian content. At one point the narrator compares these disquisitions to "an endless song" (76), a comparison meant to intimate that they are, perhaps, operatic arias and/or swan songs.

The Professor calls on the narrator various times and each time launches into one of these disquisitions that together compose his ongoing monologue. On one of these occasions, he shows the narrator a photo album of the young men, "the angels," whose "love" he tried to keep by buying them desired gifts and taking them on trips. The narrator describes the pictures in the photo album:

128 The Sentimental Mode

> There were other photographs—youngmen in Spain, France, Italy, Germany, Mexico, America ... several sailors, servicemen, various youngmen in trunks: all staring at the world with a look strangely in common: a look which at first I thought was a coldness behind the smile and then realized must be a kind of muted despair, a franticness to get what the world had offered others and not extended readily to them ... [77–78].

The Professor describes the photo album as part of his "Research" and poses several rhetorical questions to himself and the narrator. He book-ends these questions with two definite postulates about "love": "Yes, Love, indeed [...] which has many forms. Who loved the most? I? They? Who was the taker, who the giver? Who can tell? Someday—at the last of my Research—I shall know.... Now [...] take the chair and come stand near me—please" (78). The latter statement is directed at the narrator and presumably concerns some sexual act that the Professor wants him to perform. When the narrator leaves, the Professor sighs after him: "God is Love!" The two postulates about love are that it takes various forms and that God is Love. Both postulates are eminently Swedenborgian since Swedenborg affirmed both these postulates numerous times across all of his many works, including, for example, in his *Soul-Body Interaction*. About the "kinds of love," Swedenborg writes:

> There are three kinds of love: love of heaven, love of the world, and self-love. Love of heaven is spiritual, love of the world is material, and self-love is physical. When a love is spiritual, then all the elements that follow from it, the way forms follow from an essence, derive a spiritual nature from it. The same principle applies if the love is for the world or for wealth and is therefore material. All the elements that follow from it, the way corollaries follow from a premise, derive a material nature from it. In the same way, if the chief love is self-love, or a love of being exalted above everybody else, then all the elements that follow from it derive a carnal nature from it. This is because the individual characterized by a given love focuses solely on himself and therefore stops the mind's thoughts in the body. For this reason, as we have just stated, if we recognize someone's ruling love and also the sequences of purposes to means to results (which three elements follow in a sequence according to the vertical levels), then we recognize the whole person [252].

Swedenborg also explores the God-as-Love concept in *Soul-Body Interaction* when he writes, "Spiritual things cannot come from any source but love, and love cannot come from any source but Jehovah God, who is love itself. So the sun of the spiritual world, from which all spiritual things flow as from their source, is pure love that comes from Jehovah God, who is its center" (232).

These two postulates lace the Professor's disquisitions but in the form of a lamentation, a lamentation for his lost loves, for his angels who have taken flight from him—hence the subtitle of the chapter: "The Flight of Angels."

He thus reiterates his love for these young men, "his angels" to whom he gave his attention, money, and gifts in exchange for sexual favors and for the illusion of a relationship. In particular, the Professor laments the departure of "My Robbie!" (75):

> [...] my Robbie's wings began to feel for the breeze, wings are meant for flying, and before I knew it he was Gone. [...] He had wings; he had to fly away.... Or perhaps," he [the Professor] said cautiously, almost in a whisper, "could it be that Love had indeed touched him powerfully—Love for me—and that that Love, at war with his angel's love of flight—had—lost out? ... I don't know." He went on dully now. "I have heard hes now in Los Angeles—Im not sure—Ive heard he works in a bar—.... Its been so many years.... Maybe he has soared to Heaven to bring Beauty to that drab place" [75-76].

This passage illustrates how the Professor actually employs Swedenborg's theory of competing loves to explain the demise of his assumed relationship with Robbie—the angel's love of flight won out over Robbie's "love" of the Professor. The Professor also reiterates the primary Swedenborgian postulate on God, gleaned from the New Testament: "God is Love" (60, 67, 72, and 78). As for the Professor himself, readers, along with the narrator, are left to ponder what kinds of love motivate him. The Professor seems to be driven by a complicated and self-contradictory mixture of loves: a penchant for ideals (God, Love) and idealization (of harsh and some might say sordid realities) that could be analogized to love of heaven and the spiritual; love of the world—in that there is no doubt that the Professor is a "worldly" man in all senses of that word; and love of self—in that he has blinded himself to the exploitative and unequal socio-economic terms of his relationships with these "angels," young men from poor or working class backgrounds whose photographs reveal a "franticness to get what the world had offered others and not extended readily to them" (78).

The Professor also allows himself to be exploited by these young men who use him for his money and his connections. The narrative reveals that not only did the Professor go to Yale (62) but that he was there for years and that he has accumulated "foreign service appointments, honorary titles, publications in scholarly reviews, foreign publications, books he had written, citations awarded him ..." (79). Readers are invited to see him not as a somewhat marginal character but as the very embodiment of privilege and power: a diplomat, a foreign service agent, in the service of American Empire—Yale University being classic training grounds for such a career. In his last interview with the narrator before his sudden death—possibly from suicide via pills (78)—the Professor attempts to impress the narrator with his credentials. However, his performance brings the Professor no joy. Rather, the narrator conveys: "the balloon face, pitiably tilted like a sad dog's, is staring at me with something that could be only racking pain" (79). The very next moment, the Professor bursts out with a mixture of anguish, pain, and contempt over "[t]he voracious angels" (including the narrator) who have "drained" his life (79).

The comparison of the Professor to a "sad dog" is hardly accidental or off-hand and constitutes one of the reminders of the central question that haunts the narrator himself: "Why can't dogs go to heaven?" However, the emotional range evoked by the Professor episode differs considerably from that evoked by the narrator's dog Winnie's death. Whereas readers were apt previously to be inclined toward complete sympathy for Winnie and for the narrator who has been told that dogs cannot go to heaven (presumably because they do not have souls), here the reference to a "dog" resonates in more complicated and potentially contradictory ways for readers, just as the narrator alternately pities the Professor and is repulsed by him. When the Professor tries to hug the narrator during what turns out to be the last encounter between them, the narrator pushes him away and moves back quickly (79), a gesture that suggests repulsion. By this time, Rechy has had ample space in which to build up reasons for misgivings about the Professor, and his rhetoric about "angels" and "Love" now appears to be serving as an elaborate mystification of his actual relations with his rent boys.

Furthermore, the Professor (fat, more than middle-aged, and disabled) triggers what the narrator fears most: the loss of the beautiful, narcissistic image in the mirror, the end of self-reliance on the cherished "Me!" When the narrator pushes the Professor away, he is pushing away a figure of abjection: of all that falls, for the narrator, within the realm of what he decidedly wishes to maintain will never be himself—the not–Me. The Professor can be the sad dog, but the narrator does not want to be. Still, the very mention of "dog" inevitably harkens back to the ruling question that haunts the book. This question not only encompasses Winnie, but also all the human characters, including the narrator, to the extent that they exist on or have been relegated to the margins of normative society. Society condemns these characters, but they nevertheless want what it (society) wants: they are marked through and through by its value system, lusting (speaking of kinds of "love") for fame, money, glory, possessions, and desirability, to be an object of others' desire (*sans* pity and contempt).

The adaptation of Swedenborgian sentimentalism functions on a number of levels in the episode of the Professor. First, as previously discussed, Swedenborgian rhetoric about love and the central notion of people as angels or becoming angels permeates the episode as it does (more subtly but still pervasively) much of Rechy's work—as can be seen in his treatment of his adoptive city, Los Angeles, as the City of Lost Angels. Secondly, the Professor's dramatic monologue is, among other things, an act of self-mythologization in which his relationship as a client of a series of young hustlers is transformed—via sentiment, feelings, and strong desires to be loved—into a Swedenborgian scenario (with touches of Rilkean lyricism) of a man visited by angels. The more the Professor elaborates on his self-deluding confession, the more the reader experiences his narrative about himself and his young men or rent boys as "sentimentalism"—not the multi-faceted nineteenth-century trope but the pejorative, ordinary parlance version meaning, essentially, false consciousness: misplaced emotion rendering a situation in a false light. Of course, this aspect of the adaptation and manipulation of sentimentalism might lead (and indeed has led) reviewers to consider *City of Night* an anti-sentimentalist novel or simply one that has nothing to do with sentimentalism in any profound way.

But, I argue, the novel does not allow readers to dismiss the Professor or what he has to say so easily. "THE PROFESSOR: The Flight of Angels," a twenty-three page episode divided into five parts like a Shakespearean tragedy, shows the Professor to be a truly tragic figure, somewhat like King Lear lamenting his demise. Rechy portrays the Professor as both extraordinarily learned/discerning and deeply selfish. He is self-divided, painfully insightful yet also certainly blind to the devotion of the young male nurse named Larry who, Cordelia-like, cares for him to the point of procuring "angels" for him and whose love he overlooks in pursuit of those other men. The last experience the narrator has in connection with the Professor is the sound, over the telephone, of Larry's voice "shaken; controlling tears" (80) and declaring that "The Professor is dead [...]. The interviews are over" (80). The narrator himself appears to be deeply affected by the whole episode because he resolves to leave New York and "return to El Paso" (81): "once again I got a job—determined that the money I would go home with would not be street money" (81). His resolutions are short-lived; however, the fact that he makes them at all suggests that despite his tough-guy street stance, the episode with the Professor has shaken the foundations of his own rebellion against God, against "Love," and against feeling much of anything except the measure of his desirability in other people's eyes.

The sentimentalist implications of *City of Night* do not stop with the narrator or with the other characters. As previously indicated, an investigation of the novel's Swedenborgian sentimentalism leads readers toward *City of Night*'s philosophically and theologically "heretical" ambitions in relation to the cultural critique it unfolds. The ultimate effect of employing Swedenborgian sentimentalism in the novel is to create a vertically affecting sense in readers of the painful gap between the ideal and the real—between the ideal

America of spiritual and material fulfillment and the real America that the narrator opens the novel by describing:

> LATER I WOULD THINK OF AMERICA as one vast City of Night stretching gaudily from Times Square to Hollywood Boulevard—jukebox-winking, rock-n-roll moaning: America at night fusing its darkcities into the unmistakable shape of loneliness.
> Remember Pershing Square and the apathetic palmtrees. Central Park and the frantic shadows [...] the streets of America strung like a cheap necklace from 42nd Street to Market Street, San Francisco.... One-night sex and cigarette smoke and rooms squashed in by loneliness.... And I would remember lives lived out darkly in that vast City of Night, from all-night movies to Beverly Hills mansions [9].

By "vertically affecting" I mean that through the Swedenborgian rhetoric, images, and paradigms, the novel invokes a sense of and a longing for the utopian heights of intimacy, love, and community only to plummet readers down not only into marginalized and persecuted underworlds, but moreover into underworlds whose denizens have incorporated the value system and value judgments of normative society—thereby competing against, labeling, and abjecting one another rather than accepting and cooperating with one another. Adjectives in the opening paragraphs of *City of Night*—adjectives such as "gaudily," "tawdry," and "cheap" along with the last street name provided, "Market Street, San Francisco" (9)—suggest that the dominant values of "America" (whatever those are) are mired in superficial materialism and mercenary motives. The result of living according to these values is nothing less than spiritual deprivation experienced as a suffocating "loneliness" (9).

Swedenborgian sentimentalism was a driving force of social reform, justice, and the extension of civil rights in the United States during the nineteenth century (and even into the twentieth century) to the extent that it encouraged "reflective sentimentalism" (Frazer 3–18). This "reflective sentimentalism" advocated reflecting on and harnessing feelings of empathy with and compassion for human and animal sufferings to the altruistic and benevolent pursuit of the greater good and of of justice for those who had historically been deprived of it. *City of Night*'s re-enactment of Swedenborgian rhetoric, images, and paradigms borders on the parodic in that it often provides distorted and grotesque mirror images of Swedenborgian ideals of intimacy, love, and community. But, Rechy's uses of Swedenborgian sentimentalism are by no means merely or even primarily parodic. The fundamental question posed—Why can't dogs go to heaven?—is one that Swedenborgian philosophy and theology addresses in ways far more nuanced than doctrinal Catholicism or other versions of mainstream Christianity. Swedenborgian sentimentalism suggests that animals have souls, and if those souls, like the souls of humans, "love" Heaven,

Heaven is not barred to them. If, on the other hand, those souls reject Heaven and love something else—the Kingdom of this world or self—then they will be trapped in that "something else." And, as readers are reminded through the omnipresent "tape-measure" (58, 60, 61, 67, 68, 70, 78, and 80) in the episode of "THE PROFESSOR: The Flight of Angels," the measure by which we both love and judge others shakes us to the ground or transports us elsewhere.

Works Cited

Ahlstrom, Sydney E. *A Religious History of the American People*. New Haven, CT: Yale University Press, 2004. Print.
Casillo, Charles. *Outlaw: The Lives and Careers of John Rechy*. Los Angeles: Advocate Books, 2002. Print.
Frazer, Michael L. *The Enlightenment of Sympathy: Justice and the Moral Sentiments in the Eighteenth Century and Today*. New York: Oxford University Press, 2010. Print.
The Holy Bible. New International Version. East Brunswick, NJ: International Bible Society, 1978. Print.
Horowitz, Mitch. *Occult America*. New York: Bantam Books Trade Paperbacks, 2010. Print.
Rechy, John. *Bodies and Souls: A Novel*. New York: Grove Press, 1983. Print.
_____. *City of Night*. 1963. Reprint, New York: Grove Press, 1984. Print.
Rose, Donald L. *Debates with Devils: What Swedenborg Heard in Hell*. Trans. Lisa Hyatt Cooper. West Chester, PA: Chrysalis Books, 2000. Print.
Splendors of the Spirit: Swedenborg's Quest for Insight. Color film. 60 minutes. Produced and directed by Penny Price for the Swedenborg Foundation. 2001.
Swedenborg, Emanuel. *Soul-Body Interaction* in *Emanuel Swedenborg: The Universal Human and Soul-Body Interaction*. Ed. and Trans. George F. Dole. New York: Paulist Press, 1984. Print.
Viswanathan, Gauri. "'Have Animals Souls?': Theosophy and the Suffering Body." *PMLA* 126.2 (2011): 440–447. Print.
What Dreams May Come. Color film. Directed by Vincent Ward. 1998. Polygram Films.

"Shame, thas a shame"

The Anti-Sentiment of Sapphire's Push *and* The Kid

Erica D. Galioto

In the nineteenth century, authors used sentimentalism to provoke sympathy in readers who might use that emotion to inspire large-scale social change. While some were successful in producing compassion and mobilizing change, the route taken to achieve these effects has been deeply contested and rightfully so. Most importantly, the project of nineteenth-century sentimentalism often relied on the identification between a white female reader and a black female character. For this identification to occur, authors writing in this mode assimilated race to maternity, and in so doing, removed the constitutive otherness of the character with whom readers were encouraged to identify. This false identification, or (mis)identification as this author has called it elsewhere,[1] is untrue on two levels: not only are the black character and white reader very different from one another, but the unconscious also subverts the conscious mirroring of sameness perpetuated by these authors.

This essay argues that the goal of sentimentalism—using feeling to inspire change—is still valuable, though it can only be achieved through anti-sentimentalism's deliberate blocking of reader identification. This blocking of reader identification shifts the roles of reader and text. Instead of the nineteenth-century assumption that the reader is spectator and the text is object, readers of twentieth- and twenty-first-century anti-sentiment are objectified and moved to shame: the affect associated with the exposure and impossible covering of otherness. Whereas sentimentalism wipes away otherness, the twenty-first-century anti-sentimentalism used by authors like Sapphire demands its inclusion as a precursor to the shame that may inspire change on the individual level.

Push (1996) and *The Kid* (2011) both represent and enact this antisentimental movement from blocked identification to shame. Precious and Abdul suffer unspeakable, unimaginable abuse and are physically, emotionally, and psychologically shattered. Reader identification with these mistreated kids is simply impossible; instead, we are forced to bear witness to their repetitive, varied, inassimilable trauma as both adolescents attempt to heal. Our desire for distance is constantly thwarted, and through Precious and Abdul, we are pushed deeper into ourselves and feel shamed by the exposure we also suffer through witnessing the discomfiting truth of these two lives. This shame demands that readers respond to that which they may never encounter. Their responses are deeply personal and often internal and may be no more than "I see you," but they stem from the authentic identification with their own otherness: not like Precious's nurse who looks upon her with shame and forces her to feel it too, but like a witness who has heard and acknowledges an otherness that can never be accounted for, although it is exposed.

Responses to Push, Precious *and* The Kid

It is important to begin by acknowledging the vexed public reactions to *Push, Precious*[2] (*Push*'s 2009 film adaptation directed by Lee Daniels), and *The Kid*. A clear binary is evident in these responses: either Sapphire's works admirably expose a hidden reality that must be confronted or they should be spurned with contempt for that same exposure. Due, in part, to this polarized reaction, critical attention directed toward *Push* and now *The Kid* has been slim. What little attention there is focuses on this bifurcated audience response rather than on the difficulty of identification embedded therein. The paralysis caused by public and private reactions of outrage, ironically, gives readers an entryway into *Push, Precious*, and *The Kid* because the texts and the reactions to them employ the same vectors that demand our critical attention: shame and truth.

Negative reviews of Sapphire's work often cite feelings of shame as justification, as in Ishmael Reed's iconic movie review of *Precious*: "This use of movies and books to cast collective shame upon an entire community doesn't happen with works about white dysfunctional families" (1). Sapphire, in her own response to this review, attests to the importance of truth-telling, especially if that reality is difficult and shameful: "Silence will not save African Americans. We've got to work hard and long, and our work begins by telling our stories out loud to whoever has the courage to listen" (1). In this exchange, Reed and Sapphire establish the foundation for the anti-sentiment that provokes shame. Sapphire, for her part, commits herself to writing about difficult realities that are so dark that audiences don't want to see them because they require the simultaneity of naked exposure and ineffectual covering that comprises shame. Exposing these silenced lives as truth coincides with her vision of art, which "pulls us into truths and realities completely outside ourselves. We are uncomfortable in the world that Sapphire creates, even as we share those truths with burning intimacy" (Wilson 31). Reed's negative review chronicles that discomfort—that "psychological assault"—in response to the confrontation of a reality he would rather not see and be shamed by (1).

Sapphire's truth-telling exposes the invisibility and voices the silence of those we have not seen and have not heard. When readers do finally see and hear, their responses are visceral because the confrontation is all those things negative respondents suggest: disgusting, violent, unbelievable, and/or shameful. Here, audiences are affected by *lack* of identification, by difference or otherness, rather than by the sameness of false identification. Sapphire's truth moves readers to a shameful discomfort that should be embraced and not avoided, in her view. In a recent interview on *The Kid*, a novel that follows Precious's son Abdul through the cycle of abuse, Sapphire responds to characteristic negative commentary by asserting,

> I don't know how to write about these things without being as poetic and as graphic as possible.... A lot of these stories are written in this clinical journalism. Why do we have to hear about these things in language that deadens us? What I have attempted to do as an artist is to make people not be able to forget it, not be able to turn away and say, "Well, that's just how it is" [Coffey 1].

Here, once again we see the joining of difficult truth and feeling. Sapphire admits that her dual intent is to write the truth and to make audiences feel. "It's not my job to satisfy you," she admits in another interview (James 44). But neither is it her job to "[explain] something to the outsider" (43). In other words, Sapphire is telling the truth through the full range of literary language, and she seeks neither reader satisfaction nor understanding; she is not going to ease readers in with "dead" language or prepare them for what is to come; she is not going to force the sentimental identification of an "outsider" with an insider by assuaging difference.

Instead, she just tells her stories; the stories prompt difficult feelings; the difficult feelings prompt, in her words, "expansion of consciousness" (James 42). In this line of thought, it is possible to say that negative reactions to Sapphire's work reflect not her writing's subpar quality or glorification of sexual violence and racial stereotypes, but rather a deliberate defense against the "expansion of consciousness" she intends. Rather than expanding through the purposeful provocation of shame, Reed and others short-circuit her trajectory.

At the moment when *Push*, *Precious*, or *The Kid* sends a reader or viewer into the self, through the internal gaze of objectification, these negative commentators stop the process. Perhaps they cease the process of looking when they themselves are seen and "push" their own shame, along with that of Precious and Abdul, out of sight. They block their expansion and return to the safety of viewing rather than seeing.

Sapphire's art diametrically opposes this fleeing, and instead pushes readers and viewers, like she pushes herself, to expand instead of retreating. "There is a drive," she says, "a push out of chaos, despair, and madness, a compulsion to make sense of the pain and beauty of the world. There is a deep desire to be an artist, to create, generate, grow, and improve" (Wilson 38). Indeed, amidst the darkness, Precious and Abdul are model artists, expanding their own consciousnesses as they make sense of their own traumas through writing and dance, the vehicles of their own growth and improvement. Just as Precious and Abdul must literally embody their own discomfort as a prerequisite to their growth, so too must their readers.

It is obvious that Sapphire inspires difficult negative reactions, and these responses oppose the sentimental mode that is often employed when writing about tough subject matter, especially when race is a factor. Often, these works rely on the traits of nineteenth-century sentimentalism that elicit sympathy or compassion. Sympathy, in this framework, includes a distinction between self and other, establishes a hierarchy, and contains an element of pleasure on the side of the compassionate. While there is nothing perverse about sympathy, it does operate through a scheme of simplicity. It makes audiences think, in essence: *there is an other, who is not that much different from myself, who is suffering; I feel badly about this suffering, especially because this other is very much like myself; therefore, to make myself feel better, I will respond sympathetically with my thoughts and resources.*

Fundamental to this project of sympathy, of course, is the requirement that the compassionate one not turn away in rejection of the suffering other. To counteract this desire to refuse the other's suffering altogether, the other must be viewed as like the self; only through the self can we approach these ultimately self-serving acts of sympathy. Overcoming negative feelings of rejection, then, is primary in sentimental literature. The reader must not come too close to feeling that the reading is disgusting, violent, unbelievable, and/or shameful, or else the bridge between self and other will not attach. Sapphire, obviously, engages these negative feelings directly and therefore opposes a sentimental economy dependent upon the smooth identification of self and other. As Sapphire proves, though, anti-sentiment may be just as transformative as sympathy, and perhaps more so. By intentionally blocking the palliative identification encouraged by sentimental literature, Sapphire forces readers to endure negative emotions that prefigure the expansion of consciousness her appalling realities demand.

"I do know what REALITY is and it's a mutherfucker, lemme tell you"

Sentimental literature seeks to form a bond of identification between self and other, where readers are able to see themselves reflected back in the character they gaze upon. This sameness facilitates sympathy and compassion. Typically, these bonds of identification are encouraged by unmediated access to the other's consciousness, descriptions of reality that are similar to their own, thematic engagement with a universal leveling experience such as mothering, and direct addresses to the reader that emphasize the intended similarity between self and other. Sapphire's anti-sentiment blocks this identification based on false sameness—or (mis)identification—and often twists these same traits for her own anti-sentimental purposes. The first line of *Push*, for example, thwarts reader identification even as it references sentimental technique: "I was left back when I was twelve because I had a baby for my fahver," writes Precious (*Precious* 3). This opening sentence makes it clear that the reader is in the consciousness of Precious, a teenager who is twice impregnated by her father, a reality many, if not most, readers have not endured. A few lines later, the reader is addressed directly but ambiguously: "My name is Claireece Precious Jones. I don't know why I'm telling you that. Guess 'cause I don't know how far I'm gonna go with this story, or whether I'm gonna start from the beginning or right from here or two weeks from now" (*Precious* 3).

And so Precious's truth, her story, begins, but it is a truth the reader cannot assimilate because it is shockingly dissimilar and thus cannot be identified with. Precious, an obese, semi-literate, poor, African American female, suffers traumatic sexual and physical abuse by both her father and mother, births a daughter with Down Syndrome at twelve and a healthy son at sixteen, and contracts the AIDS virus from her father. Readers are granted unmediated access to Precious's consciousness, but internally she is as shattered with pain as her external body is swollen with excess. Her truth is written in her own often illegible language, the timeline of her story jumbles the past and present without warning, and her internal defense mechanisms routinely interrupt her consciousness with dreams, hallucinations, and fantasies. Her truth vividly and repetitively replays childhood sexual trauma and physical abuse. In mind and body, Precious is not just other, but Other. Her reality is not often her readers,' but is no less real for being different.

The reader is presented with the truth of a reality that is so abhorrent it appears inhuman and of a consciousness that is so disordered it appears impenetrable. Likewise, the bastion of sentimental sameness, motherhood, is demented and abusive. Not only is the reader's role unclear but reader identification is blocked outright because readers are liable to think: *this reality is not my reality, this vision of family is not my family, this language is not mine,* and/or *this mind is not inhabitable.* Even Precious herself questions her own existence, with "Why can't I see myself, feel where I end and begin" (*Precious* 31). Stripped of the comfortable position of easy active identification, readers passively bear witness to Precious's truth. Coalescing with the general "You" of her journal entries, poetry, and recovery writing, readers see and hear and feel, not out of false sameness, but out of acknowledged difference. The second appearance of reader direct address, "I bet chu one thing, I bet chu my baby can read," joins the reader with Precious's second child, Abdul, whose story in *The Kid* also actively blocks reader identification (*Precious* 63).

In the opening of *The Kid*, we meet Abdul on the day of Precious's funeral. He is nine years old and his twenty-seven-year-old mother has died of AIDS. Like *Push*, *The Kid* also actively blocks reader identification. In the first section, readers are incorporated into the consciousness of a child narrator as he struggles to make sense of his mother's death. His internal thoughts frequently blur the past and present and slip without warning into the italic reminiscences of his mother and her exact words. An exemplary passage reads, "I know you don't have what they're saying because you're good we're good I'm good we don't have that, we're, I'm a boy who's *going somewhere, gonna be something*" (*The Kid* 19). Through Abdul's mind, we see Precious and her mothering; he can and does read and has been raised until her death with self-worth and high expectations. Precious loves Abdul, and he carries that love with him through four books that chronicle his life as a second-generation AIDS orphan at ages nine, thirteen, fourteen, and eighteen. Though he internalizes his mother's voice, his reality takes a sharp turn after Precious's death, when his life experiences and his internal disintegration mirror his mother's and thus thwart reader identification. As in *Push*, reality in *The Kid* is also "a mutherfucker" unlike the reader's own.

After Precious's death, Abdul enters a broken social system that soon renders him as invisible as it did his mother. He moves from a foster placement where he is physically abused and violently raped by another boy, to St Ailanthus School for Boys where he is educated but routinely raped by the brothers, to his great-grandmother's apartment where he is forced to confront a past he refuses to acknowledge, to Roman's apartment where he consents (at age fourteen) to being his dance instructor's "boy" (*The Kid* 221). As in *Push*, *The Kid* unflinchingly depicts acts of sexual violation and physical violence that block reader identification through their graphic nature, jumbled timeframe, and shocking severity. Abdul consciously blocks their reality himself, chanting and reciting to remove himself from the present moment and often blacking out during these traumatic encounters and their aftermath. The reader is left to parse reality and hallucination and often can only make sense of Abdul's past when it emerges into the present. Like Precious, Abdul's inner thoughts are splintered and unbound. "Feel like I'm disappearing with every step I take, like my bones radioactive, like in cartoons, glowing," he thinks (*The Kid* 102). Abdul's constant name changes reflect his shifting identity. Whenever he goes somewhere new, the authority figures change his name: from Abdul to Jamal Abdul to J.J. to Arthur Stevens/Crazy Horse to his final mistaken identity of Abdul-Azi Ali. Not only do these constant name changes reflect the violent assault on his identity from the outside, but they also point to his lack of psychological and emotional stability. With no constant identity to use as a foundation, readers cannot locate a core with whom to attach and identify.

Also like his mother, Abdul frequently dissociates or dreams, sometimes in response to trauma, which makes it difficult for readers to reconstruct the chain of events that led to such dissociation. Sometimes these dreams are covers for trauma he himself inflicts on others: "Maybe I am in my dreams. Maybe this is not real. It is a dream [...]. In the dream I'm naked at the end of the hall in Dorm One, the little kids' dorm [...]. He doesn't wake up, I want him to wake up even though I'm scared for him to wake up [...]. But the dream is over. I can finally go to sleep" (*The Kid* 74–5). In passages such as this one, Sapphire places Abdul in a hallucinatory state where he fails to acknowledge his actions, but the reader is not as protected. Through Abdul, Sapphire takes her deliberate blocking of reader identification one step further. If identifying with Precious and Abdul in their moments of trauma is repellent, identifying with Abdul as he traumatizes other children is unthinkable. Full access to shattered consciousnesses does not allow for identification with that which we cannot assimilate through an axis of sameness.

Readers who follow Precious and Abdul from *Push* to *The Kid* and who once coalesced with the general "You" of her notebooks—those journal entries of poetry and prose that move from semi-literacy to signification of abuse to art—find even that tentative thread broken. Abdul eventually comes into possession of the notebooks that house Precious's burgeoning selfhood. As the notebooks progress, it is possible to align the "You" with Abdul himself, especially since it is through these notebooks that he can come to know his mother's story. Disallowing the reality contained in her writings, however, he not only criticizes and discredits her words but destroys them: "Sitting on the grass, the notebooks stacked beside me, I start tearing them page by page into tiny bits. I shred them over my backpack, scooping any pieces that fall onto the grass up and into the pack. By the time I'm through, my fingers hurt" (*The Kid* 239). This destruction is not only symbolic of Abdul's desire to destroy the evidence of his own reality, but is also representative of the intentional blocking of reader identification fashioned by Sapphire. The "You" addressed in Precious's notebooks, the "You" readers thought they were in *Push*, has been violently removed, not only through the displacement of "You" onto Abdul, with whom audiences are hesitant to find similarity, but also through the complete annihilation of the "You" Precious envisioned as her own audience. With *The Kid* the reader's involvement is even more undefined. Even the passive "You" bearing witness to Abdul's truth seems too uncomfortable to inhabit.

"Shame, thas a shame"

With reader identification deliberately blocked and rejected due to the nature of the "truths" Sapphire tells, readers do not respond to these novels with the sympathy and compassion of sentimental literature, but with the shame of anti-sentiment. As is characteristic of anti-sentimental works that engender shame in the reader, shame is also a powerful affect at work within the bounds of these narratives; Precious and Abdul are shamed from within the context of their stories, and readers experience similar shame that extends outside of them. Building on the work of Eve Kosofsky Sedgwick, this essay argues that Precious and Abdul, and then the readers of *Push* and *The Kid* themselves, experience transformational shame: a "free radical" that can make "structural changes in one's relational and interpretive strategies toward both the self and other" (62). Before this shame can be transformative, though, its presence must be acknowledged.

Shame, as defined by Silvan Tompkins, whose groundbreaking work in affect theory Sedgwick builds upon to make her own argument, "is the affect of indignity, of defeat, of transgression, and of alienation" (133). Whether the shaming comes from an external other or its internalization, the individual "feels himself naked, defeated, alienated, lacking in dignity or worth" (133). As Tompkins theorizes, shame first occurs in infancy when a baby finds that the reciprocal gaze of a caretaker is broken. This categorical example marks many of shame's distinguishing features. The shame-humiliation response, as Tompkins calls it, arises through the removal or absence of external feedback and the simultaneous desire to repair that loss. As Sedgwick explains it, "Shame floods into being as a moment, a disruptive moment, in a circuit of identity-constituting identificatory communication" (36). Since shame arises during instances of mutual communication that reinforce identity formation, shame, and one's experience of it, marks identity itself by locating that intra-psychic space between self and other where consciousness resides. Shame "strikes deepest into the heart of man" because it is fundamental to individual identity and enacts the power of relational interdependence (Tompkins 133). If shame exists first when the gaze of an other is broken, then future shameful experiences align with being seen in vulnerable postures or, even more severely, not being seen at all.

Precious admits to her own shame four times in *Push*, at points where she reconstructs vulnerable exposure or hateful feelings. When she starts at the Higher Education Alternative/Each One Teach One, she remembers being in elementary school during the time when she was first raped by her father. At school in her tiny desk, she was frequently incontinent and literally immobilized, regressing to a more primitive stage of development, which she describes as, "My head is big 'lympic size pool, all the years, all the me's floating around glued shamed to desks while pee puddles get big near their feet" (*Precious* 40). She also remembers an older version of herself, shamed by the simultaneous feelings of hatred and pleasure during her rapes, when her body would respond without her conscious intent: "I start to feel good [...]. I feel shamed" (*Precious* 24). These experiences of shame represent Precious's own internalization of a mechanism that comes first from the outside, from the gaze of others who look upon her without seeing her and who perceive her naked vulnerability and expose it without offering cover.

This external shaming is individualized in the nurse who humiliates twelve-year-old Precious when she names Carl Kenwood Jones, her father, as her baby's father. Precious writes, "She quiet quiet. Say, 'Shame, thas a shame. Twelve years old, twelve years old,' she say over 'n over like she crazy (or in some shock or something)" (*Precious* 12–13). Whereas this nurse looks at Precious but does not see her, and thus shames her, a whole system made up of individuals averts its eyes and does not even acknowledge her existence. "I see the pink faces in suits look over top of my head [...]. I sometimes look in the pink people in suits eyes, the men from bizness, and they look way above me, put me out of their eyes" (*Precious* 31–2). This deliberate, systematic shaming forces Precious to question her own existence as she strains to meet the gaze of an individual who will not shame her into alienation and indignity but validate her existence: "I watch myself disappear in their eyes, their tesses. I talk loud but still I don't exist" (*Precious* 31).

These examples serve to emphasize Precious's otherness or strangeness, which Tompkins argues is characteristic of shame. He calls shame's lack of reciprocity a barrier that is suddenly erected, blocking the mutual communication of two individuals. He writes, "Such a barrier might be because one is suddenly looked at by one who is strange, or because one wishes to look at or commune with another person but suddenly cannot because he is strange, or one expected him to be familiar but he suddenly appears unfamiliar, or one started to smile but found one was smiling at a stranger" (Tompkins 135). Precious, in her descriptions of her own invisibility, references this barrier and the strangeness that likely precedes it. She is strange in embodiment, language, and truth, and because this strangeness is apprehended, Precious is ignored and avoided and thus shamed. Likewise, readers feel Precious's shame as their own, as they are reminded of their own shameful strangeness through Precious's exposure.

Precious is subsequently caught in a debilitating shame cycle that begins with her parents, as she says, "My fahver don't see me really. If he did he would know I was like a white girl, a *real* person, inside" (*Precious* 32). The cycle then replicates in the outside world that fails to see her or even her family more broadly: "My whole family, we more than dumb, we invisible" (*Precious* 30). The system fails to see the abuse even when Precious finds herself shamed by its markers in the real world. Unseen and unvalidated, Precious internalizes the outer shame and shames herself. She hates herself for behaviors and feelings that shame her and acknowledges that the external ugliness she wears has penetrated her inner self. "But I am not different on the inside," Precious admits; the ugliness exists beneath the skin (*Precious* 125). The only way for the ugliness to have not penetrated her core, in Precious's view, was to have had someone see her—such as that shaming nurse—and acknowledge her much earlier: "I just want to say when I was twelve, TWELVE, somebody hadda help me it not be like it is now" (*Precious* 125). Instead of looking at Precious and shaming her or turning away altogether in rejection, someone should have seen and helped.

Now, without that relational support, Precious is alone and ashamed and outside. The accumulation of shame makes "[her] more shy of the next stranger [she] encounter[s]" and it also forces her to feel shamed by her own shame (Tompkins 141). Precious admits to this accumulation by writing,

> So much pain, shame—I never feel the loneliness. It such a small thing compared to your daddy climb on you, your muver kick you, slave you, feel you up. But now since I been going to school I feel lonely. Now since I sit in circle I realize all my life, all my life I been outside of circle. Mama give me orders, Daddy porno talk me, school never did learn me [*Precious* 62].

Although Precious successfully creates that circle for her son Abdul—"In his beauty I see my own"—her untimely death forces him to repeat the shame cycle experienced by his mother (*Precious* 140). As Precious felt unseen and unheard by the "pink faces in suits," Abdul is not just unacknowledged by the system, but shamefully abused by it. Brother John says, "*We'll take care of you. It's a shame you've lost your mother and father. But you have a mother and father in us here at St Ailanthus. We love you and will take care of you until you're a man and can take care of yourself, J.J.*" (*The Kid* 108–9). In a reconfiguration of Precious's parental abuse, Brother John both acknowledges Abdul's shameful parentage and adopts the role that will ultimately shame him through repetitive abuse. Not only do the brothers shame him through ritualized rapes under the guise of parental care and love, but they also publicly shame him by controlling his body nonsexually with physical assaults and refused bathroom trips. Peeing on himself like the young Precious, Abdul visibly carries the hunch of shame with a bowed back and averted eyes.

Abdul takes Precious's internalization of shame one step further in his own pursuit of shameful experiences that replay the sexual abuse perpetrated against him. This revictimization puts Abdul in positions where he uses his sexuality for financial benefit; the acts themselves are so demeaning that they clearly repeat the external shame cycle on the inside, such as when he receives only one dollar for an anonymous sex act at Marcus Garvey Park, consents to being Roman's kept "boy" for shelter, and prostitutes himself for appallingly small amounts of money. Abdul's extended stay with Toosie is a pervasive experience of shame; not only does he expose himself in the middle of the night as he sleeps, but he also openly masturbates in front of his great-grandmother as she reveals the history of his family tree. Shame circulates throughout Toosie's apartment and into Abdul's internal being. He is shamed by Toosie for his unintentional somnolent exposure, but he also induces his own shame through his transgressive autoerotic act. Furthermore, he feels shame opposite her own lack of shame and thinks, "She ain't human. Her being human makes me ashamed" (*The Kid* 181). Like Precious, whose shame forces her into a painful loneliness in which she questions her own existence, Abdul feels like he is a phony, a false projection of who he wishes he were inside. His internalization of shame is a female voice that constantly challenges his sense of self. She says, "And you're shit, do you think anybody would want you if they knew what you did? Phony, phony, phony," to which Abdul silently responds, "I hate her, whoever she is, and she not me. She's just a … a stupid voice in my head. She's in me; she's not me" (*The Kid* 275).

Shame, once outside, is now inside both Precious and Abdul; it challenges their "essential dignity" and is felt "as a sickness within the self" (Tompkins 136). Their mutual self-loathing stems from this internalization of shame and pain, but their equal lack of acknowledgment from the outside contributes to an alienating loneliness. Abdul poignantly expresses, "I feel so full and totally empty at the same time" (*The Kid* 147). Full of pain, but empty of acknowledgment and love, Abdul's life experiences metaphorically recapitulate Precious's force feeding by her mother. Like her son many years later, Precious is forced to fill herself beyond satiety with abject food, and this filling serves to highlight the pain of her emptiness. She explains this paradoxical relationship between fullness and lack when she writes, "Eating, first 'cause she make me, beat me if I don't, then eating hoping pain in my neck back go away. I keep eating till the pain, the gray TV light, and Mama is a blur; and I just fall back on the couch so full it like I'm dying and I go to sleep, like I always do" (*Precious* 21). For both Precious and Abdul, death is an attractive option: a possible cessation of all the shame and pain they experience on a daily basis. Yet neither chooses this route. Instead, each decides, like Sapphire herself, to create art as a way of reclaiming their identities. Through writing and dance, Precious and Abdul sublimate their pain and create audiences that see them without looking away. Their art allows them to transform their pervasive shame into Sedgwick's structural change; as Precious and Abdul transform, so too do the readers who experience shame and its transformation through the art that Sapphire herself has created. "Transformational shame *is performance*," explains Sedgwick, and this is what Precious and Abdul do through their writing and dancing respectively (38).

"*I think how* alive *I am*"

After their persistent mutual acknowledgement of shame and its attendant emptiness, both Precious and Abdul choose to remove their cloaks of humiliation. This conscious step is important because it pushes both mother and son to reclaim their identities by reclaiming the past and seeking new relational bonds through their art and relationships. Rather than stagnating in pain, Precious and Abdul use shame's transformative capacity to perform shame on the outside and grow "skin side out," in the words of Sedgwick, rather than endlessly repeating the initial movement of outer shame turned inward (38). In their transformations, both Precious and Abdul look to their readers as they bring their shame out in affirmation and pride and thus invite readers to transform our own shame. When these moments occur, readers have a choice to either shut our eyes in rejection or to meet the eyes of Precious and Abdul and move from shame to recognition. If we see Precious and Abdul, we have moved beyond our own shame to the empowerment of relational acknowledgement.

Although Precious and Abdul successfully transform their own shame, they do it by following two different paths. For Precious, this movement starts on the outside through her relationship with Ms Rain; for Abdul, this change starts on the inside (like the reader's own) when he finds himself shamed through his conversation with great-grandmother Toosie. Ms Rain, in her desire to teach her students to read and write, forms important interpersonal relationships with them as they write to her about their lives. In a pedagogical technique reminiscent of a dialogue journal, Precious writes to Ms Rain in her own infantile literacy, and Ms Rain writes back, questioning and affirming Precious's words even as she writes them correctly within the context of Precious's own writing. In this way, Ms Rain functions as that outside term that never acknowledged Precious before. Not only does she see and hear Precious's truths, but she models appropriate linguistic structures as she communicates with her.

Although these truths may in fact be the shameful experiences that mark Precious's identity, by drawing out of herself and into a relationship with another person and into language, Precious starts to move from shame to affirmation, from paralysis to narrative integration. Ms Rain, explicitly addressing the content of all her students' writings in class, repeats the imperative, "Say no shame. No shame" (*Precious* 76). Precious, as she reflects on Ms Rain's command in relation to her own life, affirms it back: "Most time it seem like hype, 'cause she say it so much. But that why she say she say it—to reprogram us to love ourselves. I love me" (*Precious* 76). In Precious's case, the overlap of an acknowledging adult, language development, and writing the past allows her to transform her shame into love for herself, her children, her classmates, and Ms Rain. She creates a new circle that reinforces her growth.

Significantly, this transformation is observable in Precious's art. In this way, her writing fulfills the traits of Sapphire's own definition. It is clear that the seed of improvement and of positive transformation of shame was always within Precious. Indeed, her fantasies of pop stardom and a glamorous life function doubly as a defensive mechanism against utter psychological debilitation and as the foundation for their material production in her writing. First internal and then external, these fantasies "push" Precious out of herself and out of her shame: "What is a normal life? A life where you not shamed of your mother. Where your friends come over after school and watch TV and do homework. Where your mother is normal looking and don't hit you over the head wif iron skillet. I would wish for in my fantasy a second chance. Since my first chance go to Mama and Daddy" (*Precious* 115). To generate and grow, Precious must first envision a fantasy version of her life as a prerequisite for her eventual transformation, an outside that might occasion a more pleasing inside.

Through her journal entries, her notes to Ms Rain, her poetry, and her copying of the art of others, such as Hughes's "Letter to Son," Precious expands herself and sheds her shame. Her art, language, and sense of self all improve at once as she emerges from her shameful disappearance to her more confident revelation. In this self-expression, Precious exerts not only her own authority but also her own pleasure and pride. Precious sees herself in her art and asks the reader to see her too because desire for positive affect is also a prerequisite for shame. Precious wants to be seen, or else she would not be shamed by her invisibility. Tompkins explains, "In the response of shame, be it to the stranger, to the censor external or internal, or to defeat, the self remains somewhat committed to the investment of positive affect in the person, or activity, or circumstances, or that part of the self which has created an impediment to communication" (138). She looks to the readers, hoping to be seen, even if that seeing acknowledges the sight of someone strange.

When the eyes of the reader and Precious meet, the previous shame transforms into a positive relational bond. In her notebooks, Precious turns her gaze out to the reader by drawing eyes alongside her poetry. She literally looks out to and at her readers, inviting them to return her gaze. It is important that at both moments she is also conceptualizing the mutuality of seeing and being seen and the coalescence of identity around that reciprocation. In the first poem to use this multi-modal writing approach of text and eye, Precious writes and Ms Rain corrects in parentheses: "see the i/ey (eye) see/see me/liv (live)" and alongside, there is a wide open eye with eyelashes looking out to the reader (*Precious* 91). In this synchronicity, Precious is relating her "I" to the "eye" that "sees" and ultimately to the "I" that "sees" Precious live. That "I" is the reader who both gazes and is gazed upon, who affirms and is affirmed, who acknowledges and is acknowledged.

The next time an eye looks out to the reader, the long eyelashes are gone and in their place are two tears, alongside the lines: "wallk throo Harlem in/morning to school/mostly pepul goin/to work/faces faces/iron brown/ black glas/tears/not jazzee/Harlem/of Langston Huges/Harlmen Poet Laureeyet!" (*Precious* 102–3). Here, Precious models for her reader the type of seeing she expects. Her eye demands a returning eye; readers oblige, and then they see Precious seeing that "Harlem done/took/a beating" (*Precious* 103). She doesn't turn away in rejection or bow her head in shame, but she too sees Harlem as she wants to be seen, as someplace strange that invites her reciprocal acknowledgement.

Whereas Precious first responds to the "No shame" call of Ms Rain on the outside and it transforms her inside, Abdul responds on the inside first. Betrayed, abused, and finally abandoned by an unseeing system, Abdul finds himself in Toosie's home, where he finally hears Toosie's story and his own genealogy. In this truth-telling, he faces successive generations of early sexual abuse, childhood pregnancy, forced prostitution, violence, and death.[3] Although at first Abdul actively disallows the truth of his family background using the same strategies he uses when he encounters a reality he does not want to face or a trauma he does not want to be present for, eventually he looks back at his great-grandmother, whom he calls "Slavery Days," and sees and hears her. "Now I'm really listening [...] 'Well?' I say" (*The Kid* 207). This unfortunate seeing and hearing confronts Abdul with the shame of his entire family, as well as himself, in the body of a stranger, and he quickly moves from acknowledgement to transformation.

Affirming Toosie first by giving her his treasured kaleidoscope, Abdul thinks, "Bye, Toosie. Bye, Great-Gran'ma. I close the suitcase. Where? I don't know—I don't want to live like her, I don't want to *be* like her—I do know I'm outta here" (*The Kid* 209). He then leaves, shedding his shame so he can focus on its sublimation in his art: his dance, which he calls "ascension" (*The Kid* 211). Through his dance, like Precious's writing, Abdul is able to own his identity, reclaim his past, and join a community that has members and an audience. "Here my body is my own [...]. Here I am music [...]. Here in the beat is my life," he claims (*The Kid* 116). Abdul is alive and, like his mother, desires "to have the other look with interest or enjoyment rather than with derision" (Tompkins 138). Precious and Abdul cannot get rid of their shame or pain, but they can use both for transformative purposes that expand and reclaim their identities and once again invite our interest and pleasure.

Abdul does not open his eyes onto his readers as Precious does through her writing, but Roman makes a similar analogy with Abdul's dance and invites the same kind of reciprocal seeing encouraged by Precious. He pushes Abdul to tell the truth of his story through his dance, the vehicle of his pain: "Every time you move, you should be saying something. People look at you and read your story like a book. Did you know that? That's all we have is our bodies, dancers, and you can't hide or lie. If you do, nobody want to look at you" (*The Kid* 342). Audiences are reading a book, and they are reading the character Abdul through his art and through his body. When he shows the readers his truth, they should not reject or shame him, but rather acknowledge him by holding his gaze. This mutuality is what Sapphire intends, and it is the movement of anti-sentiment that allows audiences to do so, to "see" what others do not. She does not intend for them to employ a "set of strategies" used to avoid shame like her detractors, but rather to confront it directly and allow its transformative capacity to work (Sedgwick 115). This expansion of consciousness is possible because shame is both catching and indeterminate, universal and individual; audiences experience shame when they observe others in their shame, but the feeling is intimate and hearkens back to internal otherness, a shame-based identification, a core strangeness. Ironically, readers need to be seen and heard by Precious and Abdul, just as they need the readers' seeing and hearing.

Like Dr Sanjeev, or Dr See as Abdul aptly renames him in the dreamlike ambiguity of *The Kid*'s last section, who simply asks, "Who are you?" and "Why are you here?" Sapphire's intended reader responds by acknowledging that the young man before the doctor is the accumulation of all his traumatic, shameful, and abusing experiences. Wide-eyed, like Precious's drawing, the reader hears, "All I need is Abdul and Jones," a direct affirmation of who he is in the face of an unfamiliar other (*The Kid* 353). Readers are not supposed to "look" in the manner of the blinding lights of penetration and examination that Abdul eventually shatters, freeing himself from their binding judgment, but in the manner of the open eyes and ears that have witnessed his truth. When the book closes as the door opens, sending him back into the world, the reader simply needs to acknowledge, "I see" like Precious and "I hear" like Abdul (*The Kid* 374).

Notes

1. See Galioto, "Female (Mis)Identifications: From *Uncle Tom's Cabin*'s Jealousy to *Beloved*'s Shame." This article on Sapphire's *Push* and *The Kid* moves this argument about (mis)identification, shame, and anti-sentiment into the 21st century.

2. In-depth analysis of *Precious* is outside the bounds of this current article; however, the film's interrogation of processes of looking and being seen literalizes *Push*'s conceptual center. Likewise, audience response to the film mimics responses to the books: Daniels' film has either been praised for its representation of a difficult reality or criticized for dramatizing disgusting stereotypes.

3. In total, this family lineage represents what Alice Walker calls the collective internalized shame that passes through the generations of African American families: "Our shame is deep. For shame is the result of soul injury" (55).

Works Cited

Coffey, Laura T. "Follow Precious' Son in Sapphire's New Book, *The Kid*." www.TODAY.com. www.NBCNews.com, 11 July 2011. Web. 18 January 2013.
Galioto, Erica D. "Female (Mis)Identifications: From *Uncle Tom's Cabin*'s Jealousy to *Beloved*'s Shame." *Women Writers* January 2010 (Themed Scholarly Issue: "Psychoanalysis and *La Femme*"): n. pag. Web. 18 January 2013.
James, Kelvin Christopher. "Sapphire." *BOMB* 57 (Fall 1996): 42–5. Print.
Precious. Dir. Lee Daniels. Lionsgate, 2009. Film.
Reed, Ishmael. "Fade to White." *New York Times*. NYTimes.com, 5 February 2010: 1–2. Web. 23 January 2013.
Sapphire. *The Kid*. New York: Penguin, 2011. Print.
———. *Push*. New York: Vintage, 1996. Print.

———. "Why Stories Like *Precious* Need to Be Told." *New York Times*. NYTimes.com, 12 February 2010: 1. Web. 23 January 2013.

Sedgwick, Eve Kosofsky. *Touching Feeling: Affect, Pedagogy, Performativity*. Durham, NC: Duke University Press, 2003. Print.

Tompkins, Silvan. *Shame and Its Sisters: A Silvan Tompkins Reader*. Ed. Eve Kosofsky Sedgwick and Adam Frank. Durham, NC: Duke University Press, 1995. Print.

Walker, Alice. *The Same River Twice*. New York: Scribner, 1996. Print.

Wilson, Marq. "'A Push Out of Chaos': An Interview with Sapphire." *MELUS* 37.4 (Winter 2012): 31–9. Print.

Profitable Sentiments
HBO's The Wire *and* Harriet Beecher Stowe's Uncle Tom's Cabin

KRISTIN J. JACOBSON

"This sentimental motherfucker just cost us money."—Clinton "Shorty" Buise, *The Wire*, season five, episode ten

"I don't sell dead niggers."—Simon Legree, *Uncle Tom's Cabin*, chapter 41

After Slim Charles (Anwan Glover) shoots Calvin "Cheese" Wagstaff (Method Man) in the final episode of HBO's acclaimed series *The Wire* (aired 2002–2008), Clinton "Shorty" Buise (Clinton "Shorty" Buise) laments the loss of funds promised by Cheese and needed by the co-op to buy drugs. In Buise's eyes, Slim Charles's murder of Cheese to avenge another co-op member's death has no monetary value; in fact, sentimentalism creates a deficit. Cheese is worth more alive than dead. Cheese himself had asserted moments before that the Baltimore drug dealers in *The Wire* occupy post-nostalgic, post-sentimental terrain: "There ain't no back in the day, nigga. Ain't no nostalgia to this shit here. There's just the street and the game and what happen here today." Defying this unsentimental logic, Slim Charles appears to be a throwback to an earlier era that at least some find fiscally unprofitable. In comparison, Simon Legree also "count[s] the cost" before his deadly beating of Tom in Harriet Beecher Stowe's *Uncle Tom's Cabin* (serialized 3 June 1851 to 2 April 1852; published 1852), and Legree ultimately refuses to take money for Tom's corpse (Stowe 421; 427).[1] While the motivation for the unprofitable murders is distinct, both men's dead bodies represent lost capital and ask the reader to weigh these fiscal losses against the men's moral and social value.

The charged exchanges underscore sentimentality's linchpin role in both narratives and raise questions about sentimentality's economic and social profitability. The scenes also raise questions about sentimentality's role in postmodernity. After all, if the sentimental results in "the emasculation of American men" (Fiedler 89), what is any semblance of the sentimental doing in *The Wire*'s gritty, realist narrative? Is sentimentality a rogue force or a systematic player with which all the characters in *The Wire*—drug dealers, drug users, lawyers, elected officials and police—must contend? This reading focuses on *The Wire*'s fifth and final season to flesh out the show's use of sentimental narrative structures. While all five seasons of *The Wire* deploy sentimental tactics, the fifth season's fictional serial killer, manufactured by detective Jimmy McNulty (Dominic West) and exploited by McNulty as well as other characters to garner political and public (economic) support, produces a metafiction about what elicits profitable sympathy among contemporary audiences.[2]

Comparing the use of sentimentality in *Uncle Tom's Cabin* and *The Wire*—particularly representations of sentimental masculinity's social and economic value—measures the degree to which sentimentality has and has not changed since the serialization and publication of *Uncle Tom's Cabin* in 1852. While *The Wire*'s overt references to Dickens beg comparison with this British novelist's works, *The Wire*'s sentimentalism is also deeply grounded in a specifically American sentimental tradition represented by America's sentimental urtext, *Uncle Tom's Cabin*. Measuring *The Wire* against *Uncle Tom's Cabin* underscores sympathy's enduring potential and failure to increase social awareness and motivate change; the comparison also expands our understanding of American sentimentality's—to borrow Nancy Armstrong's phrase—"racial logic."

"The Dickensian Affect": American Sentimentality *in* The Wire *and* Uncle Tom's Cabin

Comparing *The Wire* with *Uncle Tom's Cabin* reads *The Wire* against and with the grain of current criticism. *The Wire*, building on creator/writer David Simon's description, is often understood as a postmodern Greek tragedy or as a social realist "visual novel."[3] *The Wire*'s gritty, violent masculine realism does not summon sentimentality's conventional association with "mawkish, affected, or extravagantly emotional" women's writing (Davidson, "Sentimental Novel" 786). Leigh Claire La Berge, for example, notes "*The Wire* has correctly been labeled unique to the televisual medium for its use of a realist mode. It tends to eschew melodrama, sentimentality, romance, and excessive individualism, and it minimizes their associated techniques of nondiegetic sound, flashback, voice-over, dream sequence, and dialogue-dependent jump cuts" (550). However, contemporary rethinkings of sentimentality by such authors as Lauren Berlant (*The Female Complaint*, 2008), Leonard Cassuto (*Hard-Boiled Sentimentality*, 2009), and Elizabeth Barnes (*Love's Whipping Boy*, 2011) as well as *The Wire*'s ironic references to Victorian fiction—namely Charles Dickens—suggest we need to broaden further *The Wire*'s generic terrain. While this essay does not allow the space to trace the distinct literary histories of and connections among melodrama, sentimental fiction, crime fiction, the protest novel, and literary realism, *The Wire*'s "mixed-code" narrative links these various traditions (Davis 2).

Teasing out the series' specific narrative connections to sentimentalism challenges the "largely accepted [...] gendering of sentiment as feminine" (Chapman and Hendler, "Introduction" 7). The comparison counters critical reluctance to reconsider men's relationships with feminine forms and rethinks the conventional gendered boundaries that maintain a firm hold on our understanding of genre:

> The continuing lack of attention to male writers', artists', and philosophers' engagement with American sentimental culture suggests, even now, a critical unwillingness to imagine the American man of sentiment, as if this subject position is too paradoxical, too unstable, too threatening to discuss; as if critics fear the results of deconstructing the alignments of reason, commerce, and the public sphere with men, and feelings, domesticity and the private sphere with women [Chapman and Hendler, "Introduction" 7].[4]

Answering Chapman and Hendler's call, this reading reconsiders *The Wire*'s largely masculine drama—a result of its violent plotlines and focus on male politicians, criminals and police—to uncover the narrative's broad and deep connections to sentimentality.[5]

Leonard Cassuto's argument about the relationship between sentimental and crime fictions helps flesh out *The Wire*'s specific use of the sentimental. Cassuto argues that this generic and gendered dichotomy reveals itself to be more mutually dependent than distinct: "both sentimentalism and crime fiction depend on the marketplace-household (that is, public/private) division established by capitalism. Each genre seeks to emphasize one pole at the expense of the other; yet each also ruptures the divide, showing it to be untenable and yet also inextinguishable" (Cassuto 11). *The Wire*'s crime fiction likewise combines detective work with sentimental features such as sympathetic characterizations and a narrative focus on familial and social politics. Its refusal to paint characters that are fully good or bad, furthermore, results in an interrogation of these gendered generic dichotomies. As a result, familial plots can only be artificially separated from the criminal storylines in *The Wire*. The family and domestic sphere's relationship to the marketplace is as key to the characters in *The Wire* as it is to those in *Uncle Tom's Cabin*. Jimmy McNulty's family troubles, for instance, are directly related to his work. The ideological boundaries the texts draw between the public and private spheres, however, help distinguish their sentimental forms.

Domestic stability in *Uncle Tom's Cabin* is endangered, if not destroyed, by the economic institution of slavery. The marketplace, in this case, dangerously infringes on the domestic sphere. Families are literally torn apart due to financial need. Mr. Shelby sells Uncle Tom, who is separated from his wife and children. The same fate threatens the enslaved Eliza and George Harris, compelling them to escape to the North. Yet these same family ties are what allow the families to persevere. Whether inhabited by black or white families, the home in *Uncle Tom's Cabin* locates "a center of virtue [and] an arena of progressive politics" (Reynolds 43). The novel encourages faith in an idealized picture of domestic stability and morality. Stowe, furthermore, writing against the stereotype of black sexual promiscuity, "Forcefully challeng[es] such racism": "*Uncle Tom's Cabin* makes marital fidelity between blacks the driving force of its two main plots: the escape of Eliza and George Harris, and the separation of Tom from his family" (Reynolds 67). The threat to the stability of these domestic relations elicits sympathy. While *Uncle Tom's Cabin* narrates the intimate connections between the marketplace and the domestic sphere, it simultaneously constructs key moral differences between these spheres. As a result, the sentimentality in *Uncle Tom's Cabin* is less ambiguous than that found in *The Wire* and other twenty-first-century fictions.

Whereas the home in *Uncle Tom's Cabin* ideally offers "a constant haven of virtue that forwards a progressive political point" (Reynolds 266), domesticity in *The Wire* "renovate[s] the ideal home's usual depiction by positioning instability—as opposed to stability—as a key structure of quotidian American home life" (Jacobson 2). As George Lipsitz points out, *The Wire* portrays the family and the marketplace as more institutionally similar than different: *The Wire* "[depicts] both institutions as traps that constrain individuals and cultivate greed and envy rather than promote initiative or affection" (97). Stephen Lucasi similarly argues that the family in *The Wire* demonstrates globalization's destructive power (its trap), but he also suggests that the family simultaneously offers refuge from that power: "*The Wire* [...] employs familial narratives for contrasting purposes. The family continually operates as a guardedly optimistic site for the (re)valuation of human life against capitalism's global march" (138).

The final episode's montage particularly exhibits *The Wire*'s characteristic ambivalent sentimentality that concurrently portrays the home as a vicious trap and a circumspect haven.

Season five's final montage concludes narrative strands: we see what becomes of the main characters. Just prior to the montage, McNulty retrieves the homeless man he "disappeared" as part of the contrived serial killer plot. On their way back to Baltimore, McNulty pulls off to the side of the road just outside the city limits. McNulty looks out at the city and the camera shifts from McNulty and the homeless man to various scenes in the city. The images we see as viewers are representative of both McNulty's musings as he looks out over the city and the perspective of the omniscient visual narrator that sees beyond any individual character. *The Wire*'s final montage, however, frustrates the montage's association with the sentimental narrative practices of catharsis and closure.[6]

We see where the preceding action has left important characters, but in these conclusions there is as much injustice and lack of closure as there is justice and resolution. For example, Reginald "Bubbles" Cousins's (Andre Royo) sobriety is finally rewarded with a place at his sister's dinner table, satisfying a sentimental reformative character arc that takes him from druggie hustler to trusted family man; the show ends with home serving as a refuge for Bubbles. However, the young Duquan "Dukie" Weems (Jermaine Crawford) has taken Bubbles's place on the streets; when we last see Dukie he is doing drugs, unable to escape or reverse his declining domestic security. Bubbles reunites with family and home whereas Dukie's downward spiral results from a lack of domestic stability and legal employment options. Just as the series asks viewers to see institutional parallels between, for example, the police and drug dealers, its narrative also constructs various parallels among the characters. Based on the other characters we have seen, Dukie is as likely to die as to beat addiction and even Bubbles's sobriety and security is an hour-by-hour struggle: "It's a thin line 'tween heaven and here" (season one, episode four). Home for these characters may trap or empower.

Conversely, "UNCLE TOM'S CABIN," at the novel's conclusion serves as a memorial to the deceased Tom's steadfast honesty and fidelity and as a universal emblem of domesticity destroyed by slavery (Stowe 447). Tom's martyrdom offers an explicit lesson about "your freedom" and holds the potential to produce change so the same injustices are not passed on "to his wife and children" (Stowe 447). The conclusion emphasizes the immoral marketplace's violent infringements on the domestic sphere's stability. Both North and South are named "guilty before God" and the Union will only be saved "by repentance, justice and mercy" (Stowe 456). *The Wire*'s Baltimore, however, does not similarly serve as a didactic memorial to a city destroyed by drugs. *The Wire*'s conclusion does not offer religion as a source of redemption. Bubbles and Dukie's contrasting fates emphasize that the war against drugs is a deception: fighting drugs only addresses a symptom rather than the root causes grounded in capitalism's greed. When McNulty declares at the end of the final montage, "Let's go home," his remarks are cast in the context of the final montage's variant images, which present a visual story of Baltimore's contradictions: this home is neither fully a haven nor a trap.

As a result, the domestic sphere in *The Wire* is a more ambiguous space, what this writer has elsewhere described as neodomestic, what Lauren Berlant describes in *The Female Complaint* as a "countersentimental narrative," and what Kimberly Chabot Davis defines in *Postmodern Texts and Emotional Audiences* as "sentimental postmodernism." *The Wire*'s ambiguity produces a narrative that "engages and then denies or subverts" (Klein 179) sentimental pleasure in order "to subvert the passive, satisfied viewing position typically established by the primetime social melodrama" (Klein 188). *The Wire*'s dual engagement and denial of the sentimental results in a story "lacerated by ambivalence: they [countersentimental narratives] struggle with their own attachment to the promise of a sense of unconflictedness, intimacy, and collective belonging with which the U.S. sentimental tradition gifts its citizens and occupants, whether or not they are politically exhausted, cynically extended, or just plain diffident" (Berlant 55). Ambivalence, especially in regard to the home's idealized stability, distinguishes nineteenth- and twenty-first-century sentimental texts.

While the stories deploy sentimentality in more or less ambiguous ways, their critics share similar concerns regarding sentimentality's authenticity. Notably, white authors created these texts largely set in stereotypically black domestic spaces—the slave cabin and urban ghetto, respectively. As a result, authenticity becomes an implicit or explicit part of the sentimental realism and its narrative analysis: critics emphasize or question the authors' authority to represent these Other spaces and/or the authenticity of the representations. Critical emphasis on the narratives' realism, furthermore, underscores the representations' political stakes: to produce political change the fictions must be real. A sense of the explicit and implicit challenges to the texts' authenticity can be seen in Stowe's *A Key to Uncle Tom's Cabin* (1853), which she wrote to defend the novel's authenticity, and in *The Wire: The Last Word*, a short film included among the fifth season's special features that similarly emphasizes the show's realism.

Like the contemporary responses to *Uncle Tom's Cabin*'s representations of slavery, initial scholarship on *The Wire*'s portrayal of a drug-infested city also emphasizes its sociological realism. For example, *Critical Inquiry* published a series of articles examining *The Wire*'s grounding in sociological research.[7] *The Wire* encourages this line of inquiry through a variety of techniques. For example, the series blurs the line between fiction and reality in its select use of actors who play themselves—or, at least, retain their own names. Joseph Christopher Schaub, in fact, argues that *The Wire*'s fiction is more real or authentic than reality television (124). Penfold-Mounce et al. similarly argue that *The Wire* offers a "new take on reality TV," what the authors describe as "authentic television" (159). The final montage emphasizes this blurred boundary between fiction and reality by turning the lens from the fictional characters to focus on footage from the streets of Baltimore and its inhabitants. In doing so, the closing gesture continues to invite the viewer to understand the fictional drama as reality. Representational authenticity is key because if the sentimental text is found to persuade by deception, then its political message is invalidated.

Authenticity alone, however, may not be enough to validate the political message. Critics question what social profit is to be gained if an individual is only required to "*feel right*," as suggested in *Uncle Tom's Cabin* (Stowe 452). Likewise, *The Wire*'s ambivalence leads some critics to bemoan the show's lack of solutions and sense of powerlessness. Such concerns, as expressed by Ann Douglas, align sentimentalism with the status quo: "Sentimentalism provides a way to protest a power to which one has already in part capitulated" (12). In contemporary parlance, this skepticism toward sentimentalism questions whether sentimentality results in neoliberalism, a "stripped-down, nonredistributive form of 'equality' designed for global consumption during the twenty-first century, and compatible with continued upward redistribution of resources" (Duggan xii). Countering this logic, Rebecca Ann Wanzo contends "sentimentality *cannot* easily be understood as progressive or conservative" (9). In this view, the individual text and its socio-political grounding rather than the mere presence or absence of sentimentality produces a "progressive or conservative" narrative.[8] Comparing *The Wire* with *Uncle Tom's Cabin* grounds *The Wire*'s narrative within slavery's specific historical and aesthetic legacies, revealing *The Wire*'s neoliberal as well as progressive politics.[9]

Looking at *The Wire* alongside *Uncle Tom's Cabin* underscores that contemporary Baltimore, the setting of *The Wire*, is not simply a product of twenty-first-century globalization. Stowe, in fact, pointed out in *A Key to Uncle Tom's Cabin* that Baltimore housed an important slave market (149) as well as fostered abolition (197).[10] Comparing *The Wire* with *Uncle Tom's Cabin* and its socio-historical setting reminds viewers that Baltimore—a city at the geographic crossroads between North and South—continues to foster these contradictions. Baltimore's legal and illegal global trafficking of bodies and goods is not a new phenomenon or the sole result of twenty-first-century global capital. Rather, it is a global and national legacy as old as the city itself, with roots in the (transatlantic) slave trade.[11]

The Wire's turn to Victorian England rather than the United States and the resulting lack of explicit reference to Baltimore's historical connections to slavery speaks to creator David Simon's claim that the series is not about race:

> I understand that you may perceive a racial message in the fact that the lives so depicted are African-American. Race is a touchy subject and for that reason, many people struggle with the world we are depicting on *The Wire*. But I can only assure you that the message of *The Wire* has precious little to do with race. It is about class, and capitalism, and how money and power route themselves. It is about who has a future in America and who is denied a future. This is a show, in fact, about the other America—as distant from the viable black middle class as from the white middle class. It is a show about people whose lives are worth less every day, because we as a nation have constructed an economic model that assures certain classes luxury and profit while failing to address the basic dignity and relevance of many other Americans trapped at the lowest rungs of that economic model [King et al.].

Rather than outline the complex ways in which racial and class inequality relate, Simon claims "the message of *The Wire* has precious little to do with race," disconnecting race from how "money and power route themselves." This stance requires him to distance the show from slavery's socio-political legacies—hence, the references to Victorian Britain rather than the Victorian United States—and elide racial difference and oppression in favor of class struggle.[12] Simon's critique of capitalism suggests a Marxist lens. Furthermore, the recognition that race, particularly as a representation of black culture, constitutes a "touchy subject" but not the primary theme, asks the viewer to reconsider the role of race in the series. To what degree does racial difference matter in a series about class inequalities?

The reference to Dickens relocates attention to British Victorian sentimentalism and is a telling narrative ploy enabling Simon to not include slavery and its legacies among "all the pieces [that] matter."[13] Doing so also furthers Simon's claim that *The Wire* is more about class than race. However, this tactic also depends on race operating outside of or despite class, but as the terms "white trash" or "ghetto" often signify, class and race/ethnicity are frequently co-dependent. Furthermore, class and race/ethnicity do not always "match" in expected ways, a tension exploited by *The Beverly Hillbillies* and other comedies about the nouveau riche. More seriously, as David Wilson argues in his book *Cities and Race: America's New Black Ghettos* (2006), race often plays an essential role in justifying neoliberal policies that disproportionately impact black communities. Geographers David J. Roberts and Minelle Mahtani take Wilson's argument further, arguing "neoliberalism modifies the way race is experienced or understood in society" (250). By shifting sentimentalism's sociopolitical grounding to Dickens's England, *The Wire* effectively rewrites slavery out of the black experience. The telling omission documents *The Wire*'s (conscious) refusal to connect the city's and the characters' problems to this much longer history of predatory capitalism. Simon, following this neoliberal vein, suggests that race ultimately creates "precious little" difference among people.

Thus, while critics sing the praises of *The Wire*'s sociological realism, pedagogically—if we take Simon at his word—*The Wire* teaches viewers "precious little" about race. These claims seem to be at odds with each other. Simon's narrative strategies resemble the neoliberal tactics described by David Theo Goldberg in *Racist Culture: Philosophy and the Politics of Meaning*: "modern racist culture is marked, fundamentally, by its refusal to acknowledge the role that racism plays in everyday structures of society and how these structures work to fundamentally disguise and, simultaneously, reify the power of racism within society" (Roberts and Mahtani 253). The privileging of class over race results in, as George Lipsitz argues, the crime *The Wire* "cannot name." Where Lipsitz names the crime as housing inequality based on racial discrimination, this essay suggests this unnamed "crime" can be traced back even further to slavery. Simon's framing and narrative choices—especially when set within the American sentimental tradition—expose key blanks in *The Wire*'s narrative; nevertheless, a close reading of *The Wire*'s characters, especially the male cast, reveals that the characters embody key racial differences, even among members of similar economic classes.

These differences, as Berlant argues in *The Female Complaint* and as this essay has begun to suggest here in relation to *The Wire* and *Uncle Tom's Cabin*, indicate the persistence of sentimental structures and critiques. In the case of *The Wire*, tracing "the *Uncle Tom* genealogy" recovers denied literary ancestry (Berlant 20). As the next section examines in more detail, the characters themselves are also a part of this sentimental legacy. Wanzo points out in *The Suffering Will Not Be Televised* that *Uncle Tom's Cabin*'s characters have become "rhetorical shorthand" for an array of stock sentimental characters (24). How *The Wire* contends with this representational legacy further demonstrates its balance of neoliberal and progressive politics.[14]

Sentimental Identification and Masculinity: McNulty and Murdered Black Men

Both *Uncle Tom's Cabin* and *The Wire* focus on "Life Among the Lowly," presenting a range of characters from various classes and races/ethnicities that demonstrate an array of gendered behaviors and sexualities. The narratives use characterization as a persuasive means to bring about desired social change: support for the end of slavery in *Uncle Tom's Cabin* and an indictment of capitalism in *The Wire*. Sentimentalism's power rests in the characters' ability to produce sympathetic identification among different social classes within the text and between the characters and the reader/viewer. Glenn Hendler names the "classic example of this gesture" as "[t]he oft-cited moment in *Uncle Tom's Cabin* when the escaped slave Eliza Harris wins the senator's wife, Mrs. Bird, over to her cause by asking, 'Have you ever lost a child?'" (6). Motherhood and especially the loss of a child connect the women across their racial and class differences. *The Wire* encourages similar moments of sympathetic recognition among characters.

Critics such as George Lipsitz frequently highlight the parallels *The Wire* draws between the police and drug dealers (95). Like the shared experience of motherhood that connects a senator's wife and a runaway slave in *Uncle Tom's Cabin*, the shared experiences of these professions challenge the moral distinctions that normally separate these groups. Arguably the most memorable, explicit cross-identification between characters in *The Wire* occurs in a courtroom scene in which Omar Little (Michael K. Williams) is testifying for the prosecution (season two, episode six). In this scene, Omar draws an explicit comparison between his livelihood of robbing drug dealers and the defense lawyer's job: "Just like you, man [...]. I got the shotgun. You got the briefcase. It's all in the game though, right?" This uncomfortable moment of recognition for the corrupt defense lawyer, Maurice "Maury" Levy (Michael Kostroff), nevertheless results in a validation that both men profit from the drug trade and its associated violence. As the camera pans the room, the jury, prosecution, judge, and courtroom observers nod in agreement; the jury ultimately finds the defendant guilty. The viewers may also experience a moment of uncanny recognition while watching this scene, realizing that their entertainment is similarly predicated on exploiting drug violence. Those that suffer under such violence rarely reap the social or economic profits.

The Wire, like *Uncle Tom's Cabin*, shifts narrative focus to encourage a range of fluctuating alliances and identifications between characters and the viewer. Jimmy McNulty's character fosters one of the most powerful identifications. While *The Wire*'s ensemble cast includes powerful female characters, male characters such as Jimmy McNulty and Marlo Stanfield (Jamie Hector) provide the narrative's core, particularly in the fifth season. Their rivalry fosters a protagonist-antagonist relationship. As described above, McNulty also provides the focal point for the final montage. As a result, viewers are particularly hailed via McNulty's character as the (anti-)hero. *The Wire* subverts and confirms this identification through McNulty's (anti-)heroic actions. McNulty, lacking the resources to investigate Stanfield, creates a fictional serial killer in order to obtain police resources, which he in turn diverts to building the case against Stanfield. Like Captain Ahab in *Moby-Dick*, McNulty's consuming desire to catch Stanfield ultimately corrupts.[15] When the serial killer is revealed to be a ruse and an illegal wiretap is discovered, the Stanfield case falls apart. Focusing on the sentimental tradition reveals that McNulty's character arc also resembles the female protagonists of much nineteenth-century sentimental fiction.

The white female protagonists in much sentimental domestic literature map literal or metaphoric journeys to find home.[16] Characters such as Ellen Montgomery in *The Wide, Wide World* or Jo March in *Little Women* must overcome individual flaws in order to achieve home and family. McNulty's struggle to find and make a home throughout the five seasons creates a parallel with these sentimental protagonists. For example, when confronted by his girlfriend, Officer Beatrice "Beadie" Russell (Amy Ryan), about his increasing absences from home and the mounting evidence of his drinking and infidelities, McNulty attempts to describe his good intentions: "You start to tell the story, you think you're the hero, and then when you get done talking..." (season five, episode eight). He cannot finish. McNulty recognizes that he is not the hero; he has made mistakes. His hangdog body language throughout Beadie's dressing down suggests that he agrees with her claims about the importance of family; McNulty simply has a knack for screwing up.

Significantly, women in *The Wire* such as Beadie or McNulty's ex-wife do not primarily exist as "entrappers and domesticators," and the male protagonists are not running from these "civilizing" forces (Baym 133). As a result, *The Wire* most clearly develops feminine, not masculine, narrative structures. Unlike "the entrammeling society and the promising landscape" of the masculine narratives Nina Baym describes in "Melodramas of Beset Manhood," the institutional forces and urban landscape in *The Wire* are not "depicted in unmistakably feminine terms" (133). McNulty's infidelities are not so much a rejection of or a revolt against domesticity—he loves his family—but a character flaw that he, like the female protagonists in much sentimental fiction, must overcome.

McNulty's work particularly inhibits his relationship with his family. As Gerardine Meaney points out in "Not Irish Enough? Masculinity and Ethnicity in *The Wire* and *Rescue Me*," "[t]he incompatibility of work and family is a recurrent theme of *The Wire* and an implicit theme in a vast array of crime fiction" (11). William "Bunk" Moreland (Wendell Pierce) and Shakima "Kima" Greggs (Sonja Sohn), for instance, share many of McNulty's struggles. When

McNulty asks Kima if she misses her ex-girlfriend, she responds, "I still got too much dog in me to be settled like that" (season five, episode eight). Lester Freamon (Clarke Peters), furthermore, warns McNulty that their "natural police" efforts will not result in "a shining Jimmy-McNulty-day moment" and that "[t]he job will not save you, Jimmy. It won't make you whole. It won't fill your ass up" (season three, episode nine). McNulty does not heed Lester or Bunk's warnings and, following the sentimental logic of the sacrifice, can only return home after his "death." Female protagonists in domestic and sentimental fiction are often rewarded with home and family (marriage) or punished and/or redeemed with death. McNulty's final line and the last line spoken in the series—"Let's go home"—underscores this sentimental narrative arc. The series finale emphasizes McNulty's status as a flawed, feminized hero in search of home.

McNulty's character flaws and his creation of the fictional serial killer in season five link him especially with Jo March from *Little Women*. Like Jo March's sensation stories, McNulty's fictional serial killer brings in needed money. When McNulty is unable to generate the resources to investigate the twenty-two murdered bodies found in vacant buildings and arrest prime suspect Marlo Stanfield for these crimes, he cooks up a fake serial killer. However, unlike Jo, who heeds Professor Bhaer's warning and stops writing the sensation stories, McNulty ignores detective William "Bunk" Moreland's advice and his sensation story spins out of control. As a result, McNulty leaves the police force, which functions as a symbolic death. The fake wake held for McNulty to roast his police service further connects his character to nineteenth-century sentimental protagonists.

McNulty's "death" invokes both Eva's and Tom's deaths. In the first case, McNulty's arc resembles the sentimental tradition Nancy Armstrong describes in "Why Daughters Die: The Racial Logic of American Sentimentalism." Armstrong understands the death of white daughters, such as Eva in *Uncle Tom's Cabin*, as the logical outcome for a nation concerned with miscegenation. Eva's purity and innocence is never "soiled" through a maturation of her innocent love for Tom and Topsy. In this light, McNulty would seem to represent Eva's impure, modern doppelganger. McNulty's stereotypically Irish vices—drinking and womanizing—place him at odds with Eva's angelic character. Yet Sergeant Jay Landsman's (Delaney Williams) eulogy for McNulty's fake wake proclaims that McNulty is "natural police" (season five, episode ten). Like Eva, McNulty acts as "a kind of fetish that allows readers both to acknowledge and to deny" socially suspect desires (Armstrong 7). Landsman's "golden throat[ed]" eulogy paints a legend, positioning McNulty as a hybrid "black sheep" and white savior. McNulty, then, embodies, through his racialized whiteness as an Irish American, a transgressive miscegenation that Eva cannot.

Landsman describes McNulty as an obstinate "black sheep" that "brooked no authority." He also says, "when you were good, you were the best we had." McNulty's symbolic death is the price he pays for overstepping bounds whereas Eva's death, as Armstrong argues, forecloses transgressive possibilities.[17] Yet McNulty's revered status as "natural police" also establishes his authenticity—his own version of Eva's purity—which necessitates his (symbolic) death. Like Eva, he is too good for this world. Similar to Tom's murder, furthermore, McNulty's sacrifice exchanges economic value (in McNulty's case, a pension) for symbolic value. Just as Tom, according to sentimental logic, might be said to be too good a slave to continue to live as one, McNulty's "natural police" abilities mean that he, too, becomes a symbolic sentimental sacrifice. *The Wire's* nihilism gives way here to sentiment. Just as Eva's death, as Armstrong argues, "establishes her status as an 'inalienable possession,' a literary figure whose meaning could not be touched by the social-historical environment of slavery," McNulty's symbolic death ultimately transcends the social-historical environment of corruption and greed through the "natural police" inscription (13).

McNulty's and Eva's deaths suppress potentially radical solutions in favor of sentimental sacrifices.[18] The narratives' "racial logic" demands that the characters do not reconcile their familial conflicts related to the marketplace. Their deaths allow McNulty to continue to signify "natural police" and Eva to maintain "natural" or unadulterated whiteness. Their deaths take the characters out of circulation, out of material possession to the realm of a sentimental symbolic fetish that depends on white privilege to function. Notably, Lester Freamon, the black rogue detective who also leaves the police force as a result of his involvement in McNulty's scheme, does not join McNulty and lie in state on the pool table at the wake. Rather, the assembled officers make homoerotic jokes about McNulty and Freamon. Their secret miscegenation, now public knowledge, must—nevertheless—be kept quiet: Freamon says, "Keep our secrets, Jimmy" (season five, episode ten). Ultimately the white bodies of Eva and McNulty preserve some semblance of sentimental stability and, as a result, maintain the status quo; the bodies of black men in the narratives, however, elicit appeals for political change. The deaths of black characters are handled differently than the deaths of white characters in both *Uncle Tom's Cabin* and *The Wire*.

McNulty's "death" results in a return home; however, the deaths of black men brook no such individual transformations. The dead bodies of black men in both *The Wire* and *Uncle Tom's Cabin* occupy different symbolic terrain than those of their white counterparts. *The Wire* expands this racial logic in the differences it maps between the bodies of black drug dealers in the vacant buildings, who do not garner the public's attention, and the fictional white serial killer with a sexual fetish who murders white homeless people and captures the media's and the public's attention. The white victims of the fictional sadistic killer elicit public outcry and paternalistic concern from the mayor, who uses the attention to further his ultimately successful bid for governor.[19] The narrative juxtaposes the deaths of these similarly "disposable people"—black drug dealers and white homeless—and presents two very different reactions. Where the white homeless victims elicit sympathy and concern, the black drug dealers are, in the words of *Baltimore Sun* reporter Mike Fletcher (Brandon Young) "dead where it doesn't count" (season five, episode three).[20] While the white homeless occupy this same geographic region and economically many of the low-level drug dealers are not much better off than the homeless, the vacant dead's connection with the illegal drug trade and the fact that they are black make them unsympathetic.

The violent crimes committed by Marlo or in his name do not categorize him or his hired guns as serial killers; these behaviors fold into stereotypes about black male violence. In McNulty's words, "Upstairs wouldn't jump on a *real* serial killer. Fuckin' Marlo, whose got bodies all over him. Well, maybe they need the make believe" (season five, episode three). This "make believe" produces metafictional commentary on the raced nature of American sentimentalism. The more sympathetic "make believe" is white: white male killer and white victims. La Berge explains the violent deaths of the vacant murders and the fictional serial killer as key to distinguishing the difference between realism and melodrama: "violence committed in the commission of accumulation produces realism, whereas violence committed in the commission of gratification produces melodrama" (La Berge 560). Notably, racial identity also plays a role in how these violent actions are viewed.

The narrative self-consciously addresses race's role in American sentimentalism in the conversation that sparks McNulty's creation of the fictional serial killer. McNulty, sitting at a bar with Bunk and Freamon, states, "The guy [Marlo Stanfield] leaves two dozen bodies scattered all over the city and no one gives a fuck." Paralleling the scene in the newsroom, Freamon replies, "It's who he dropped." The conversation continues:

> BUNK: "True dat. You can go a long way in this country killing black folk. Young males, especially. Misdemeanor homicides."
> McNULTY: "If Marlo was killing white women..."
> FREAMON: "White children..."
> BUNK: "Tourists..."
> McNULTY: "One white, ex-cheerleader tourist missing in Aruba."
> BUNK: "Trouble is, this ain't Aruba, bitch."
> FREAMON: "You think that if 300 white people were killed in this city every year, they wouldn't send the 82nd Airborne? Negro, please" [season five, episode two].

If white bodies, such as Eva and McNulty, most readily elicit sympathy, what do the bodies of black men signify? The vacant murders suggest that little has changed in the sympathetic portrayal of black men since the nineteenth century. For black bodies to elicit sympathy they must be killed despite their moral *and* economic value. Black bodies perceived to be without moral and economic value—such as those entombed in the vacants—elicit no sympathy from the public. By contrast, Proposition Joe's unjust murder elicits sympathy in Slim Charles, who murders Cheese in revenge. In this sense, Proposition Joe is most like Tom, while Marlo Stanfield—who orders and is present at Proposition Joe's murder—is most like Simon Legree.

Tom's and Joe's illogical, sympathy-producing murders depend on the reader/viewer recognizing that the men are killed despite their loyalty and economic value, though Joe's murder does not achieve the degree of sympathetic impact ascribed to Tom's death: Joe's death does not transform characters beyond provoking Cheese's murder. Cheese, lacking a moral code, is not mourned by the drug co-op members or the viewer. The loss of his money is lamented more than his death, and no one moves to exact revenge for Slim Charles's actions. *The Wire*'s metafiction critiques this racism, troubling our understanding of the raced distinctions between realism and sentimentalism. In this sense, the metafictional "serial killer kills the series by destroying for the viewer the fantasy of this, or perhaps of any, realism" (La Berge 560). Extending this logic further, these contrasting representations of sentimental masculinities suggest that black male characters cannot be both realistic and sympathetic.

Uncle Tom's capacity to elicit sympathy depends on several "unrealistic" factors. He, of course, has more than economic value for George Shelby, who after his father's death searches for Tom but arrives too late to save him from Simon Legree's clutches. Were it not for a letter detained "by some unfortunate accident," George would have arrived in time to save Tom's life (Stowe 423). This near miss heightens the pathos of Tom's senseless death. Tom's pure ethics and Christian worldview, furthermore, produce a selfless martyr: "I loves every creatur' everywhar!—it's nothing *but* love! O, Mas'r George! what a thing 't is to be a Christian!" (Stowe 426). The negative stereotype that emerges from Tom's feminine passivity and profound Christian faith—the "Uncle Tom" insult—capitalizes on his Christ-like forgiveness and nonviolence, especially toward his white owners, rather than on the ways Tom's actions trouble other racist stereotypes about blacks' inhumanity, criminality, and savage masculinity. Keffrelyn D. Brown and Amelia Kraehe describe the "Uncle Tom" stereotype as the industrious black "servant […] who is devoted and loyal to serving White people and their interests, while posing no threat to, nor seeking to challenge, the existing status quo" (78). Thus, the Uncle Tom stereotype emphasizes the character's cloying characteristics in the service of whites while downplaying how Tom's sacrifice first helps Emmeline and Cassy escape and then results in the freedom of all slaves on the Shelby farm.

In addition to its complex portrayal of domesticity, *The Wire* paints its characters in ambiguous terms in other ways as well. Brown and Kraehe argue that *The Wire* "troubles [a] one-dimensional reading of the Black masculine and its implication on larger discourses about Black community" (76). They discuss Lieutenant Cedric Daniels (Lance Reddick) as a character that combines the "devoted servant," trickster, and "sexual superman" figures (Brown and Kraehe 79–82). As a result, "*The Wire* presents a complicated black masculinity that defies easy categorization [...]. [S]tereotypes [...] exist alongside counter-tropes that make more complex the messages embodied in [...] traditionally racialized characterizations" (Brown and Kraehe 85). Jason Vest agrees that black masculinity in *The Wire* straddles progressive and conservative representations: "*The Wire*'s black leaders may be far more sophisticated characters than the shucking-and-jiving African Americans found in the 19th- and 20th-century American minstrel shows but [...] Burell, Royce, and Davis nonetheless bear faint minstrel traces" (Vest 189). The life and death of the queer gangster Omar Little perhaps best represents this ambiguous blending of sophistication and minstrelsy.

Omar mixes Wild West bravado and verbal acuity with a Robin Hood–type ethics. He earns his living by stealing from drug dealers, never pulls his gun on a "citizen" (someone not engaged in the drug trade), and does not shoot children. His open homosexuality amid the virulently homophobic gang culture emphasizes his extreme outsider status. However, he is not simply a violent Uncle Tom; rather, his steadfast ethics and "feminized" sexuality queer this and other black male stereotypes. As with Tom, Omar's ethics contribute to his death: a child, Kenard (Thuliso Dingwall), eventually kills Omar. Omar's view of children as nonthreatening means he does not draw his gun when Kenard enters the corner store. The viewer does not see Kenard enter, but hears the door jingle and sees Omar make eye contact and then turn his back to the door. Omar's death shocks the viewer because we trust that Omar would not let his guard down. Kenard's murder breaks down Omar's (and the viewer's) moral understanding of the world.

Unlike McNulty's and Uncle Tom's deaths, Omar's death does not reinforce stability or purity. He does not die as a symbol of the "natural gangster" or as a (feminized) martyr. No eulogy is spoken for him, his body is incorrectly identified in the morgue, and his death does not even merit a brief mention in the "Metro Digest" section of the *Baltimore Sun* (season five, episode eight).

The word on the street cannot believe that a child alone brought down such a legendary gunslinger. As a result, Omar's death is simultaneously the logical end to a violent life and the senseless death of a man shot unawares by a small boy no more than twelve years old. Omar's death paints an individual picture of one of the hundreds of "misdemeanor homicides" and the lack of economic and social investment in the twenty-two vacant murders. Little, if any, social or economic capital is invested in these deaths. Omar's death highlights the collective lack of sympathy for the overwhelmingly disproportionate number of violent deaths experienced by black males. This version of sentimentality does not present "death as a positive substance, as a property, that can be turned to 'profit' by producing a community of like persons, but, rather [...] render[s] death unconceptualizable and absent while at the same time [...] recogniz[ing] 'death' as the 'inner' possibility of shared singularity" (Michaelsen 74). Rather than (de)constructing a profitable martyr in Omar, *The Wire* demonstrates through his character why the black male is unable to occupy a sympathetic position in contemporary culture, while simultaneously producing an unrealistic character that elicits sympathy from the viewer.

Omar's larger-than-life gunslinger bravado and wit connects him more closely with unrealistic legend than with realist character traits. Harvey Cormier "eulogiz[es]" Omar's "implausible" character (206) in "Bringing Omar Back to Life": "The heavy realism of *The Wire* is leavened by this bit of magic. Omar is a fantasy figure" (209). Cormier goes on to describe Omar as a "superhero" and "a figure more likely to be found in a comic book, or at least a graphic novel, than roaming the actual streets of Baltimore. He therefore contrasts strikingly with the other characters on the show in their lovingly laid-out and ultrarealistic scenario" (210). As a result, despite his violent actions and outsider status, Omar appeals to many viewers for the ways in which he fights against the status quo: "Can we Omar wannabes really fight this unending battle with the *status quo*? How can we keep going? How can we hold on to hope? 'A day at a time, I suppose,' would be Omar's own answer, and that answer is an important truth of real life. It is not a fantasy, even if Omar is— for the time being" (212). Cormier's reading underscores sentimentality's "unrealistic" profitability: its capacity to engender hope. Omar, in this light, must die before the series ends in order to perform his contradictory role as a sympathetic black male character: the viewer must see his death largely ignored by the social milieu he inhabited, and must simultaneously mourn Omar's death and potentially the deaths of all the "misdemeanor homicides" with which his death is connected.

Omar's fantastically violent character and sudden death also play into the long history of the black male's bodily threat and simultaneous "corporeal vulnerability," which Cassandra Jackson outlines in *Violence, Visual Culture, and the Black Male Body* (50). Omar's death, in this respect, simultaneously "contain[s] and ultimately make[s] palatable his supposed hyper-maleness by objectifying and eroticizing black male bodies" (45):

> While images of black male woundedness may be viewed as acts of testimony that make visible the suffering of young black urban men, they can just as easily be interpreted as visualizations of the alterity of black bodies. For audiences who see their own bodies as essentially different from those pictured, the image of the wounded black man confirms not only the equation between blackness and suffering, but also the equation between whiteness and bodily integrity [45].

Jackson's reading of wounded and crucified "Uncle Tom" black male bodies (54–59) underscores the idea that "violence is the only means through which black men become subjects," and that even this tactic frequently fails (55–56).

Conclusions

As the contrasting deaths of the black and white male characters reveal, *The Wire* provides a foundation for exploring the relationship between nineteenth- and twenty-first-century sentimentalism and sentimentalism's relationship to American capitalism. *The Wire*'s failure to reproduce within the text a realistic Uncle Tom or sympathetic black male martyr underscores Bunk's claim that "young [black] males, especially" cannot be viewed as sympathetic characters, only violent, greedy ones. Omar's sentimental potential relies on the viewer identifying with his character while the unsympathetic public within *The Wire* ignores his death. As Susan A. Bandes argues, "[t]he feat *The Wire* achieves is to draw us deeply into the lives of individual characters while at the same time drawing back and showing us the roles these characters occupy in a larger system. This systemic focus doesn't work against the viewer's ability to empathize with individual characters" (444). Comparing *The Wire*'s supposed post-sentimentalism with the avowedly sentimental *Uncle Tom's Cabin* reveals how these sentimental scripts from the nineteenth century continue to operate today.

Reading *The Wire* against *Uncle Tom's Cabin* also supports Brown and Kraehe's contention that *The Wire*'s sentimental realism is grounded in an ahistorical neoliberalism in which "blackness is stripped of its historical-political context and collective responsibility" (86). *The Wire*'s turn to Dickens's Victorian England and the contrasting deaths of black and white males reveal how "[t]hese re(-) presentations, then, fall short of fashioning a Black male persona that is human, complex *and* politically aware of/concerned with his place in the larger Black community. Instead, *The Wire*'s Black male exists precariously in and between two worlds that he alternately desires and repels, supports yet neglects" (Brown and Kraehe 86). *The Wire*'s dramatized masculinity considers the limits and raced differences of individual sacrifice in a "rigged game."

Preston "Bodie" Broadus (J.D. Williams) concludes in "Final Grades" (season four, episode thirteen), "[t]his game is rigged, man. We like the little bitches on a chessboard." Within its manipulated environment *The Wire*'s pawns—the flawed heroes and outcasts—cannot rely on the Protestant moral structures associated with nineteenth-century sentimental empowerment. Prayer, trust in God, and fear of "the *day of vengeance*" do not provide *The Wire*'s moral compass, as they do in *Uncle Tom's Cabin* (456). As a result, *The Wire*'s "mixed-code" narrative "work[s] both within and against postmodernism to offer an antidote to the nihilism, emotional disconnection, antipopular spirit, and masculinist values evident in some strains of postmodern culture and theory" (Davis 2). The sentimental keeps *The Wire* from falling into complete postmodern nihilism: sentimentalism keeps the hope for change—even in this rigged game—alive.

In doing so, *The Wire* also shows the racial limits of the sentimental imagination. As Cassuto notes, "sentimentalism dramatizes the fight between group-oriented sympathy and hard-boiled individualism against a setting provided by market-driven capitalism. The achievement of renunciation in sentimental stories, of living for others, demonstrates the superiority of self-sacrifice to life according to the market, where you simply grasp after what you want" (10). Cassuto suggests that profitable social sentiments depend on the renunciation of capitalism. *The Wire* embodies this argument while demonstrating that social profit rarely wins against economic profit. Furthermore, the contrast between the individual symbolic deaths of McNulty, Cheese, and Omar and the mass vacant deaths and fictional serial killer murders demonstrate that renunciation is often a racialized function of white privilege—a key factor to understanding how this rigged game is wired.

NOTES

1. Leonard Cassuto suggests "[p]erhaps the quintessential hard-boiled character in sentimental fiction is Simon Legree of Stowe's *Uncle Tom's Cabin*, who literally costs out human life, calculating that it's most economical for him to work his slaves to death and buy new ones" (Cassuto 9–10).

2. Leigh Claire La Berge does not use the term metafiction in "Capitalism and Serial Form"; however, La Berge's essay similarly argues that the fifth season is distinctive due to its self-reflective (557) and didactic format (549). Like La Berge's discussion, this analysis reads *The Wire*'s fifth season as the most sentimental in form. While this reading, which draws from contemporary rethinking of sentimental forms and views the previous four

seasons' "eschew[ed] melodrama" differently, the readings ultimately share an interest in the ways *The Wire* cannot escape sentimental eruptions and how those eruptions are related to capital (La Berge 550). For a discussion of sympathy and "utopian sentiments" (Bell 533) in *The Wire*'s fourth season, see Robert LeVertis Bell's "'Precarious Lunch': Conviviality and Postlapsarian Nostalgia in *The Wire*'s Fourth Season."

3. For a discussion of genre and *The Wire*, see Paul Allen Anderson's "'The Game Is the Game': Tautology and Allegory in *The Wire*"; Leigh Claire La Berge's "Capitalist Realism and Serial Form: The Fifth Season of *The Wire*"; Adrienne Brown's "Constrained Frequencies: *The Wire* and the Limits of Listening"; Jameson's "Realism and Utopia in *The Wire*"; Chris Love's "Greek Gods in Baltimore: Greek Tragedy and *The Wire*"; C.W. Marshall and Tiffany Potter's "'I am the American Dream': Modern Urban Tragedy and the Borders of Fiction"; Alasdair McMillan's "Dramatizing Individuation: Institutions, Assemblages, and *The Wire*"; Ted Nannicelli's "It's All Connected: Televisual Narrative Complexity"; Ruth Penfold-Mounce, David Beer and Roger Burrows's "*The Wire* as Social Science-fiction?"; and Liam Kennedy and Stephen Shapiro's *The Wire: Race, Class, and Genre*.

4. Dana D. Nelson makes a similar claim in "'No Cold or Empty Heart': Polygenesis, Scientific Professionalization, and the Unfinished Business of Male Sentimentalism": "We need to let go of assumptions that accompany the 'feminization of sentiment' model— that male texts need not be read for evidences of sentimentalism" (47).

5. This claim is not meant to diminish the female characters, such as detective Shakima "Kima" Greggs (Sonja Sohn), assistant state's attorney Rhonda Perlman (Deirdre Lovejoy) and muscle Felicia "Snoop" Pearson (Felicia Pearson), that appear in the narrative. Nevertheless, of the eighty-four characters listed on HBO's *The Wire* cast and crew website (http://www.hbo.com/the-wire/cast-and-crew/index.html), only ten are female. The plot, as a result, carries a masculine feel even as characters such as the queer gangsters "Snoop" and Omar Little broaden the bounds of masculinity.

6. Sentimental literature itself is associated with montage: "standard works by Brown and Petter [view] the sentimental novel as formula literature, as an epigonic montage of already established components" (Hansen 39). This association is furthered by sentimental film's use of the montage. For a discussion of the relationship between literary montage and the development of sentimental cinema, see Timothy Johns's "Birth of a Medium: Dickens, Griffith, and the Advent of Sentimental Cinema." In regard to closure, Robyn R. Warhol points out in *Having a Good Cry: Effeminate Feelings and Pop-Culture Forms* that the serial resists closure and the romance seeks it (76). Serial sentimental texts thus exploit the tension created by a resistance to closure and the desire for (familial) unity: "sentimental plots are built around the quest for unity, and sentimental tears are shed over sundered unions" (Noble 65). Dobson explains, "[w]e can recognize sentimental literature by its concern with subject matter that privileges affectional ties, and by conventions and tropes designed to convey the primary vision of human connection in a dehumanized world" (268). The montage assists the sentimental serial by recapping events and maintaining sentimentalism's dynamic use of catharsis and closure.

7. The articles are available online: http://criticalinquiry.uchicago.edu/essays_on_the_wire. The book *Tapping into The Wire: The Real Urban Crisis* by Peter L. Beilenson and Patrick A. McGuire also presents *The Wire* as a realist "road map" for understanding urban life and public policy.

8. Likewise, *The Wire*'s characteristic ambiguity and complexity do not automatically craft a progressive or conservative narrative.

9. Neoliberalism, as Wendy Brown argues in "American Nightmare," is not sutured to a particular ideology: it can be aligned with progressive as well as conservative politics (691).

10. Stowe mentions in the latter reference the Sharp Street United Methodist Church,

which formed Baltimore's first black congregation. Frederick Douglass was a member of the congregation.

11. See Seth Rockman's *Scraping By: Wage Labor, Slavery, and Survival in Early Baltimore* for a more in-depth discussion of Baltimore's hybrid economy. *The Wire* also explicitly addresses a version of the modern slave trade in season two. In this season, thirteen women are found dead in a shipping cargo container.

12. Simon is aware of Baltimore's historical connections to slavery. In fact, he relates a "useless history lesson" in an interview with Nick Hornby (74).

13. Freamon states "all the pieces matter" in episode six of the first season. The following reading of *The Wire*'s connection to neoliberalism and race draws heavily from David J. Roberts and Minelle Mahtani's introduction to their article "Neoliberalizing Race, Racing Neoliberalism: Placing 'Race' in Neoliberal Discourses."

14. For a more in-depth discussion of black male stereotypes in *The Wire*, see Brown and Kraehe's article "Sociocultural Knowledge and Visual Re(-)Presentations of Black Masculinity and Community: Reading *The Wire* for Critical Multicultural Teacher Education." Chaddha and Wilson argue that *The Wire* undermines urban stereotypes in "'Way Down in the Hole': Systematic Urban Inequality and *The Wire*" (187). Jameson also briefly discusses the role of racial (black) stereotypes in his article "Realism and Utopia in *The Wire*" (361; 370). James Braxton Peterson's "Corner-Boy Masculinity: Intersections of Inner City Manhood" details "the proliferation of various complex representations of urban black masculinity detailed in *The Wire*" (108). James S. Williams's "The Lost Boys of Baltimore: Beauty and Desire in the Hood" argues that *The Wire* "blows apart the traditional limits in depicting African Americans on television" (58).

15. McNulty's own "*mētis*," or cunning intelligence, also likens him to Odysseus. Focusing on the tragic and epic natures of McNulty's character arc, one might productively compare him to Odysseus in the *Odyssey*, who is known for his cunning and also struggles with a variety of roadblocks before finally returning home.

16. See Jacobson, *Neodomestic American Fiction* for a discussion of this trope, especially pages 46–47.

17. P. Gabrielle Foreman similarly argues "death in *Uncle Tom's Cabin* acts as an insistent sign not of redemption but of the consequence of sexual transgression" (51).

18. Stowe's "solution" to move George and Eliza to Liberia (Stowe 440–442) and Topsy to Africa (443), where she works as a missionary, could also be read as narrative displacement: "Let us imagine black people making English families there, Stowe seems to say" (Armstrong 14). Likewise, McNulty's corrupt police work means the guilty are not punished to the full extent of the law. Notably, the criminals' displacement appears to impede them only temporarily. For example, when we last see Stanfield, he has taken over a new corner.

19. As is often the case with how whiteness is marked, the show itself does not emphasize the homeless victims' race. The cases McNulty doctors are all white. McNulty stages the first "victim"—a white male—at the end of season five, episode two. The homeless victim McNulty discovers in the unsolved files with a red ribbon as well as Raymond Cole's unsolved homeless case are also white (season five, episode three). The homeless man whose picture is sent to the *Baltimore Sun* reporter is white, and the victim's family whom Kima interviews in season five, episode seven, is white.

20. In this scene Alma Gutierrez (Michelle Paress) laments the fact that her triple-homicide story did not make the front page. Mike Fletcher explains why her story was bumped.

Works Cited

Anderson, Paul Allen. "'The Game Is the Game': Tautology and Allegory in *The Wire*." *Criticism: A Quarterly for Literature and the Arts* 52.3–4 (2010): 373–98. Print.

Armstrong, Nancy. "Why Daughters Die: The Racial Logic of American Sentimentalism." *The Yale Journal of Criticism: Interpretation in the Humanities* 7.2 (1994): 1–24. Print.

Bandes, Susan A. "And All the Pieces Matter: Thoughts on *The Wire* and the Criminal Justice System." *Ohio State Journal of Criminal Law* 8.2 (2011): 435–45. Web. 21 September 2011.

Barnes, Elizabeth. *Love's Whipping Boy: Violence and Sentimentality in the American Imagination*. Chapel Hill: University of North Carolina Press, 2011. Print.

Baym, Nina. "Melodramas of Beset Manhood: How Theories of American Fiction Exclude Women Authors." *American Quarterly* 33.2 (1981): 123–139. Web. 29 October 2011.

Beilenson, Peter L., and Patrick A. McGuire. *Tapping into* The Wire: *The Real Urban Crisis*. Baltimore: Johns Hopkins University Press, 2012. Print.

Bell, Robert LeVertis. "'Precarious Lunch': Conviviality and Postlapsarian Nostalgia in *The Wire*'s Fourth Season." *Criticism* 52.3–4 (2010): 529–46. Web. 20 August 2011.

Berlant, Lauren. *The Female Complaint: The Unfinished Business of Sentimentality in American Culture*. Durham, NC: Duke University Press, 2008. Print.

Brown, Adrienne. "Constrained Frequencies: *The Wire* And The Limits Of Listening." *Criticism: A Quarterly for Literature and the Arts* 52.3–4 (2010): 441–59. Print.

Brown, Keffrelyn D., and Amelia Kraehe. "Sociocultural Knowledge and Visual Re (-) Presentations of Black Masculinity and Community: Reading *The Wire* for Critical Multicultural Teacher Education." *Race, Ethnicity and Education* 14.1 (2011): 73–89. Web. 20 September 2011.

Brown, Wendy. "American Nightmare: Neoliberalism, Neoconservatism, and De-Democratization." *Political Theory* 34.6 (2006): 690–714. Web. 22 November 2011.

Cassuto, Leonard. *Hard-Boiled Sentimentality: The Secret History of American Crime Stories*. New York: Columbia University Press, 2009. Print.

Chaddha, Anmol, and William Julius Wilson. "'Way Down in the Hole': Systematic Urban Inequality and *The Wire*." *Critical Inquiry* 38.1 (2011): 164–188. Web. 20 September 2011.

Chapman, Mary, and Glenn Hendler, eds. *Sentimental Men: Masculinity and the Politics of Affect in American Culture*. Berkeley: University of California Press, 1999. Print.

Cormier, Harvey. "Bringing Omar Back to Life." *Journal of Speculative Philosophy* 22.3 (2008): 205–213. Print.

Davidson, Cathy N., Linda Wagner-Martin, and Elizabeth Ammons. *The Oxford Companion to Women's Writing in the United States*. New York: Oxford University Press, 1995. Print.

Davis, Kimberly Chabot. *Postmodern Texts and Emotional Audiences*. West Lafayette, IN: Purdue University Press, 2007. Print.

Dobson, Joanne. "Reclaiming Sentimental Literature." *American Literature: A Journal of Literary History, Criticism, and Bibliography* 69.2 (1997): 263–288. Print.

Douglas, Ann. *The Feminization of American Culture*. New York: Knopf, 1977. Print.

Duggan, Lisa. *The Twilight of Equality: Neoliberalism, Cultural Politics, and the Attack on Democracy*. Boston: Beacon Press, 2004. Print.

Fiedler, Leslie A. *Love and Death in the American Novel*. New York, Stein and Day, 1966. Print.

Foreman, P. Gabrielle. "'This Promiscuous Housekeeping': Death, Transgression, and Homoeroticism in *Uncle Tom's Cabin*." *Representations* 43 (1993): 51–72. Print.

Hansen, Klaus P. "The Sentimental Novel and Its Feminist Critique." *Early American Literature* 26.1 (1991): 39–54. Web. 21 November 2011.

Hendler, Glenn. *Public Sentiments: Structures of Feeling in Nineteenth-Century American Literature*. Chapel Hill: University of North Carolina Press, 2001. Print.

Hornby, Nick. "David Simon [Creator-Writer-Producer of HBO's *The Wire*]." *Believer* 5.6 (2007): 70–78. Print.

Jackson, Cassandra. *Violence, Visual Culture, and the Black Male Body*. New York: Routledge, 2011. Print.
Jacobson, Kristin J. *Neodomestic American Fiction*. Columbus: Ohio State University Press, 2010. Print.
Jameson, Fredric. "Realism and Utopia in *The Wire*." *Criticism* 52.3–4 (2010): 359–72. Web. 20 August 2011.
Johns, Timothy. "Birth of a Medium: Dickens, Griffith, and the Advent of Sentimental Cinema." *Victorian Studies: An Interdisciplinary Journal of Social, Political, and Cultural Studies* 52.1 (2009): 76–85. Print.
Kennedy, Liam, and Stephen Shapiro, eds. The Wire*: Race, Class, and Genre*. Ann Arbor: University of Michigan Press, 2012. Print.
King, Jim, et al. "3rd Exclusive Q&A with David Simon." *The Wire on HBO: Play or Get Played in David Simon's Baltimore*. 4 December 2006. Web. 21 November 2011. http://www.borderline-productions.com/TheWireHBO/exclusive4-1.html.
Klein, Amanda Ann. "'The Dickensian Aspect': Melodrama, Viewer Engagement, and the Socially Conscious Text." The Wire*: Urban Decay and American Television*. Ed. Tiffany Potter and C. W. Marshall. New York: Continuum, 2009. 177–189. Print.
La Berge, Leigh Claire. "Capitalist Realism and Serial Form: The Fifth Season of *The Wire*." *Criticism* 52.3–4 (2010): 547–67. Web. 20 September 2011.
Lipsitz, George. "The Crime *The Wire* Couldn't Name: Social Decay and Cynical Detachment in Baltimore." *How Racism Takes Place*. George Lipsitz. Philadelphia: Temple University Press, 2011. 95–113. Print.
Love, Chris. "Greek Gods in Baltimore: Greek Tragedy and *The Wire*." *Criticism: A Quarterly for Literature and the Arts* 52.3–4 (2010): 487–507. Print.
Lucasi, Stephen. "Networks of Affiliation: Familialism and Anticorporatism in Black and White." The Wire*: Urban Decay and American Television*. Ed. Tiffany Potter and C. W. Marshall. New York: Continuum, 2009. 135–48. Print.
McMillan, Alasdair. "Dramatizing Individuation: Institutions, Assemblages, and *The Wire*." *Cinephile: The University of British Columbia's Film Journal* 4 (2008): 41–49. Print.
Meaney, Gerardine. "Not Irish Enough? Masculinity and Ethnicity in *The Wire* and *Rescue Me*." *Irish Postmodernisms and Popular Culture*. Ed. Wanda Balzano, Anne Mulhall, and Moynagh Sullivan. New York: Palgrave Macmillan, 2007. 3–14. Print.
Michaelsen, Scott. "Toward a Critique of Sentimentalisms in Cultural Studies." *Aztlán* 23.2 (1998): 47–80. Print.
Nelson, Dana D. "'No Cold or Empty Heart': Polygenesis, Scientific Professionalization, and the Unfinished Business of Male Sentimentalism." *Differences: A Journal of Feminist Cultural Studies* 11.3 (1999–2000): 29–56. Print.
Nannicelli, Ted. "'It's All Connected': Notes on the Teleplays." The Wire*: Urban Decay and American Television*. Ed. Tiffany Potter and C. W. Marshall. New York: Continuum, 2009. 190–202. Print.
Noble, Marianne. *The Masochistic Pleasures of Sentimental Literature*. Princeton, NJ: Princeton University Press, 2000. Print.
Penfold-Mounce, Ruth, David Beer, and Roger Burrows. "*The Wire* as Social Science-Fiction?" *Sociology* 45.1 (2011): 152–167. Web. 20 September 2011.
Peterson, James Braxton. "Corner-Boy Masculinity: Intersections of Inner-City Manhood." The Wire*: Urban Decay and American Television*. Ed. Tiffany Potter and C. W. Marshall. New York: Continuum, 2010. 107–121. Print.
Potter, Tiffany, and C. W. Marshall. "'I am the American Dream': Modern Urban Tragedy and the Borders of Fiction." The Wire*: Urban Decay and American Television*. Ed. Tiffany Potter and C. W. Marshall. New York: Continuum, 2009. 1–14. Print.
Reynolds, David S. *Mightier Than the Sword:* Uncle Tom's Cabin *and the Battle for America*. New York: W. W. Norton, 2011. Print.

Roberts, David J., and Minelle Mahtani. "Neoliberalizing Race, Racing Neoliberalism: Placing 'Race' in Neoliberal Discourses." *Antipode* 42.2 (2010): 248–57. Print.
Rockman, Seth. *Scraping By: Wage Labor, Slavery, and Survival in Early Baltimore*. Baltimore: Johns Hopkins University Press, 2009. Print.
Schaub, Joseph Christopher. "*The Wire*: Big Brother Is Not Watching You in Body-more, Murdaland." *Journal of Popular Film & Television* 38.3 (Fall 2010): 122–32. Print.
Stowe, Harriet Beecher. *A Key to Uncle Tom's Cabin*. Boston: J.P. Jewett & Co., 1853. Print.
———. *Uncle Tom's Cabin*. 1852. New York: Oxford University Press, 1998. Print.
Vest, Jason P. *The Wire, Deadwood, Homicide, and NYPD Blue: Violence Is Power*. Santa Barbara, CA: Praeger, 2011. Print.
Wanzo, Rebecca. *The Suffering Will Not Be Televised: African American Women and Sentimental Political Storytelling*. Albany, NY: SUNY Press, 2009. Print.
Warhol, Robyn R. *Having a Good Cry: Effeminate Feelings and Pop-Culture Forms*. Columbus: Ohio State University Press, 2003. Print.
Williams, James S. "The Lost Boys of Baltimore: Beauty and Desire in the Hood." *Film Quarterly* 62.2 (2008–2009): 58–63. Print.
Wilson, David. *Cities and Race: America's New Black Ghettos*. New York: Routledge, 2007. Print.
The Wire. Seasons 1–5. HBO. June 2002-March 2008. Television.

Thank you to Vorris Nunley at the University of California–Riverside and to Lisa Honaker at the Richard Stockton College of New Jersey for their feedback on this essay. Thank you also to Ken and Nancy Tompkins who encouraged me to watch and then brainstormed with me on several occasions about The Wire's *relationship to* Uncle Tom's Cabin.

Race, Religion and Sentimentalism in Marilynne Robinson's *Gilead* and *Home*

Elizabeth A. Ellis

> There is no group in history I admire more than the abolitionists, but from their example I conclude that there are two questions we must ask ourselves—what do we choose not to know, and what do we fail to anticipate? The ultimate success of the abolitionists so very much resembled failure that it requires charity, even more than discernment, to discover the difference.—Marilynne Robinson

> The memory of the early anti-slavery days is very sacred to me. The Holy Spirit did actually descend upon men and women in tongues of flame. Political and theological prejudices and personal ambitions were forgotten in sympathy for the wrongs of the helpless, and in the enthusiasm to keep the fire of freedom from being extinguished on our national altar.—Lydia Maria Child

In her most recent collection of essays, *When I Was a Child I Read Books* (2012), Marilynne Robinson describes her belief in the value of fiction as, "whatever else, an exercise in the capacity for imaginative love, or sympathy, or identification" (21). The essay in which she makes this statement, "Imagination and Community," draws connections between what Robinson describes as the great value of writing and the benefits it offers to communities. For Robinson, community consists "very largely of imaginative love for people we don't know or whom we know very slightly" (21). The broadest possible exercise of imagination, she claims, is "the thing most conducive to human health, individual and global" (26). While hardly a new argument for fiction, essential to Robinson's characterization is the term "imaginative love," which for her is synonymous with sympathetic identification.

Robinson's description of the work of fiction, the value of community, and the definition of the individual echoes the terms employed by another group: the nineteenth-century abolitionists. Convinced that sympathetic identification would change society, much sentimental abolitionist fiction took broadening an individual's capacity for imaginative love as its very purpose. Harriet Beecher Stowe gives perhaps the most famous explanation in her preface to *Uncle Tom's Cabin*:

> The poet, the painter, and the artist now seek out and embellish the common and gentler humanities of life, and under the allurements of fiction, breathe a humanizing and subduing influence, favorable to the development of the great principles of Christian brotherhood. The hand of benevolence is everywhere stretched out, searching into abuses, righting wrongs, alleviating distresses, and bringing to the knowledge and sympathies of the world the lowly, the oppressed, and the forgotten [3].

As this passage indicates, much sentimental abolitionist rhetoric developed around concepts of imagination, sympathy, and community as integrally linked. The charges against their perspective may perhaps by now seem familiar: these writers forward a universal subjectivity, usually white, female, and middle-class; they fail to anticipate the consequences of a postslavery America; they rely on a naïve conception of families based on the white middle-class experience; they ignore the significance of racial prejudice; and they manipulate black enslaved characters for these purposes, to name some of the more familiar criticisms.

From the perspective of the twenty-first-century scholar, then, Robinson's view of fiction and the sentimentalists' perspective may not appear to be contiguous. Contemporary critics might assume contemporary novelists have learned their lessons: to draw on sentimentalism now would be to appear naïve or, worse, nostalgic. The work of this essay is to suggest that Marilynne Robinson's novels *Gilead* (2004) and *Home* (2008) challenge this perspective. This essay argues that these novels work with, and not against, the strand of sentimental writing associated with abolitionists such as Harriet Beecher Stowe and Lydia Maria Child. Revising many of the tropes of abolitionist rhetoric and intensely engaged with its vision, Robinson draws on the abolitionist tradition while also exposing what from the twenty-first-century vantage point appear as its failures. Thus *Gilead* and *Home* pose a double-sided critique. From one side, the novels trace sentimentalism's inability to account for race directly into domestic space. Jack Boughton, as the returned Prodigal Son, suffers from unresolved conflicts between Ames, his father, and his paternal grandfather, illustrated most clearly in his inability to find a "home" that is accepting of his interracial marriage. From the other side, however, *Gilead* and *Home* interrogate the contemporary culture that supposedly rejects influence through sympathetic identification, or in Robinson's terms, "imaginative love." This interrogation specifically works to challenge portrayals of religious experience, religious communities, and faithful individuals as anti-intellectual, insular, and disengaged from social critique.

To illustrate both sides of Robinson's challenge, this essay moves first through the novels' engagement with the tropes and vision of abolitionist fiction. Section one illustrates how the narrative framing in *Gilead* revises one of the most common sentimental tropes: direct address. Section two examines the narrative frame's connection to another sentimental trope: deceased or absent family members. Section three demonstrates how these tropes ultimately trace the blind spots of abolitionists' reform vision into 1950s domestic space. The essay concludes by considering how this engagement poses its own challenge to the contemporary milieu that might be tempted to ignore the continuity between *Gilead* and *Home* and the tradition of abolitionists' writing now assessed as "sentimental."

"My Dear Son": John Ames's Deathbed Epistle

Gilead opens, "I told you last night that I might be gone sometime, and you said, Where, and I said, To be with the Good Lord, and you said, Why, and I said, Because I'm old, and you said, I don't think you're old" (1). *Gilead*, Marilynne Robinson's second novel, foregrounds the relationship between the narrator, Congregationalist minister John Ames, and his imagined reader, the adult version of his seven-year-old son, Robby. Ames has recently discovered he is dying from a heart condition. As this epistolary novel unfolds, Ames explains the things he realizes he will never be able to share with his son, including, among other things, wisdom from his past sermons, explanations of his theological views, memories of courting and marrying Robby's mother Lila, stories of his relationship with his grandfathers, father, and brother, and a history of Gilead, Iowa, the place where generations of Ameses have lived and worked. Much of the novel, then, deals with Ames's and Gilead's immediate past. Equally important for Ames to convey to Robby, however, is a sense of their daily interactions. In this way, his letter is meant as a record of his perspective of their last days together. While the novel is apparently an intimate (and to a certain extent plotless) conversation between father and son, woven into this account is Ames's friendship with neighbor and Presbyterian minister Robert Boughton. The story of Boughton's estranged son, Jack, provides the central conflict for *Gilead* as well as for Robinson's third novel, *Home*. Jack, as the returned Prodigal Son, provides the narrative expression of the historic conflicts both Ames and Boughton have experienced in Gilead.

While many critics have considered the significance of domesticity for Robinson's first novel, *Housekeeping*, scholarly discussion of *Gilead* and *Home* has not yet taken up the interplay of the novels with domestic themes. Laura E. Tanner considers *Gilead* through contemporary theories of neuroscience to illuminate the novel's depiction of sensory perception. Christopher Leise and Christopher Douglas, however, see *Gilead*'s undertaking as revisionary and historical. Leise reads *Gilead* in conversation with seventeenth- and eighteenth-century writers such as Anne Bradstreet, Thomas Shephard, and Jonathan Edwards. Through this reading Leise argues that Robinson's novel attempts to legitimate a re-reading of both Calvinism and Puritanism (351). Concerned with questions of history and multiculturalism, Douglas situates *Gilead* alongside the "postsecular," highly spiritual fiction of writers such as Thomas Pynchon, Don DeLillo, Toni Morrison, N. Scott Momaday, and Leslie Silko. Douglas claims that *Gilead* perpetuates a reductive view of history that ignores Christian slavery (339). This essay's reading of the novel contributes to this discussion by demonstrating how the novel also works with nineteenth-century discourses of abolitionism, particularly those considered the domain of women in the abolitionist movement.

Through their engagement with nineteenth-century sentimental abolitionist rhetoric, *Gilead* and *Home* expose what critics consider the failure of tropes such as direct address and epistolary forms. Particularly with regard to the rhetoric of white women in the abolitionist movement, critics claim that these tropes forward a universal subjectivity, usually white, female, and middle-class. Abolitionists built their case against slavery by appealing to this imagined universal identification, focusing particularly on how enslavement disadvantaged the white middle class. Thus often the enslaved person's experience was manipulated to illuminate the problems slavery posed for the nineteenth-century middle-class family (Bacon, Samuels). In Angelina Grimke's "Appeal to Christian Women of the South," for example, her argument takes the form of an epistle and opens with appeals to familial ties forged through religious and geographic unity:

> Respected friends,
> It is because I feel a deep and tender interest in your present and eternal welfare that I am willing thus publicly to address you. Some of you have loved me as

a relative, and some have felt bound to me in Christian sympathy, and Gospel fellowship; and even when compelled by a strong sense of duty, to break those outward bonds of union which bound us together as members of the same community, and members of the same religious denomination, you were generous enough to give me credit, for sincerity as a Christian, though you believed I had been most strangely deceived. I thanked you then for your kindness, and I ask you *now*, for the sake of former confidence and former friendship, to read the following pages in the spirit of calm investigation and fervent prayer. It is because you have known me, that I write thus unto you [1].

Employing direct address, Grimke writes through the epistolary form to an audience of white women living in the southern United States. As this passage demonstrates, she creates an imagined community of which she and her audience are all a part, one that is held together by the bonds of Christianity and a white, middle-class conception of family. Grimke's text serves as one example among many others. Jacqueline Bacon, in *The Humblest May Stand Forth*, considers Grimke's appeal alongside Lydia Maria Child's story "Miss G." As Bacon argues, "Appeal to the Christian Women of the South" opposes slavery by emphasizing the perils it poses for white middle-class women and by appealing to an imagined unity between them. In the form of an epistle directed to Grimke's "former friends," "Appeal" works through the strategy so common among nineteenth-century women in reform movements, appealing to a "sympathy between women, while purporting to valorize universal qualities" yet "often normaliz[ing] the experiences of particular women, marginalizing those women who are less privileged" (120). bell hooks argues that white women abolitionists not only failed to confront the racism that upheld slavery, but through appeals such as the one cited by Grimke above, they perpetuated it (125).

How then does the Reverend Ames's epistle to his son expose this failure as it also draws on the forms of Grimke, Child, and other women writing abolitionist texts? *Gilead* transforms the epistolary form and direct address employed by Grimke and others first through its singular and familial reader. Direct address and the epistolary form are directed in this case toward only one reader, Robby, the narrator's son. Through this revision *Gilead* subverts convention by highlighting the father-son relationship within the home and by placing the audience directly in between these two perspectives. After several pages devoted to memories of his past, Ames inserts a story about Robby set in the present:

> You and Tobias came trudging home at dawn and spread your sleeping bags on your bedroom floor and slept till lunchtime. (You had heard growling in the bushes. T. has brothers.) Your mother had fallen asleep in the parlor with a book in her lap. I made you some toasted cheese sandwiches, which I cooked a little

too long. So I told you the story you like very much, about how my poor old mother would sleep in her rocker by the kitchen stove while our dinner smoked and sputtered like some unacceptable sacrifice, and you ate your sandwiches, maybe a little more happily for the scorch. And I gave you some of those chocolate cupcakes with the squiggle of frosting across the top. I buy those for your mother because she loves them and won't buy them for herself. I doubt she slept at all last night. I surprised myself—I slept pretty soundly, and woke out of a harmless sort of dream, an unmemorable conversation with people I did not know. And I was so happy to have you home again [37].

As this passage indicates, the epistolary form works as Ames's attempt to explain and record his relationship with his son and to foreground the significance of domestic space for their relationship. Ames's voice as he writes to his son Robby provides the narrative frame, with the important distinction that Ames continually emphasizes the limitations of both of their perspectives, foreshadowing the story of Jack told in *Gilead* and in *Home*. The deployment of "you," then, comes to stand both for the reader and for the son in communion with an unseen father—a sort of "holy trinity" narrative strategy grounded in an emphasis on the partiality of any one perspective. In Ames's words, his perspective is partial and limited, and his language may miss his point or lose its power simply as a result of the passage of time: "I have thought about that very often—how the times change, and the same words that carry a good many people into the howling wilderness in one generation are irksome or meaningless in the next" (171). Besides conveying his vulnerability and limited view of his relationship to his son, his past, and his interactions with the Boughtons, Ames's fervent attention to the relationship between language, perspective, and time creates an epistolary form grounded in the mysterious encounter with the other.

Besides its emphasis on the father-son relationship within the home, *Gilead* exposes the limitations of nineteenth-century abolitionists' employment of direct address by blending the epistolary form with a number of others significant to the abolitionist movement. While on one level the novel works as a letter, to do so it blends the sermon, the jeremiad, the prayer, and the journal—combining genres taken up by sentimental writers with those employed by male abolitionists. Manipulating and blending genres, the novel references the many audiences Ames has encountered as a pastor, thus drawing his vocation as a preacher into what is on one level simply a letter.

Here the novel mediates intertextually between various abolitionist discourses, putting sentimentalist forms like the letter, the novel, and the journal in conversation with those such as the sermon and the prayer—forms taken up by white male abolitionists including William Lloyd Garrison and Theodore Weld—as well as with the jeremiad and kairotic epideictic employed by African American abolitionists including David Walker and Frederick Douglass. Here the novel challenges those who would critique abolitionist rhetorics as it also poses a critique of those like Weld and Garrison who employed such modes. As this list of genres and writers indicates, abolitionist rhetoric made use of the language of social conscience for a variety of ends: the reformers above did not agree on the best road to eradication of slavery, and the arguments they employed demonstrate this complexity. *Gilead*, as well as *Home*, attempts to respect this complexity while demonstrating the limits of it.

For the purposes of considering how Robinson revises direct address, it is perhaps most useful to examine how *Gilead* works as a *deathbed epistle*. This form draws on the rhetorical work surrounding death in nineteenth-century culture to expose how Ames's letter foregrounds his suffering, aging body and the significance of male absence in domestic space. As numerous critics have noted (most famously perhaps in the Ann Douglas-Jane Tompkins debate), the deathbed was crucially important to sentimentalist writers. Stowe's depiction of Eva's death serves as the commonplace example here, and as critics have noted, it was a crucial moment for sentimentalists. As Winfried Herget puts it, "Scenes of parting and reunion are prominent structural devices of the sentimental text. A stock situation of that type, and one with a long-standing tradition of awakening conscience, particularly in sermon literature, is the deathbed scene which also carries the feeling of loss and separation to the extreme" (7). *Gilead* works as an extended parting scene, leading up to Ames's final exit from his home and family. Rather than focus on a victim's death, though, *Gilead* illuminates Ames's perspective on his own death and what he wishes he had been able to accomplish while he lived but instead leaves to Robby and the men who follow after him.

Viewing *Gilead* as a deathbed epistle brings to light two of Robinson's significant revisions to sentimental abolitionism's employment of deathbed scenes: this exit foregrounds Ames's *aging* body, particularly his failing heart. While at times Ames mentions physical ailments and draws attention to how his heart condition limits him, he spends far more time considering what has been possible for him and what he regrets leaving behind. In this way, *Gilead* revises the perspective so common to nineteenth-century deathbed sermons and rhetoric, which employed religious ideology to undermine and dismiss earthly suffering in favor of an eternal perfection. Little Eva's deathbed scene turns on this ideology, and it appears in many other examples of deathbed rhetoric. *Gilead,* though, works to revise this form: if any one should be looking forward to a religious afterlife, presumably it is the suffering preacher on his deathbed. Ames, however, expresses his own sadness over leaving his body and the world as he has known it. This passage exemplifies how Ames's deathbed epistle draws on nineteenth-century religious ideology in order to then revise it:

> Today was the Lord's Supper, and I preached on Mark 14:22, "And as they were eating, he took the bread, and when he had blessed, he brake it, and gave it to them, and said, Take ye: this is my body." Normally I would not preach on the Words of Institution themselves when the Sacrament is the most beautiful illumination there could be. But I have been thinking a great deal about the body these last weeks. Blessed and broken. I used Genesis 32:23–32 as the Old Testament text, Jacob wrestling with the Angel. I wanted to talk about the gift of particularity and how blessing and sacrament are mediated through it. I have been thinking lately how I have loved my physical life [69].

This passage demonstrates how Ames's deathbed epistle engages with and revises the sentimentalist view of dying and the cultural work surrounding death. Here we see how this form enables *Gilead* to draw on a number of genres at once: Ames refers to his sermon, expounds upon it, and connects it to his perspective on his ailing body. Besides enabling the amalgamation of genres, the deathbed epistle is centered on an aging, male body in domestic spaces. Exposing his own inability to anticipate leaving his body and his life behind, Ames's deathbed epistle revels in the daily occurrences taking place in his home and church, both spaces that according to nineteenth-century separate spheres ideology were considered the domains of women.

Thus *Gilead* subverts the gendered expectations associated with the form Robinson employs, the epistolary novel. Moreover, through its singular audience, emphasis on a partial point of view, and blended genres, *Gilead* revises the epistolary form to expose how its narrow focus naïvely reveals only the perspective of the middle-class white family. When considered together with Robinson's third novel, *Home*, the two works illuminate the connections between the failure of abolitionist tropes and the limits of the sentimentalists' reform vision. *Gilead* and *Home* also reveal the limits of the sentimentalist trope of absent or lost family members, further interrogating and revising forms that privileged middle-class white subjectivity.

Fathers and Sons: Abolition and Views on War

Besides *Gilead*'s revision of direct address, *Gilead* and *Home* together employ and revise the sentimentalist trope of absent family members. *Home* tells its own account of life in Gilead during the 1950s; this novel, however, focuses on the perspectives of Jack and Glory, both of whom have come back to the Boughton home after years away. Where *Gilead* focuses on the Reverend Ames's memories, *Home* describes other characters' perspectives on the same period of time. And while *Gilead*'s narrative frame foregrounds the father-son relationship within the home and makes Ames's imminent exit central to its epistolary form, *Home* draws its central conflict from Jack Boughton's presence in and absence from Gilead even as the elder Boughton's frail body signals his impending death.

Sentimentalists often relied on impending deaths or references to absent family members for sympathetic effect. Lydia Maria Child's short story "Charity Bowery," for example, sets an entire story around Charity's list of lost family members. Here in the final passage from the story, Charity explains to the narrator her perspective on the final resolution of her family:

> About a year after this conversation, I again visited New York, and called to see Charity Bowery. I asked her if she had heard any further tidings of her scattered children. The tears came to her eyes. "You know I told you," said she, "that I found out my poor Richard was sold to a Mr. Mitchell, of Alabama. A white gentleman, who has been very kind to me, went to them parts lately, and brought me back news of Richard. His master ordered him to be flogged, and he wouldn't come up to be tied. 'If you don't come up, you black rascal, I'll shoot you,' said his master. 'Shoot away,' said Richard; 'I won't come to be flogged.' His master pointed a pistol at him,—and,—in two hours my poor boy was dead! Richard was a spirity lad. I always knew it was hard for him to be a slave. Well, he's free now. God be praised, he's free now; and I shall soon be with him" [18].

This passage illustrates a trope characteristic of many abolitionists' writing: a family broken apart by slavery. In Child's version, the resolution for Charity and her children will come only in a religious afterlife. This trope once again assumes a middle-class white understanding of family, and it perpetuates the belief that once slavery is abolished, people of color will have access to the familial experience slavery has made impossible. As many critics have noted, in this regard, the white abolitionist vision of reform failed to anticipate the problems that would persist long after slavery ended. Through their characterization of racial prejudice and segregation as issues separate from the elimination of slavery, many abolitionists oversimplified such issues and perhaps unknowingly perpetuated a racist vision of America.

Through their engagement with the absent family members trope, Robinson's novels *Gilead* and *Home* expose what from a twenty-first-century perspective appears clearly to be the failure of the abolitionists' vision: the belief that eradicating slavery was an issue separate from and superior to the elimination of prejudice and segregation. By connecting a burned African American church with the absence of fathers from domestic space, the novels establish a link between families broken apart by racial prejudice and segregation and the limits of the abolitionists' vision of reform.

The principle event that illustrates this revisionist project is the African

184   The Sentimental Mode

American church in Gilead's presence and its subsequent burning. In Ames's narration of the burning, the event encourages his grandfather to leave the town where he has lived and worked nearly his entire life:

> Then he was terribly lonely, no doubt about it. I think that was a big part of his running off to Kansas. That and the fire at the Negro church. It wasn't a big fire—someone heaped brush against the back wall and put a match to it, and someone else saw the smoke and put the flames out with a shovel. (The Negro church used to be where the soda fountain is now, though I hear that's going out of business. That church sold some years ago, and what was left of the congregation moved to Chicago. By then it was down to three or four families. The pastor came by with a sack of plants he'd dug up from around the front steps, mainly lilies. He thought I might want them, and they're still there along the front of our church, needing to be thinned. I should tell the deacons where they came from, so they'll know they have some significance and they'll save them when the building comes down. I didn't know the Negro pastor well myself, but he said his father knew my grandfather. He told me they were sorry to leave, because this town had once meant a great deal to them) [36–37].

This event highlights the tensions due to racial prejudice and segregation that have existed in Gilead since before the Civil War. The burning of the African American church illustrates the enduring presence of racism in a town consistently known as a haven for abolitionist sentiment. In both *Gilead* and *Home* the burning of the church symbolizes the failures of the abolitionist vision to account for such hatred or to respond to it in an effective way. In the 1950s (the temporal setting of both *Gilead* and *Home*) Iowa was one of only three states that had legalized interracial marriage. The destruction of this church in Gilead, Iowa, and the eventual departure of the entire congregation signifies the enduring presence of racism and how it is connected to the abolitionist vision of reform.

The burned church as impetus for Ames's grandfather's absence illuminates the novels' focus on a particular and specific Christian response to slavery, one defined by place: the only response to slavery in Gilead, Iowa, was abolition. Thus, the conflict was not over whether to abolish slavery, but how. Ames's father and grandfather were both abolitionists and ministers in Gilead. The conflict between them was not about *whether* Christians should participate in the abolition of slavery; rather, they disagreed about the *proper* way to participate in it. Ames's grandfather, a friend of John Brown, believed in guerrilla warfare as the appropriate abolitionist response, whereas Ames's father was a resolute pacifist. The unresolved conflict between Ames's grandfather and father accounts for the loneliness Ames's grandfather experiences and his decision to leave the town. Through his exit he severs his ties to his son, grandson, church, and the town he had long called home. Disillusioned by the failure of his efforts in Gilead and the disagreement with his son, the elderly Ames is the first of the novels' fathers to depart from home due to unresolved conflict among abolitionists and the effect of the limits of their vision.

For Jack, the burned church signifies the precarity of his own life and his absence as a father to Robert and partner to Della, the son and the woman he was to provide a home for. Jack Boughton's absence from Gilead gives *Home* its title. In returning to his father's house, Jack leaves his own family behind. We learn that he has an African American partner, Della, and that they have a son, Robert. The memory of the burned church serves as a reminder to Jack, Ames, and Boughton that despite Gilead's longstanding abolitionist tradition, racism is still very real. Ultimately the abolitionists' reform vision failed to account for homes and churches, so that even in Gilead, Jack, Della, and Robert have no promise that they will be able to live as a family.

Both novels, then, turn on the absence of fathers from their families. One of the effects of this is to demonstrate the persistent conflict that the burned church, now gone altogether, represents. Through connections between this space and various absent fathers, *Gilead* and *Home* expose the failure of the abolitionist vision of reform by drawing on tropes that were important to the movement.

Coming Home: The Case of Jack Boughton's Marriage

Both *Gilead* and *Home* are historical novels, but *Home* spends more time in the novels' 1950s present. It is Jack's story, set in this period, that creates all of the central conflicts: in *Gilead* it is his relationship to Ames, and in *Home* his relationship to his father, particularly his inability to find a home for his partner and child. These conflicts become an extension of the New Testament parable of the Prodigal Son. Jack, as returned Prodigal, seeks a new life, while the fathers (Ames and Boughton) who receive him seek to do all they can to enable this quest. Jack is hesitant to ask for their help in regard to Della and Robert for a number of reasons; one important among them is that he does not know how they will feel about his interracial relationship. Jack's story, then, traces the novels' engagement with the failures of sentimental tropes and of the abolitionists' vision directly into 1950s domestic space. Where *Gilead* revises direct address to expose this sentimental trope's naïve view of audience, and where both *Gilead* and *Home* draw attention to fathers' absences from their families to expose the limits of the abolitionists' reform vision, all of these revisions ultimately work toward illuminating what has torn Jack's family apart—the residual effects of racial prejudice and segregation on the 1950s "home."

Through its interplay with nineteenth-century sentimental ideals of "home as a haven," *Gilead* and *Home* show the effect of abolitionist rhetoric and reform on domestic life: Jack's residual homelessness causes him to enter and ultimately leave Ames's home and church as well as his father's home and church, creating conflict with each entrance and exit. Here the novels subvert the sentimental vision of the home and church as feminine spaces with the potential to "redeem" individuals from within. According to nineteenth-century domestic ideology, the home was to be guarded by a woman and preserved as a refuge from the "other world." As Harriet Beecher Stowe puts it:

> Home ought to be so religiously cheerful, so penetrated by the life of love and hope and Christian faith, that the other world may be made real by it. Our home life should be a type of higher life. Our home should be so sanctified, its joys and sorrows so baptized and hallowed, that it shall not be sacrilegious to think of heaven as a higher form of the same thing—a Father's house in the better country, whose mansions are many, whose love is perfect, whose joy is eternal [333].

Appealing to religious language, Stowe and others saw caring for the home as a sacred task. According to nineteenth-century ideals of domestic space, if presided over by an "angelic woman" the home might become nothing short of "heaven on earth." This ideology was of course also central to the abolitionists' arguments, as seen in the essays and fiction of Grimke and Child. Drawing on familial bonds through direct address and decrying the dissolution of those bonds through the removal of family members are both tropes that emerge from the perspective Stowe outlines above.

Ultimately, *Gilead* and *Home* work together toward one end: exposing how what the abolitionists failed to anticipate or refused to know has affected one man and his family—Jack, Della, and Robert—in the 1950s. These effects can be traced from Jack's inability to find a home to share with Della and Robert and back into the homes from which he and Della came: the Boughton house in Gilead, Iowa, and Della's parents' home in Tennessee.

Gilead and *Home* offer different perspectives on the same story. In both, Jack's return to Gilead is prompted by his inability to become a husband and remain a father, despite falling in love with Della and having a son with her. Thus Jack arrives back in Gilead after years away, weary, disheveled, and carrying the secret of Della and Robert that he cannot imagine sharing with his sister or his father. In the version *Gilead* provides, eventually Jack confesses his story to Ames in the hope that Ames can offer the possibility of a home for him to share with Della and Robert in Gilead. Relating his story to Ames, Jack describes the short period of time during which he, Della, and Robert lived together in St. Louis. Unable to keep his African American partner and biracial son a secret from his boss, Jack lost his job. Shortly after this incident,

Della left with Robert for Tennessee. Jack's ultimate quest in returning to Gilead is to secure a new home and life for his family. The effects of Jack's broken family can be traced into both the African American home and church where Della and Robert live in Tennessee as well as the Boughton and Ames homes in Iowa. As Robinson's novels have it, ultimately every family and home is implicated in the racial conflicts of 1950s-era America. Jack, as returned prodigal with no home for his partner and child, demonstrates the limits of a vision of social reform that turns on white middle-class subjectivity. Through a sustained examination of the connections between domestic space in pre- and post–Civil War America and the conflicts Jack, Della, and Robert face in seeking to live together, *Gilead* and *Home* revise the "home as haven" trope by interrogating its limits.

Rethinking Sentimentalism: Imaginative Love or Grace?

Certainly Robinson's novels pose a weighty critique in their engagement of sentimental and abolitionist discourse. However, the critique also suggests that even though the limits of the nineteenth-century reform vision are clear now, it is perhaps equally important to acknowledge that perspective affords this clarity. As the epigraph to this essay indicates, for Robinson, enlarging one's imagination to appreciate abolitionists' efforts is central to her thought. As she puts it in *The Death of Adam* (1998), which she calls a "campaign of revisionism," she describes her interest in history thus: "[C]ontemporary discourse feels to me empty and false [...]. I propose that we look at the past again, because it matters, and because it has so often been dealt with badly" (2,4). In her more recent collection of essays, Robinson acknowledges that *Home* and *Gilead* intertwine with her interest in revisiting the past. Gilead is modeled after Tabor, a town located in the southwest corner of Iowa and founded by a group from Oberlin. She describes the importance of revisiting this particular history because it is "quintessentially American":

> Why does it matter whether or not this past is remembered? I will put the question another way: What was lost when this past was forgotten? We know from subsequent history that the ideals of equality these reformers lived out were not an aberration, that they lay along the grain of American cultural development, that they expressed an understanding of the implications of the founding documents which has been affirmed through legislation and Supreme Court decisions and has come to be acknowledged, by most of us, as quintessentially American [181].

As Robinson claims here and in numerous other essays, central to her understanding of American literature and culture is the spirit of reform and the language of social conscience that she so admires in the abolitionists. Thus her own engagement with their ideals and rhetoric, much of which is now characterized as inextricably intertwined with sentimentality, encompasses critique as well as respect and a desire to revisit the urgency of the abolitionists' cause.

To return to Robinson's characterization of fiction for a moment, perhaps the crucial difference between her understanding of the purpose of fiction and the one cited by Stowe is what Robinson refers to as a "sense of mystery": "I think everyone would, seen properly, have a meditative space around them. Our understanding of the world is fragmentary and we are extremely prone to over-interpret it. The sense of mystery may itself be the great missing value" ("Further" 488). While *Gilead* and *Home* engage in social critique, ultimately Robinson's faithfulness to her belief in restoring or renewing a sense of mystery plays out in a commitment to character, place, and history. For this reason she has far more often been compared to Emily Dickinson and Ralph Waldo Emerson than Harriett Beecher Stowe and Angelina Grimke. However, in considering the significance of sentimental tropes, the abolitionists' vision, and domestic space for *Gilead* and *Home*, it is possible to see how Robinson's fiction embraces and engages all that she finds "quintessentially American."

Works Cited

Bacon, Jacqueline. *The Humblest May Stand Forth: Rhetoric, Empowerment, and Abolition.* Columbia: University of South Carolina Press, 2002. Print.

Child, Lydia Maria. "Charity Bowery." New York: American Anti-Slavery Society, 1839. Print.

Douglas, Ann. *The Feminization of American Culture.* New York: Farrar, Strauss, Giroux, 1998. Print.

Douglas, Christopher. "Multiculturalism and Unlearned History in Marilynne Robinson's *Gilead*." *Novel* 44.3 (2011): 333–353. Web. 9 September 2012.

Grimke, Angelina. "Appeal to the Christian Women of the South." New York: American Anti-Slavery Society, 1836. Print.

Hartshorne, Sarah D. "Lake Fingerbone and Walden Pond: A Commentary on Marilynne Robinson's *Housekeeping*." *Modern Language Studies* 20.3 (1990): 50–57. Web. 9 September 2012.

Hedrick, Tace. "'The Perimeters of Our Wandering Are Nowhere': Breaching the Domestic in *Housekeeping*." *Critique: Studies in Contemporary Fiction* 40.2 (1999): 137–51. Web. 9 September 2012.

Herget, Winfried. *Sentimentality in Modern Literature and Popular Culture.* Tübingen: Narr, 1991. Print.

———. "Towards a Rhetoric of Sentimentality." In *Sentimentality in Modern Literature and Popular Culture.* 1–14. Tübingen: Narr, 1991. Print.

hooks, bell. *Ain't I a Woman: Black Women and Feminism.* Boston: South End Press, 1999. Print.

Leise, Christopher. "'That Little Incandescence': Reading the Fragmentary and John Calvin

in Marilynne Robinson's *Gilead.*" *Studies in the Novel* 41.3 (Fall 2009): 248–267. Web. 9 September 2012.
Mallon, Anne-Marie. "Sojourning Women: Homelessness and Transcendence in *Housekeeping.*" *Critique: Studies in Contemporary Fiction* 30.2 (1989): 95–105. Web. 9 September 2012.
Ravits, Martha. "Extending the American Range: Marilynne Robinson's *Housekeeping.*" *American Literature* 61.4 (1989): 644–66. Web. 9 September 2012.
Robinson, Marilynne. *The Death of Adam.* New York: Picador, 1998. Print.
_____. "Further Thoughts on a Prodigal Son Who Cannot Come Home, on Loneliness and Grace: An Interview with Marilynne Robinson." Interview by Rebecca M. Painter. *Christianity and Literature* 58.3 (2009): 485–492. Print.
_____. *Gilead.* New York: Farrar, Strauss, Giroux, 2004. Print.
_____. *Home.* New York: Farrar, Strauss, Giroux, 2008. Print.
_____. *When I Was a Child I Read Books.* New York: Farrar, Strauss, Giroux, 2012. Print.
Samuels, Shirley. *The Culture of Sentiment: Race, Gender, and Sentimentality in 19th Century America.* New York: Oxford University Press, 1992. Print.
Stowe, Harriet Beecher. *House and Home Papers.* Boston: Ticknor and Fields, 1865.
_____. *Uncle Tom's Cabin.* New York: Signet, 2008. Print.
Tanner, Laura E. "'Looking Back from the Grave': Sensory Perception and the Anticipation of Absence in Marilynne Robinson's *Gilead.*" *Contemporary Literature* 48.2 (2007): 227–52. Web. 9 September 2012.
Tompkins, Jane. *Sensational Designs: The Cultural Work of American Fiction, 1790–1860.* New York: Oxford University Press, 1986. Print.

Madea's Middle Class

Sentimental Spaces in Tyler Perry's Madea's Family Reunion *and* Why Did I Get Married?

ASHLEY REED *and* JENNIFER LARSON

In 1992, Tyler Perry lost his meager life savings producing a play that flopped. He then struggled, living in his car, for six years until he staged the same play again, this time in churches, and this time to great success (Als). Fewer than 20 years after his first theatre failure, Perry topped *Forbes*'s list of the highest paid men in entertainment: from May 2010 to May 2011, Perry earned $130 million (Pomerantz). These earnings flowed from the ever-growing Perry media empire, which in 2011 included over a dozen films, two TV series, and ten stage plays released on video. According to *New Yorker* critic Hilton Als, this empire is built on themes that are primarily "aspirational, geared toward blacks from backgrounds similar to his, who drea[m] of Huxtable-like success and comfort in an imperfectly integrated world." But these same themes, and Perry's unprecedented success, also antagonize critics and other filmmakers including Spike Lee, who has repeatedly labeled Perry's work "coonery buffoonery."

This suspicion of Perry's motives and contempt for his aesthetic recalls the infamous January 19, 1855, letter to publisher William D. Ticknor, in which Nathaniel Hawthorne complained that the country was "wholly given over to a damned mob of scribbling women." These "scribbling women," the writers of hugely popular sentimental fiction, worried Hawthorne and his contemporaries because they changed the literary landscape—economically and socially—by forcing writers and critics alike to consider the interpolation of emotion, politics, and aesthetics in nineteenth-century American life. Perry's success similarly forces his supporters and his detractors to reconsider the role of media in general and film specifically in American culture, economics, and race and gender politics, and such a reconsideration points again to the enduring power of the "scribbling women's" tool: sentimentalism.

This essay argues that Tyler Perry's films and stage plays belong to an ongoing American sentimental tradition. The hallmark of this tradition is its implicit promise that affective bonds formed in community provide an adequate form of resistance to systems of economic and political oppression that undermine the solidarity of disadvantaged people. Specifically, this essay examines two films: *Madea's Family Reunion* and *Why Did I Get Married? Madea's Family Reunion* is the first Madea film written and directed by Tyler Perry. (The previous Madea film, *Diary of a Mad Black Woman*, was directed by Darren Grant.). *Why Did I Get Married?* is the first film written by, directed by, and starring Tyler Perry that does not include Madea. Madea, as the black matriarch/mammy played by Perry himself, provides a focal point for the intersection of race, class, and gender in many of Perry's films and has also become the subject of much anti–Perry criticism. By juxtaposing these two different but representative films from Perry's oeuvre, this essay investigates how Perry's particular sentimental investments are displayed in and through but also without the Madea character.

Any discussion of sentimental narrative requires that the critic attempt to pin down the meaning of the "sentimental," a term that has been under perpetual debate since at least the 1970s, when feminist critics including Ann Douglas, Nina Baym, and Joyce Warren began recovering nineteenth-century women's writing and subjecting it to sustained historical and contextual analysis. Rather than recapitulate the history of sentimental criticism, however, this essay offers June Howard's succinct yet thorough description of the form as a suitable starting point:

> We can organize answers to the question "what is sentimentality?" like this. Most broadly—when we call an artifact or gesture sentimental, we are pointing to its use of some established convention to evoke emotion; we mark a moment when the discursive processes that construct emotion become visible. Most commonly—we are recognizing that a trope from the immense repertoire of sympathy and domesticity has been deployed; we recognize the presence of at least some fragmentary element of an intellectual and literary tradition. Most narrowly—we are asserting that literary works belong to a genre in which those conventions and tropes are central [76–77].

By this definition Perry's work—or at least the work for which he is best known, the films that have earned him the ire of critics and cultural commentators while also earning him millions upon millions of dollars—is sentimental in every possible way. Perry's films draw on "established conventions" for evoking emotion, including sick or estranged mothers, absent or abusive father figures, dead and endangered children, greedy temptresses, and wise elders. Domesticity is the central trope of Perry's films as it was of the nineteenth-century sentimental novel: Perry's sentimental acknowledges the variety of careers engaged in by his characters (from bus driver to minister to lawyer to psychiatrist to banker) while nevertheless positioning marriage and childrearing as the center of community life. And his films, as this essay will show, belong to an intellectual and literary tradition that reaches back to the nineteenth century but has particular relevance for the twenty-first.

By positing home and family, rather than business or other competitive endeavors, as the center of communal life and women as its adjudicators, Perry's films belong to the sentimental tradition that included Harriet Beecher Stowe, Susan Warner, and Maria Susanna Cummins. But even as he invokes the middle-class aspirations and domestic concerns of the nineteenth-century white sentimental, Perry's films also hearken back to a black sentimental tradition that includes William Wells Brown's *Clotel* and Harriet Jacobs's *Incidents in the Life of a Slave Girl*. The nineteenth-century black sentimental exposed the facts behind the coy gentilities of the white sentimental novel: where Susan Warner's Ellen Montgomery was only subjected to symbolic sexual threats— an unfriendly gentleman tries to whip her horse; a teasing patriarch pays her for a kiss—Brown's Clotel Jefferson and Jacobs's Linda Brent were literally owned by the father figures in their lives, the masters who had raped their mothers and who now hover over the narratives, poised to do the same to them.

Almost one hundred sixty years after the fact, Perry's films recapitulate and combine these two narratives: the white sentimental novel, concerned primarily with escaping the economic and emotional dominance of a bad patriarch by aligning oneself with a good one, and the black sentimental novel, which baldly exposes the sad reality that under conditions in which some humans are legally and economically dependent on others, there is no such thing as a "good" patriarch.

In exploring Tyler Perry's particular innovations on the sentimental tradition, this essay reflects Cindy Weinstein's recent work, which demonstrates that sentimental narratives, rather than functioning as "a monolithic entity, a critic's white whale [...] to be confronted and destroyed," actually belong to a multifarious mode that takes different narrative forms and produces different political effects according to the communal and historical context in which they appear (Weinstein 2–3). In other words, "feeling right"—to use Harriet

Beecher Stowe's famous phrase—is a culturally conditioned act, and sentimental texts cannot be properly understood outside of the political and historical conditions under which they are produced.

The context of Perry's films is a black middle-class milieu all but ignored by mainstream film and television production companies that, when they depict communal black life (as opposed to the solitary black hero in the vein of Denzel Washington or Jamie Foxx) at all, proliferate portraits of gang warfare and drug addiction. Perry's films, by contrast, create fictional spaces in which his middle-class black audiences encounter a recognizable, if exaggerated, vision of black community. According to Hilton Als, Perry's stage plays and films fill a void left, not only by white popular culture, but by the disappointments of American political life: "By the time Perry came along, the white world had failed his future fans time and again [....] What Perry's target-audience members lacked onscreen and onstage was a lens through which to see themselves refracted, and a forum in which their religious and political beliefs would be neither challenged nor ignored."

By centering his productions on recognizable aspects of black middle-class life, Perry has created what cultural theorist Lauren Berlant calls an "intimate public"[1]:

> What makes a public sphere intimate is an expectation that the consumers of its particular stuff already share a worldview and emotional knowledge that they have derived from a broadly common historical experience [....] [E]xpressing the sensational, embodied experience of living as a certain kind of being in the world, [an intimate public] promises also to provide a better experience of social belonging—partly through participation in the relevant commodity culture, and partly because of its revelations about how people can live [...] [viii].[2]

One of the characteristics of Perry's intimate public is the shared communal knowledge that political and legal processes that favor wealthy white men are often at best irrelevant and at worst devastating to black families and communities. In Perry's sentimental fictions, the political realm—and its enforcing arm, the courts—is fraught with danger and disgrace for those who cannot claim privileged access to it. The communities depicted in Tyler Perry's films, then, are left to manage themselves, and the sentimental ways in which they do so make up the subject of this essay.

A Patriarch in a Matriarch's Clothes: Madea's Family Reunion

Madea's Family Reunion employs sentimental tropes in the film's central narrative, a story about abused black women, but then complicates its relationship to the sentimental tradition by making Madea—a black man dressed as a mammy figure—the film's ultimate heroine. Madea is the woman who "saves the day" with an alternate and superficially anti-sentimental morality based on her unique and often very physical brand of justice. The film therefore raises key questions about the locus of power in black families. While the film appears to offer a shift away from oppressive patriarchs and the women who love or serve them, this shift is paradoxical because much of the power transfers to Madea and thus, implicitly, to Perry himself—a move that reconnects the film to patriarchal tropes.

The central storyline of *Madea's Family Reunion* follows two half sisters, Lisa and Vanessa, as they plan Lisa's wedding to the physically and verbally abusive banker Carlos. Their mother, Victoria, has orchestrated the union to protect her own financial interests (she has stolen from Lisa's inheritance), and she insists that the wedding go on even after she learns of the domestic violence. Victoria and Vanessa clash throughout the film because Victoria allowed Vanessa to be raped by Lisa's father when she was a child, again for financial security. Because of Vanessa's own economic struggles, she and her two children are staying with Madea, who has recently become the foster mother to a teenaged girl named Nikki. While both Nikki and Madea initially resist the arrangement, Nikki eventually thrives under Madea's strict care. Meanwhile, Madea encourages Lisa to fight back against Carlos and call off the wedding. Since all of the wedding arrangements and guests are already in place, though, Vanessa's gentle suitor Frankie proposes spontaneously, and the pair marry with the blessing of the community.

Madea's Family Reunion bears out Cindy Weinstein's observation that the sentimental, even as it ostensibly celebrates the domestic and the familial, actually relies on the rupturing of family ties: "separations of parent and child constitute the foundational plot mechanism upon which so many sentimental texts depend" (26). In *Madea's Family Reunion*, the fathers of Vanessa's two children have abandoned her and do not pay child support. Vanessa's father did the same to her mother, Victoria. Madea's ward, Nikki, has been cycled through an abusive foster-care system that has left her feeling worthless and vulnerable, and Madea herself faces prison for removing her house arrest anklet—a metaphorical "shackle" to the domestic space.

But *Madea's Family Reunion* explores this institutional victimization most poignantly through its treatment of physical and emotional abuse. The plot emphasizes both the intergenerational nature of family violence—Victoria was abused by her own drug-addicted mother, so she allows her daughters to be abused by various men—and its ties to economic dependence. Lisa continues to subject herself to Carlos's abuse because of his wealth and its related promise of economic security. The film emphasizes this promise through the prominence of Lisa's 10-karet diamond engagement ring. The first time the audience sees Carlos hit Lisa—when he comes home and finds her in the arms of the stripper Lisa and Donna hired—the shot focuses on Lisa's hands (and thus her ring) as she leans against the wall and sobs.

Yet it is Victoria, rather than Carlos, who consistently reminds Lisa of her dependence—one of the subtle ways in which this and other Perry films decry domestic violence while often laying the blame for its perpetuation, not on abusive men, but on their victims. The shallow and money-hungry Victoria allows one daughter to be repeatedly molested and advises the other to put up with regular beatings, all in the name of financial "security." Although Victoria admits that she was "sold" for drugs by her own mother, the film nevertheless provides few moments of sympathy for her, and she is perhaps even more demonized than the actual male abusers to whom she gives her daughters. In fact, Timothy Lyle notes that in the stage play of *Madea's Family Reunion*,[3] "The father escapes any form of punishment or critique" (Lyle 953). The same is true for the film. Lisa even refuses to believe Vanessa's accusations against her father and only appears to do so after Victoria corroborates them to defend herself against Vanessa's attacks. This defense does not further indict the rapist, but further indicts the mother's failures. While Perry asserts in his director's commentary for *Madea's Family Reunion* that Carlos and Victoria play a game of "Who's the biggest devil?" in the film, to most audiences it must seem that Victoria is the clear winner.

As a counter to Victoria's poisonous matriarchal control, the film offers Madea's practical and family-centric brand of wisdom. While Madea, ironically, also uses physical violence (or threats thereof) to control others, her primary mode of influence is emotional, and in this respect she is the most sentimental character in the film despite her raunchy insults and off-color jokes. Her home is refuge, and her guidance is unfailing. Vanessa and her children live with Madea, Lisa comes to Madea's home to escape Carlos, and Madea's reputation for helping the lost leads the judge to make her Nikki's foster mother in lieu of jail. Like Victoria, Madea is often bullied by an abusive and aberrantly sexual patriarch—her brother Joe (also played by Perry); but unlike Victoria, Madea is able to subvert this power, usually through verbal prowess.

Madea therefore becomes the locus for the film's sentimental message: in the absence of effective patriarchal power to help remedy the impact of institutional oppressions, women should gather in the safety of the domestic space under the protective influence of the wise matriarch. However, Madea's true identity—Perry in drag—complicates this message. Perry's gender is unmistakable, but Lyle acknowledges the need, separate from embracing traditionally limited physical definitions of gender identity, "to analyze the degree to which Perry offers specific rhetoric that aligns him with or makes him a mouthpiece for the masculine gendered political category and its accompanying patriarchal rhetoric and sociopolitical and cultural power" (Lyle 944). Essentially, the film leads viewers to question why and to what extent Madea is just as much a symbol of actual patriarchal power as she is a representative of matriarchal power. As a matriarch, she seems to improvise on the sentimental model, positing a space such as that offered by Jacobs's *Incidents* or Fanny Fern's *Ruth Hall* in which sisterhood, rather than traditional conventions of submissive womanhood, triumphs. If the dominant voice is masculine, however, then the film simply trades a flawed patriarch for a more benign—yet still dominant—one. The challenge in *Madea's Family Reunion*, then, is to carefully examine the message that Madea delivers within the familial space and what power that message actually supports.

In most of the Madea films, that message is normative, offering a model of female strength not necessarily based in individual women's choices. Perry points out in his director's commentary for *Madea's Family Reunion* that he consciously tried to make Madea less active in his female characters' journeys of self-discovery than she was in the previous Madea film, *Diary of a Mad Black Woman*. In *Diary,* Madea accompanies her granddaughter Helen to confront her abusive estranged husband and ends up cutting his couch in half with a chainsaw. This second film's Madea is "milder," Perry says, because he wanted the story to be about "fighting your own battles and finding your own path." But according to Hilton Als, this move does not lessen Madea's overall impact on the women: "Although many of Perry's plots ostensibly revolve around the idea of female self-actualization, his heroines, instead of finding themselves, are bullied by Madea into a kind of social conformity that has little to do with whatever character traits they exhibit." That is to say, most changes in the film's female characters stem, not from any discovery of power within themselves, but rather from following Madea's advice for how to feel and act.

Madea's discourse also varies vastly from those delivered by the film's other matriarchs, Myrtle (Cicely Tyson) and May (Maya Angelou), who emphasize personal responsibility and continuity with a shared past. During the family reunion, Myrtle delivers a monologue on the steps of a former slave cabin after walking with May and 96-year-old Aunt Ruby past various family members behaving in ways that the women find shockingly inappropriate. At the climax of her speech, Myrtle says:

> What happened to us? Who are you? Do you know who you are? What happened to the pride and the dignity and the love and respect that we had for one

another? Where did it go? And how, How do we get it back? I'ma tell you. Young Black men, take your place. We need you. Your sons and daughters need you. Did you understand what I just said. You were sold off and had no choice, yes, but now it's time to stay. Take your place. Now. Starting now. Starting now. Young black women, you are more than your thighs and your hips. You are beautiful, strong, powerful. I want more from you!

Then, at Vanessa and Frankie's wedding, May reads a poem (which Angelou penned exclusively for this film) with the repeated stanza: "I was always yours to have/ you were always mine/ we have loved each other/ in and out of time." Both Myrtle's monologue and May's poem emphasize the primacy of love and acceptance as well as an awareness of history and place. Both also put value on both masculine and feminine identity—May through the absence of gender markers, and Myrtle through her unilateral call to action.

Although the film seems to centralize these characters' contributions by situating them within the family reunion from which the film takes its title, their words are far overshadowed by Madea's prominence. For one thing, the family reunion is a relatively small part of the narrative (fewer than 20 minutes in a nearly two-hour-long film), and it is Madea who orchestrates the reunion and pressures (through threat of violence) less willing family members to attend (it is, after all, *Madea*'s family reunion). More importantly, the film does not indicate that these women's words have any effect on their audience, whereas Madea's impact on the film's characters—and on its narrative as a whole—is unmistakable. Each of the film's almost fairy tale-like plot lines is either totally orchestrated or heavily influenced by Madea. Her tough love-turned-encouragement approach with Nikki eventually gives the teenager confidence to excel at school, and the climax of the film is Lisa enacting Madea's advice to not only leave Carlos, but also enact physical revenge through "gritball," a violent maneuver that must occur in the kitchen because it involves a frying pan and a pot full of hot grits.[4] Madea's "behind the scenes" role in Vanessa and Frankie's relationship, though, reveals her most compelling connections to sentimental traditions. Madea shelters Vanessa and her children, and when Frankie comes to pick up Vanessa, Madea does not question his intentions or mock the couple; she simply says, "You go on, I got these kids," thereby transferring maternal responsibility on to herself and allowing Vanessa the space to explore her emotional and physical connection to Frankie. Without this transfer, Vanessa is defensive and nervous, as evidenced by her instinct to break up with Frankie (and suspect him of abuse) after he takes her children out for ice cream while she sleeps.

Frankie and Vanessa's relationship also most closely mirrors that which audiences might find in a nineteenth-century story, so Madea's sanctioning and encouraging of this relationship further links her to this tradition. Frankie identifies himself as "Christian," and Lisa, after she had her second child outside of marriage, "gave [her] life to god" and vowed to remain celibate until she was married. Outside of Perry's non-comedic character Brian, who is the model father in *Diary of a Mad Black Woman* and who saves Madea from jail, Frankie is the only positive male character in this film. The film's narrative even subtly links Frankie with paternalistic divinity. When skeptical Vanessa asks him why he's not in a relationship, he responds that he wants "to be the chaser." Then, in her wedding vows at the end of the film, Vanessa tells Frankie, "You are a breathtaking reflection of God's love for me, of how he *pursued* me and loved me." Like the ministers who provided the ideal husbands for heroines of nineteenth-century sentimental novels, the self-confessed Christian Frankie "represent[s] both divine and worldly authority [and] provides [the heroine] with a way to live happily and obediently in this world while obeying the dictates of heaven" (Tompkins 183). Vanessa's submission to purity and piety, and the security afforded her by Madea's domesticity, bring her a husband with God-like priorities and a commitment to her happiness.

Madea's role in this wedding, though subtle, is also integral. The fact that Madea still goes to the church with Joe and Nikki, even though she clearly knows that Lisa is not going to marry Carlos, suggests that she knows there is going to be a wedding—Vanessa and Frankie's. This knowledge underscores the extent of Madea's control over the film's characters. And since sentimental plots, as Harriet Jacobs remarks at the close of her narrative, tend to end with marriage, Madea's role in Lisa and Frankie's wedding suggests her endorsement of the sentimental model.

Madea also dispenses much of her advice within the domestic sphere as her extended family members come to her home for refuge. In the sentimental model, the home is a safe feminine space, as well as a locus of feminine power. Yet, according to Lyle, Perry-as-Madea, "in the disguise of a *trusted participant* [...] subsumes the space, directs the discourse, and proffers masculinist, oppressive messages that absorb the power that could come from forming a collective, symbiotic sisterhood" (952). As such, "What was once a safe site in which one was able to nurture strategies of feminist resistance and to promote supportive dialogue among women becomes a site infected by a patriarchal rhetoric that is often packaged and disguised as feminist resistance" (Lyle 952). Madea becomes a troublesome character for many viewers because she appears to be a matriarch and thus moves freely in physical and discursive feminine spaces; yet, once in these spaces, her patriarchal message does not always fit her appearance.

Even in her message against domestic violence, the core of Perry's sympathetic appeal in the film, Madea evokes solutions that point, at least in part, to an assumption of patriarchal privilege. For Lyle, the problem with Perry's treatment of domestic violence is that, often, "the solution revolves around *more* violence" and that it is fundamentally not practical given the realities of the American legal system (Lyle 955). Rather than give women emotional and social support in the wake of their trauma or tangible tools for moving on with their lives, the film thus reinscribes violence as the normative response, regardless of effect. The film even nods to the danger Lyle describes: Madea's legal troubles stem from her vengeful destruction of an abuser's property in *Diary of a Mad Black Woman*.

The film's narrative also places Madea in a tenuous position vis-à-vis domestic violence because she employs it herself. First, shortly after the scene in which Carlos slaps Lisa, Madea slaps Nikki on the way home from the courthouse. Then, the film situates Madea at the center of two important domestic violence references from popular culture. When Nikki doesn't want to ride the bus because she is being bullied, Madea escorts her onto the bus and threatens the children. One young man yells "Shut up, old lady!," so Madea slaps him repeatedly, then quotes from the film adaptation of Alice Walker's *The Color Purple*: "I loves Harpo but I'll kill him dead afore I let him beat me!" Madea then raises her fist threateningly and says she'll be there to meet the bus that afternoon. Later, Madea and Uncle Joe are watching an episode of *Good Times* in which a young Penny Gordon (Janet Jackson) is physically abused by her mother. In the featured clip, Penny's mother burns her with an iron. Uncle Joe asks, "What make people be so mean to children?" At that moment Nikki enters, Madea asks her where she's been, and when Nikki is evasive, Madea takes out a paper bag full of belts. Just as Penny starts screaming and crying on the TV, begging her mother not to hurt her, Madea begins whipping Nikki with a thin belt.

Both *The Color Purple* and *Good Times* allusions speak against abuse while simultaneously equating Madea with the abuser. In the first example, Madea takes her lines from Sophia, a woman who has been abused by nearly every man she's ever met, and while she eventually physically fights back against her husband Harpo, this move is fundamentally a defense against a dominant force. In Madea's case, though, she is beating and threatening a child who is not only younger, but also much smaller than she is—especially since she is really a six-and-a-half-foot man. In the second example, Madea's movements even mirror the abusive mother's. And while the brutality of Madea's abuse does not equal the original, she nevertheless physically disciplines a child who has already been repeatedly "beaten down" by the foster care system, and she does so over the objection of the otherwise callous Joe.

Perry's—and Madea's—reinscriptions of domestic violence are particularly disturbing when considered in the light of Perry's enormous popularity. At the metatextual level, Perry, as writer of the films, intentionally places his fictional characters in dangerous situations. Domestic violence is not simply a social issue to be explored, but also an evocative narrative hook—a source of audience rage that can be manipulated by Perry as writer-director. In the director's commentary for *Madea's Family Reunion*, Perry describes attending a screening of the film at the Magic Johnson theatre. When Victoria, Lisa's mother, tells Lisa that she needs to "stop doing what [she is] doing to make [Carlos] angry," the crowd, according to Perry, responded with an audible "roar." At this moment, Perry reports, he thought, "OK, Tyler, you're on to something." What Perry was "on to" was not only the prevalence of domestic violence in America but its potential to elicit an exaggerated emotional response from an audience. The story of the roaring audience raises the question of whether Perry's films are popular because they offer a realistic depiction of domestic violence or, more sinisterly, because they perpetuate scenes of violence that audiences find enjoyable and entertaining.

Perry often counters criticism of Madea by claiming that he has been surrounded by Madea characters throughout his life. He says "I based Madea on my mother and my aunt," and elaborates: "When I was growing up, and for generations before, you could find Madea on every corner in every neighborhood. She used to be everywhere. [...] She's the grandmother everybody can relate to. Almost everybody knows a Madea. You know someone like this woman. If you don't, I feel sorry for you. She is the protector of all things family, of all things good" ("Conversation"). In the director's commentary for *Madea's Family Reunion*, Perry says that even the spanking is true to character for these women, and he recalls how Jenifer Lewis, who plays Lisa's wedding planner and who was unfamiliar with Perry's previous work, actually wanted to play Madea after reading the script. He recounts that she asked him, "Why do they want me to play this role? I'm Madea." But Madea's familiarity makes her potentially more insidious. In his play *The Colored Museum*, George C. Wolfe warns against the deleterious effects of "well-worn mamas" even when these characters appear in critically acclaimed and well-intentioned black productions, such as Lorraine Hansberry's *A Raisin in the Sun* (29). Audiences can stop questioning even the most damaging of stereotypes if they are used often enough, that is, if they become so well-worn that they are almost comfortable—or simply just familiar.

Lyle also challenges Perry's audiences to remember that Harriet Jacobs clashed with her grandmother over how to find agency within the confines of white patriarchal oppression. He explains, "the fact remains that the Black matriarch often serves the interest of the patriarchy" (Lyle 950). Lyle's points here suggest that just because the women are beloved and respected by their families and their communities doesn't mean that they can't also be part of a cycle of oppression that continues to subjugate these same families and communities.

Tangible evidence of this oppression can be found in a study that explores how watching characters such as Madea on screen affects black women's self-esteem. The study asked 36 African American women their feelings about Perry's Madea and similar characters played by Eddie Murphy and Martin Lawrence. These interviews revealed that even though the characters in question are played by men and black women may "find themselves different from those images," these women nevertheless "may categorize themselves as similar because the images reflect people in their in-group." The women then naturally compare these images to "dominant beauty ideals," which they have "internalized," and "as a result, their own self-identity will be affected as they realize that a beauty-worshipping society is portraying people like them in a way society considers as ugly" (Chen 122–23).

The researchers also discovered that the drag element of these characterizations was doubly harmful to black female identity because it "both reinforced the dominant beauty ideal and heightened the ridicule of Black women for violating this ideal." The women interviewed revealed that "depictions of male mammies emphasized this mockery because they usurped a familiar image of a grandmother or matriarch and turned it into an absurdity portrayed by men, robbing Black women of the positive associations the familiar images might evoke" (Chen 125). Thus, the comic Madea mammy not only invades a literal and figurative matriarchal space but also leads women to feel less "right" about themselves. In this twist, Madea is not anti-sentimental or sentimental; she is just detrimental.

Why Did I Get Married? *Managing the Black Middle-Class Marriage*

Perry's 2007 film *Why Did I Get Married?* eschews the Madea character but nevertheless participates in the policing of black affect—particularly black female affect—that *Madea's Family Reunion* and other Perry films enact. *Why Did I Get Married?* is the most self-consciously upper-middle-class of Perry's films, centering on four professional couples who vacation together every year as a way of assessing the states of their various marriages. While *Madea's Family Reunion* concerns itself with cycles of domestic abuse and a perceived loss of communal black identity, *Why Did I Get Married?* contemplates the ramifications of class identification and the difficulty of maintaining a distinct personal identity in the face of overwhelming economic and domestic expectations. In the process it echoes the middle-class aspirations of the nineteenth-century sentimental novel while simultaneously revealing the psychic distortions caused by the application of white middle-class values to black family life.

Why Did I Get Married? features four high-achieving couples who have been friends since meeting at a historically black university. Patricia (played by Janet Jackson, one of Perry's favorite actors) is a psychologist who writes about marital issues; her most recent book has just won a prestigious academic award. She and her husband Gavin (Malik Yoba) have a seemingly perfect marriage, but their relationship is strained by a tragedy that is revealed only in the film's third act. Diane (Sharon Leal) and Terry (Tyler Perry) are a lawyer and a pediatrician, respectively, who have different ideas of work-life balance: Diane works 16-hour-days and wants no more children, while Terry is home every evening with the couple's only daughter and still hopes for a son. Angela (Tasha Smith) is a successful entrepreneur with a line of women's hair care products, while her husband Markus (Michael Jai White), a former professional athlete, works in one of her salons, an emasculating post-injury job that the alcoholic Angela ridicules at every opportunity. Mike (Richard T. Jones) and his wife Sheila (Jill Scott) apparently live off of Mike's money, with Sheila a full-time homemaker. But this traditional, hierarchical marriage—closer to the nineteenth-century separate spheres model than any other relationship in the film—does not guarantee happiness; instead, Mike takes advantage of his power over Sheila, belittling her because of her weight and bringing his girlfriend Trina (Denise Boutte) on the retreat with them.

Like *Madea's Family Reunion* and other Perry films, *Why Did I Get Married?* adheres to a longstanding sentimental tradition of establishing and then policing the boundaries within which affective communities can flourish. *Why Did I Get Married?* models proper black middle-class behavior by demonstrating the domestic affections that keep middle-class families intact (or fail to); in the process it performs the sentimental mode's positioning of class as an affective status as much as an economic one. To be properly middle-class, one must not only have the right kind of job and the right amount of money (not too little, not too much), but one must behave in ways befitting the middle class, and the spectrum of appropriate behavior is both small and ever-shrinking. The women in *Why Did I Get Married?* must operate within a very contracted space if they are to be accepted as members of a paradigmatic black middle-class community: they must be successful but not cutthroat, ambitious but not emasculating, maternal but not mousy, domestic but not dependent. Their husbands, meanwhile, must be supportive but not effeminate and strong but not violent.

Why Did I Get Married?, then, despite the lack of Madea and Uncle Joe, shares the didactic concerns of Perry's other films, carefully delineating a spectrum of acceptable middle-class black life and reinforcing its normative message through both narrative resolution and the construction of audience empathy. The stories of Sheila and Angela, the homemaker and the CEO, illustrate most clearly the narrow space of acceptable black womanhood that middle-class success leaves open. As the limit cases of Sheila and Angela demonstrate, Perry's ideal black female professionalism is bounded at both ends of the economic spectrum: women should not be too ambitious or career-driven, but they must have the capacity to support themselves financially, lest they find themselves, like the demonized Victoria in *Madea's Family Reunion*, at the mercy of a wealthy but morally bankrupt man.

Sheila is the character in *Why Did I Get Married?* who comes closest to resembling the abused and broken women at the heart of Perry's other films: she has been so demoralized by Mike's coldness, insults, and sexual withholding that she makes no move to leave him, still believing that they can work on their marriage at the retreat even though he has brought his mistress. When their marriage crumbles and Mike cleans out her bank account, it becomes clear that Sheila's emotional dependence on Mike cannot be neatly severed from her economic dependence on him. Not only does Sheila feel physically and emotionally worthless—"I just need to lose a few pounds and then things'll get better for us" she plaintively tells her girlfriends—but she is also economically without value: Mike's departure with Trina leaves Sheila with an old car, a broken-down rental property, and "87 dollars to my name." When Sheila confesses to Troy, the local sheriff of the town in which Mike has abandoned her, that she "[has] no life without" her ex-husband, she is not speaking romantically; she literally has no marketable skills, and it is only through Troy's kindness (or perhaps his charity) that she secures an entry-level retail job at a hardware store.

Sheila's divorce from Mike should affect her status within the film's middle-class community, but it never does—a fact that reinforces *Why Did I Get Married?*'s construction of class as a behavioral concept rather than an economic one. So long as Sheila retains her faith in God, her friendships with Patty, Diane, and Angela, and her willingness to forgive Mike for his treatment of her, she remains safely ensconced within acceptable middle-class affective norms.

In fact, in *Why Did I Get Married?* it is the wealthy Angela, not the newly impoverished Sheila, who is in danger of betraying the film's middle-class ideals. Loud, abrasive, and frequently drunk, Angela makes a spectacle of herself in public places (where her behavior is remarked on by the judgmental white people who stand at the fringes of the story) and humiliates her husband for his economic dependence on her. It is these acts—her foul language, unmediated anger, and denigration of her husband's masculinity—that bring her dangerously close to betraying the community. At one point Patty finds it necessary to "explain" Angela's behavior to a group of students in an almost anthropological way: she points out that Angela is extremely intelligent, majored in chemistry, and started her own business when she "couldn't get a job in corporate America." Patty doesn't explain why Angela couldn't get a job, but when the audience meets Angela in the next scene she is loudly berating Markus in public while drinking from a flask, and the reason for her lack of mainstream success becomes clear: she cannot conform to the behavioral requirements of a white-collar office job. As the film's representative of academic and professional discourse, one of Patty's narrative purposes is to signal to the audience how precarious Angela's middle-class status truly is.

Although Angela is clearly among the wealthier members of the group, Perry clarifies her failure to fulfill middle-class norms by drawing parallels between Angela and her nemesis, Markus's "baby mama" Keisha. In scenes in which Keisha and Angela appear together, Keisha's casual appearance and dress contrast sharply with Angela's tailored pencil skirts and straightened hair, but their behavior is almost identical, with each woman threatening violence and hurling insults at the other. These scenes are played as theatrical comedy, but the normative implication is that, regardless of actual wealth, neither woman is exhibiting proper middle-class behavior. If Angela wants to rise to true middle-class status (and therefore rise above Keisha), she will need more than expensive clothing and a successful business: she will have to stop drinking, stop embarrassing herself in public, and treat her husband with respect—especially since he gave her the seed money for her company. Angela, Sheila, and the other women portrayed in *Why Did I Get Married?* are thus restricted to a narrow range of acceptable economic and affective behavior—one implicitly based on the middle-class expectations of white society.

Noting these and other "controlling images" of black life that appear, not only in Perry's films, but in earlier productions by both black and white filmmakers—images meant to position black Americans as "good candidates for integration"—Cherise Harris and Keisha Tassie have argued that Perry's films reify stereotypes of middle-class black Americans as "violent, criminal, and even hypersexual" while simultaneously creating new stereotypes like the "Emasculated Black Gentleman" (325, 323).[5] But the problem with analyses like Harris and Tassie's is that there is no way in which Perry (or any other black filmmaker) could avoid condemnation: black male characters who resort to violence are characterized as "Black Brutes," but those who don't are "Black Buddies," modern-day Uncle Toms. Black female characters who flaunt their education and sexuality are "Educated Black Bitches," but those who don't are "weak and ineffectual" (324–325). Like Sheila and Angela, whose behavior must fall within carefully prescribed limits, the acceptable range of black characters that critics like Harris and Tassie will acknowledge is so small as to make black creative production seem impossible.

As a filmmaker, then, Tyler Perry is subject to the same suffocating normative expectations as his characters—a problem that *Why Did I Get Married?* addresses on the metatextual level. In condemning Perry for supposedly reifying cultural stereotypes about black people, Harris and Tassie perform the very problem Perry faces as a black artist in the American cultural marketplace: his choices are so overdetermined by cultural expectations of representativeness—every black person should be the perfect black person—that the spaces within which one might create a non-stereotyped black character become vanishingly small. *Why Did I Get Married?* is a more complex film than critics like Harris and Tassie acknowledge precisely because the film does not simply prescribe norms; it simultaneously reflects on the psychological costs that compliance with those norms exacts.

In movies like *Madea's Family Reunion* the problem of representativeness is addressed through Madea herself: a wealthy young black man dressed as an old black woman of nebulous economic status performs a parody of minstrelsy (occasionally including whiteface) that seeks to short-circuit the problem of representativeness by conflating age, gender, race, and class in one explosively indeterminate figure. In *Why Did I Get Married?*, in which there is no Madea to act as a magnet for problems of signification, the pressures of black representation leak through in queer snips of dialogue and prolonged silences. In one particularly striking instance, a scene late in the film finds Patty and Gavin, the one couple with a seemingly perfect marriage, standing in their kitchen arguing over the death of their son Noah in a car accident. Patty confesses that she was tired and hurried the day Noah died; she was late for a meeting, and she strapped Noah into his car seat but didn't check to be sure that the seat itself was secured. "Perfect Patty messed up!" shouts Patty, and her third-person confession indexes not only the sense of alienation engendered by her attempts to play the ideal wife, mother, and professional, but also Perry's metatextual reflection on the problematics of framing black experience within a middle-class sentimental framework that originated in white discourse. Both Patty and Perry must constantly judge themselves against impossible standards of perfection imposed by others, requiring them to stand simultaneously both inside and outside of the norms that would enclose them.

The ever-shrinking possibilities for how one might perform blackness in acceptable ways, then, is a problem at the level of narrative—Gavin and Patty, Angela and Markus, and their friends must squeeze themselves into narrow behavioral boxes—and on the aesthetic level as well. Audiences and critics, both black and white, expect Perry—as creator of sentimental middle-class fictions—to perform an artistic persona that offers a model of black creativity that achieves success without reifying black stereotypes; these expectations would of course never be placed on a white director vis-à-vis "white" creativity or "white" stereotypes. Like "perfect Patty," with her one emotional outburst, Perry's public life sometimes displays the strain of such expectations, as when, after years of fielding questions about a trumped-up "feud" with Spike Lee, he finally told a reporter in 2011 that "Spike can go straight to hell" (Gray).[6]

Such textual and metatextual outbursts are indicative of the sentimental situation, in which the sentimental subject, having only limited access to canonical forms of political and social influence, exerts power in those realms that are more immediately accessible: the personal and the domestic. The sentimental provides its audiences "with a design for living under ... restricted conditions," but "at the same time it provides them with a catharsis of rage and grief that registers the cost of living according to that model." In scene after tearful scene, "[t]he force of those passions that must be curbed at all costs pushes to the surface" (Tompkins 173). In *Why Did I Get Married?* this paradigm is exemplified in the character of Sheila, whose only recourse against Mike's insults and ridicule comes in tears, prayers, and self-recriminations. "Jesus, make it all right," she prays under her breath while driving alone across country; "It's me. It's me. I know it's me," she repeats when her friends complain about Mike's behavior; she makes preemptive comments about her weight before Mike can do so. Sheila's character, powerless to stop Mike's abuses—at least until she breaks a bottle over his head—directs her frustrations inward, resulting in a nearly incoherent monologue that registers how completely she has internalized Mike's despotic rule.

When Sheila finally stands up to Mike it is her silence and her violence, not her tears or her speech, that indicate her emergence from the sentimental paradigm of sacrifice and self-suppression. After Mike leaves Sheila the next scene finds her sitting on the bed in a dingy motel room. The camera tracks along the floor from the door to the side of the bed, where it focuses first on Sheila's feet, then dollies slowly up her legs and past her torso, finally coming to rest on her expressionless and tear-streaked face. The camera's lingering contemplation of Scott's ample body—a sequence that is out of character for the film, which otherwise hums along in a series of medium shots showcasing Perry's dialogue rather than his actors' physical attributes—emphasizes how completely Sheila has failed to meet the physical and behavioral standards imposed by her husband. Jill Scott, the actress who plays Sheila, sits silent, allowing the camera to pass judgment on her body. The flow of excuses and self-abuse stopped, Sheila's prolonged silence heralds the beginning of her healing process but also registers a lacuna in Perry's own language—the point at which Perry, as screenwriter, stops talking and lets silence speak for itself.

Conclusion: Getting the Joke

Ann Douglas, in condemning the rise of nineteenth-century sentimental culture, portrayed her subjects as unwitting victims of their own cluelessness: "Their conscious motives were good—even praiseworthy; their effects were not altogether bad [....] Whatever their ambiguities of motivation, [they] believed they had a genuine redemptive mission in their society"; their sins were "hardly altogether their fault" (10–11). Readings of Tyler Perry's oeuvre often display a similarly patronizing attitude. Reviewing his first Tyler Perry movie, *Diary of a Mad Black Woman*, Roger Ebert wondered, "Did nobody realize that Grandma Madea [...] is playing by different rules than anyone else in the cast?" Wesley Morris notes that Perry "may not yet have mastered fluid dramatic structure or where to put the camera, but he knows how to get out of the way of good and determined women."

Such critical assessments not only fail to recognize the conventions of the sentimental genre Perry's films invoke—in which subtleties of characterization and narrative complexity are less important than didactic clarity—but also overlook the layers of possible meaning that Perry's films offer and that this essay has sought to reveal. Perry is well aware of the critical dismissal of his films but refuses to allow the white critical establishment to define the terms of his creative process. "Let me tell you what," Perry told *60 Minutes* in 2009, "Madea, Brown and all of these characters are bait. Disarming, charming, make-you-laugh bait so that I can slap Madea in something and talk about God, love, faith, forgiveness, family."

While Perry's implicit characterization of his audiences as responding to comedic "bait" carries its own patronizing implications, he also gives viewers opportunities to reflect on the stereotyped nature of his characters. The closing credit outtakes in which Perry "unmasks" his depiction of Madea by shifting in and out of character and costume offer viewers the chance to reflect on Madea as a constructed figure. These outtakes solidify Perry's sentimental strategy by subtly drawing viewers into the filmmaking process. Over the closing credits of *I Can Do Bad All by Myself*, for instance, Perry includes a practical joke he played on the film's star, Taraji P. Henson. In a scene deleted from the final film, a teenaged character named Jennifer reads aloud to April (Henson) a letter ostensibly written by April's now-dead mother. The letter admonishes April to be humble, especially when she wins her first Academy Award, at which point she should remember to thank all of the people who ever helped her, including her hair and makeup crew and Perry himself.

In this scene the camera shoots from over Henson's shoulder, framing the young actress who plays Jennifer, but as Henson comprehends the joke she turns slowly toward the camera and makes a wry face, presumably at Perry (who as director would have been standing behind the camera) but also, by virtue of the camera position, at the audience. As the audience watches Henson compress her lips and shake her head in mock disapproval, they are transformed, by virtue of Henson's slow 180-degree turn, from observers of a staged scene to participants in an unstaged one. The inclusion of such closing-credit outtakes is both a convention of comedic films and part of Perry's sentimental style. Like the church services, family picnics, and impromptu concerts that punctuate his films, it solidifies the communal relationship formed between Perry and his audiences. Everyone is in on the joke.

Notes

1. In drawing on both Weinstein and Berlant we might seem to be contradicting ourselves: Weinstein's work is in part an objection to negative critical formulations of the sentimental, including Berlant's, in which "'Feeling right' always seems to be feeling (and doing) wrong" (Weinstein 2). As Dana Nelson notes, much criticism of the sentimental boils down to "arguments about it as a (bad) female indulgence, a (bad) feminizing discipline or a (good/bad) feminizing cultural agenda" (29), and these arguments usually hinge on the critic's perception of whether and how sentimental texts perform cultural or political work. While we acknowledge that these debates are ongoing we are less concerned with condemning or praising Perry's work than we are with situating it in the larger cultural context of the late-twentieth and early-twenty-first centuries.

2. Berlant's work engages "the first mass cultural intimate public in the United States": the "women's culture" produced by nineteenth-century writers of sentimental fiction and carried on by twentieth-century authors and filmmakers. This article engages the "intimate public" of black middle-class culture that Perry's films help to create—an intimate public that is both related to and separate from the "women's culture" that Berlant identifies.

3. While this plot element follows the stage play closely, many others do not. Lisa and Vanessa (whose names are different in the play) are much less emotionally stable in the stage version; the play also ends with Lisa's marriage to another man, rather than Vanessa and Frankie's wedding.

4. The use of hot grits to punish a wayward spouse is also mentioned in *Why Did I Get Married?*

5. Harris and Tassie offer *The Cosby Show* (1984–1992) and the Eddie Murphy film *Boomerang* (1992) as examples of pop culture products that employ "controlling images"

of black men and women. Their analysis draws heavily on E. Franklin Frazier's *The Black Bourgeoisie* (1957) for its theoretical grounding.

6. The narrative of the Spike Lee-Tyler Perry "feud" is as much a media creation as an actual series of events. In March 2010 Lee posted a blog entry to his website denying that there was any feud between Perry and himself. But media outlets have continued to report on the supposed animosity between the two men—a fact that is itself indicative of racist attitudes toward successful black filmmakers. As the cultural commentator Alyssa Rosenberg notes, "feud stories" and "catfight stories" (in the case of competing women) perpetuate racist and sexist perceptions "that there [is] a limited amount of success to go around" for African Americans and other minorities "and that [those] who are allowed access to it must be held to unusually high standards."

Works Cited

Als, Hinton. "Mama's Gun." *The New Yorker* 86. 1 (2010): 68–72. Web. 8 May 2013.

Berlant, Lauren. *The Female Complaint: The Unfinished Business of Sentimentality in American Culture*. Durham, NC: Duke University Press, 2008. Web. 14 April 2011.

Chen, Gina Masullo, Sherri Williams, Nicole Hendrickson, and Li Chen. "Male Mammies: A Social-Comparison Perspective on How Exaggeratedly Overweight Media Portrayals of Madea, Rasputia, and Big Momma Affect How Black Women Feel About Themselves." *Mass Communication and Society* 15.1 (2012): 115–135. Web. 8 May 2013.

Douglas, Ann. *The Feminization of American Culture*. New York: Knopf, 1977. Print.

Ebert, Roger. "*Diary of a Mad Black Woman* Movie Review." www.rogerebert.com 2005. Web. 3 June 2013.

Gray, Madison. "After Racial Criticism, Tyler Perry Says Spike Lee Can 'Go to Hell.'" *Time* 20 April 2011. Web. 16 May 2013.

Harris, Cherise, and Keisha Tassie. "The Cinematic Incarnation of Frazier's Black Bourgeoisie: Tyler Perry's Black Middle-Class." *Journal of African American Studies* 16.2 (2012): 321–344. Web. 16 August 2012.

Howard, June. "What Is Sentimentality?" *American Literary History* 11.1 (1999): 63–81. Web. 11 July 2011.

Lee, Spike. "No Feud with Tyler Perry by Spike Lee." 40acreswww 17 March 2010. Web. 9 May 2013.

Lyle, Timothy. "'Check with Yo' Man First; Check with Yo' Man': Tyler Perry Appropriates Drag as a Tool to Re-Circulate Patriarchal Ideology." *Callaloo* 34.3 (2011): 943–958. Web. 8 May 2013.

Morris, Wesley. "Tyler Perry's Secret to Success." *Slate Magazine* 22 October 2007. Web. 3 June 2013.

Nelson, Dana D. "'No Cold or Empty Heart': Polygenesis, Scientific Professionalism, and the Unfinished Business of Male Sentimentalism." *differences: A Journal of Feminist Cultural Studies* 11.3 (1999): 29–56. Web. 22 February 2012.

Perry, Tyler. "A Conversation with Tyler Perry." *Penguin Group*. 2013. Web. 3 June 2013.

———. "Director's Commentary." *Tyler Perry's Madea's Family Reunion*. DVD. Santa Monica, CA: Lionsgate, 2006.

Pomerantz, Dorothy. "The Highest Paid Men in Entertainment." *Forbes* 12 September 2010. Web. 8 May 2013.

Rosenberg, Alyssa. "Jessica Chastain and Jennifer Lawrence Both Want an Oscar. That's Not a Catfight." *Slate Magazine* 11 February 2013. Web. 11 June 2013.

60 Minutes. Interview with Tyler Perry. CBS, October, 2009. Television.

Tompkins, Jane P. *Sensational Designs: The Cultural Work of American Fiction, 1790–1860*. New York: Oxford University Press, 1985. Print.

Tyler Perry's Diary of a Mad Black Woman. DVD. Dir. Tyler Perry. Santa Monica, CA: Lionsgate, 2005. Film.
Tyler Perry's I Can Do Bad All by Myself. DVD. Dir. Tyler Perry. Santa Monica, CA: Lionsgate Home Entertainment, 2010. Film.
Tyler Perry's Madea's Family Reunion. DVD. Dir. Tyler Perry. Santa Monica, CA: Lionsgate, 2006. Film.
Tyler Perry's Why Did I Get Married? DVD. Dir. Tyler Perry. Santa Monica, CA: Lionsgate, 2008. Film.
Weinstein, Cindy. *Family, Kinship, and Sympathy in Nineteenth-Century American Literature*. New York: Cambridge University Press, 2004. Print.
Wolfe, George C. *The Colored Museum*. New York: Dramatists Play Service, 2010. Print.

About the Contributors

Nathaniel **Cadle** is an assistant professor of English at Florida International University in Miami, where he teaches courses on American literary realism and modernism. He is at work on his first book, *The Mediating Nation: Late Realism, Globalization, and the Progressive State*.

María **DeGuzmán** is a professor of English and comparative literature and founding director of Latina/o Studies at the University of North Carolina at Chapel Hill. She is the author of *Buenas Noches, American Culture: Latina/o Aesthetics of Night* (Indiana University Press, 2012).

Elizabeth A. **Ellis** is a doctoral student at the University of Maryland, College Park, and teaches courses in rhetorical theory and history and first-year writing. Her work focuses on the interplay of rhetoric, religion, gender and culture. She is working on her dissertation, which examines the rhetoricity of the religious press in the context of the black freedom movement.

Anne-Marie **Evans** is a senior lecturer in American literature at the University of York St. John. Her main area of interest is early twentieth-century American literature. Her thesis examined the work of writers such as Edith Wharton, Ellen Glasgow, Gertrude Stein, Fannie Hurst and Zora Neale Hurston in terms of literature, consumerism and the articulation of female identity.

Erica D. **Galioto** is an associate professor of English at Shippensburg University in Pennsylvania, where she teaches classes in American literature and psychoanalysis, English education, and writing. Her research focuses on "real-world therapy": everyday experiences in fiction and life that occasion therapeutic effects outside a clinical setting.

Kristin J. **Jacobson** is an associate professor of American literature at the Richard Stockton College of New Jersey. She teaches courses in American literature, American studies, and women's, gender and sexuality studies. Her book *Neodomestic American Fiction* (Ohio State University Press, 2010) investigates manifestations of domestic fiction.

Jennifer **Larson** teaches film, literature, and writing at the University of North Carolina at Chapel Hill. She is the author of *Understanding Suzan-Lori Parks* (University of South Carolina Press, 2012) and *Understanding Walter Mosley* (University of South Carolina Press, forthcoming).

Lisa **Mendelman** is a Ph.D. candidate in English literature at the University of California, Los Angeles. Her dissertation, "Modern Feeling: American Sentimentalism and Femininity, 1915–1935," focuses on the aesthetic category of modern sentimentalism. She has contributed to the *American Women's History Encyclopedia* (2012) and *Modern Fiction Studies* (forthcoming).

Ashley **Reed** is a Ph.D. candidate in the Department of English and Comparative Literature at the University of North Carolina at Chapel Hill. Her research centers on gender, race, and formations of secular agency in the nineteenth-century United States. She is co-editing a volume of essays on medicine and religion in North American culture.

Brian **Sweeney** is an assistant professor of English and 2012–13 CREST Residential Fellow at the College of Saint Rose in Albany. He teaches courses in early and nineteenth-century American literature and periodical studies. He is working on a book about servants, professionals, and occupational affect in U.S. literature of the nineteenth century.

Julie **Taylor** is a lecturer in American studies at Northumbria University. She is the author of *Djuna Barnes and Affective Modernism* (Edinburgh University Press, 2012). Her article on "Hart Crane's Queer Intimacy" is forthcoming in *Twentieth Century Literature*. She is also editing an essay collection on modernism and affect.

Jennifer A. **Williamson** is a gender technical specialist at Counterpart International and a former instructor of English and women's studies at the University of North Carolina at Chapel Hill. She is the author of numerous articles and the book *Twentieth-Century Sentimentalism: Narrative Appropriation in American Literature* (Rutgers, forthcoming).

Michael T. **Wilson** is an associate professor of English at Appalachian State University. His interests focus on gender studies and American literature. He has published on a variety of topics, and his work has appeared in *Studies in American Fiction*, *Currents in Teaching and Learning* and *Teaching American Literature: A Journal of Theory and Practice*.

Index

Numbers in **_bold italics_** indicate pages with photographs.

abolition/abolitionists 24, 122, 157, 175–188
abuse 58, 60, 112, 135–136, 138–140, 143–144, 147–148, 176, 193–195, 197, 199, 201;
  sexual abuse/incest 60, 64, 69, 135–136, 138–140, 143–144, 147–148; *see also* violence, domestic
Adams, J. Donald 94
AIDS 138–139
Alcott, Louisa May 59–60, 65
Als, Hilton 190, 193, 196
American Medical Association 21, 22, 31–32
American Mercury 40
angels 60–61, 65, 99, 121–124, 126–131, 133, 182, 186
animals 123–127, 129–130, 132
anti–Sentimentalism 1, 8, 56, 58, 68n2, 91, 121, 123, 131, 134–135, 137–138, 141, 148, 149n1, 194, 201
"Appeal to Christian Women of the South" 178–179; *see also* Grimke, Angelina
Armstrong, Nancy 152, 162–163, 171n18
art 136, 137, 140, 145, 146, 147, 148
Atlantic Monthly 17

Bacon, Jacqueline 179
Bandes, Susan A. 168
Barnes, Elizabeth 7, 10, 29, 64–65, 153
Baym, Nina 4, 161, 191
Beegel, Susan F. 96
Bell, Michael 9–10
Benn Michaels, Walter 20
Bennett, Jill 66
Bennett, Paula 7
Berlant, Lauren 7, 39–40, 53n5, 115, 153, 156, 159, 172, 193, 208n1-2
Bodies and Souls 123–124

Boomerang 208n5
Booth, Wayne 39, 41
Bradstreet, Anne 178
Braudy, Leo 97
Brown, Gillian 7
Brown, Herbert Ross 105
Brown, John 184
Brown, Keffrelyn D. 165–166, 168–169
Brown, William Wells 192

Cannon, James P. 74–75, 85
Caruth, Cathy 68n3
Caselli, Daniela 68n2
Cassuto, Leonard 91, 153, 166, 168, 169, 169n1
Cather, Willa 8
Catholicism 123, 125, 126, 132
Chapman, Mary 153
"Charity Bowery" 183–184
Charlotte Temple 8, 112
Chesnutt, Charles 15–21, 23–32, 33n2, 33n5
Chicano 121, 122
Child, Lydia Maria 179, 183, 186
Christianity 8, 102, 114–117, 124, 126, 132, 165, 176, 178–179, 184, 186, 198
City of Night 121–133
Clark, Suzanne 9–10, 39, 53n8, 57, 68n2, 99, 108, 113, 119
Clotel 192
Coffey, Laura T. 136
Coleman, Emily 58
The Color Purple (film) 199
The Colored Museum 200
Communist Party USA 74, 79–81
Conrad, Joseph 50

213

Index

Coolidge, Susan 65
Cormier, Harvey 167
The Cosby Show 208n5
coverture 6; *see also* feme covert
Crane, Gregg 7, 96, 104
Crane, Stephen 7
Cummins, Maria Susan 112, 192

Dalí, Salvador 107
Dalton, Ann 60, 68n4
Daniels, Lee 135, 149n2
Danielson, Susan 29, 30
Das, Veena 66
Davidson, Cathy 5–6, 10, 152
Davis, Kimberly Chabot 153, 156, 169
"A Day's Wait" 105
The Death of Adam 187
deathbed epistle 181–182
Deleuze, Gilles 66
DeLillo, Don 178
Den Tandt, Christophe 7–8
Diamond Lil 108, 115
Diary of a Mad Black Woman (film) 191, 196, 198–199, 207
Dickens, Charles 152–159, 168
Dickinson, Emily 188
Dobson, Joanne 3–5
domestic labor 15–17
domestic spheres 1, 107, 109, 153–156, 180, 186–188, 206; race in 177, 186, 198; men in 181–183
domestic tragedy 28
domestic virtue 30, 33n9
domesticity 5, 7, 87n1, 154–155, 186, 191; disruptions 78, 79, 84, 154, 202; and femininity 1, 10, 30, 37, 203; and modernism 9, 68; and realism/naturalism 8; and sentimentalism 3, 5, 68, 109, 161–162, 192; *see also* neodomestic
Dos Passos, John 71–72, 80, 83–87
Douglas, Ann 4, 5, 7, 61, 157, 181, 191, 207
Douglas, Christopher 178
Douglass, Frederick 181
The Drag 1908
Dreiser, Theodore 7, 72, 80, 83, 85–87
DuBois, W.E.B. 20, 23, 26, 27, 31
Duggan, Lisa 157

Ebert, Roger 207
Edmunds, Ann 68n2
Edwards, A.S. 70–71
Edwards, Jonathan 178
Eliot, T.S. 56, 68n1
Ellison, Julie 7
Emerson, Ralph Waldo 188

Engels, Friedrich 87n1
epistolary novel 177–182
Ernest Linwood 59, 65
eroticism 62–63, 68n5

false consciousness 131
family 193–194
Farrell, James T. 70–72
Faulkner, William 40
feme covert 6; *see also* coverture
Fern, Fanny (Sara Payson Willis Parton) 3, 196
Fiedler, Leslie A. 152
Fisher, Philip 5–6, 17, 28, 75
Fisk University 23
flapper 46
Flexner, Abraham 31
Flexner Report 31–32
Foley, Barbara 81
Forter, Greg 90, 91, 93, 94, 96, 105
Foxx, Jamie 193
Frazier, E. Franklin 209n5
Freud, Sigmund 44, 54n24, 68n3
Frost, Robert H. 78

Garrison, William Lloyd 180–181
Gellert, Hugo 77, 80, 83
Gentlemen Prefer Blondes 36–55, 108
Gold, Michael 71–73, 77, 79–80, 87
Good Times 199
Good Wives 60
Goodness Had Nothing to Do with It 109, 115, 119
Gordon, Eugene 83
Grant, Cary 108
Grebstein, Sheldon Norman 105
Grimke, Angelina 178, 186, 188

Hansberry, Lorraine 200
hard-boiled fiction 91, 169
Harlan County War 80, 84–87
Harlan Miners Speak 85–87
Harlem 147
Harper's Bazaar 40
Harper's Magazine 16–17
Harris, Cherise 204–205, 208n5
Harris, Joel Chandler 17
Hawthorne, Nathaniel 3, 190
Hendler, Glenn 61, 64, 160
Hentz, Caroline Lee 59, 65
Herget, Winfried 181
homosexuality 2, 47, 49, 121–122, 127, 166
hooks, bell 179
Howard, June 191
Howard University 32

Index 215

Howells, William Dean 7, 57
Hughes, Langston 147
Hutcheon, Linda 39
Huyssen, Andreas 56

I Can Do Bad All by Myself 208
Incidents in the Life of a Slave Girl 192, 196
Industrial Workers of the World 70, 77
International Labor Defense 74–81, **76**, **82**, 85–87; *see also Labor Defender*
interracial marriage 184, 185; *see also* miscenegation

Jackson, Cassandra 168
Jacobs, Harriet 192, 196, 198, 200
Jacobson, Kristin J. 154
James, Kelvin Christopher 136
Jazz Age 45–48, 52n2
Jim Crow laws 18–21, 23–25, 31

Karsner, Rose 75
Kerr, Francis 93
The Kid 135–137, 139–140, 141, 144–146, 148–149
King, Jim 158
Klein, Amanda Ann 156
Knadler, Stephen 25, 30
Kraehe, Amelia 165–166, 168–169

La Berge, Leigh Claire 152–153, 164–165, 169n2
Labor Defender 72, 74–86, **76**, **78**, **82**, 87n5; *see also* International Labor Defense
The Lamplighter 112
Latham, Sean 80
Latino identity 11, 122, 123
Lawrence, Martin 201
Lee, Spike 190, 206, 209n6
Leise, Christopher 178
Lewis, Sinclair 7
Lewis, Wyndham 43, 54n22
The Liberator 71–74
Linder, Mark 108
Lipsitz, George 154, 159–160
Little Women 59–60, 65, 161–162
Loos, Anita 40–41, 108, 115
Lucasi, Stephen 154
Lyle, Timothy 195–196, 198–200

Maddock Dillon, Elizabeth 38, 99
Madea's Family Reunion (film) 191, 193–201, 203, 205
Madea's Family Reunion (play) 194
Mahtani, Minelle 159
market capitalism 20–22, 23–24, 25

The Marrow of Tradition 15–21, 23–32, 33n5
Marx, Karl 87n1
masochism 63
The Masses 70, 72–74
matriarchy 194–196, 198–201
McGurl, Mark 43–45
McKay, Claude 71–72
McTeague 7
Meaney, Gerardine 161
medical profession 21–24, 31–32, 33n7, 33n8
Meharry Medical College 32
Mencken, H.L. 36, 40, 52n1, 53n13
Merish, Lori 7
Mexican American 124, 125, 127
Michaelsen, Scott 167
miscegenation 162–163; *see also* interracial marriage
modernism 8–9, 37–38, 57–58, 92, 100–101, 104–106; challenges 91, 103; critics 8, 57; and femininity 93, 94, 98; influence 1, 10; and sentimentalism 7, 10, 38–39, 53n8, 58, 61, 65, 68, 71, 72, 90–92, 96–97, 100, 103
Momaday, N. Scott 178
Mooney, Tom 77–81, **77**, **78**, 87n8
Morris, Wesley 207
Morrison, Toni 178
Morrisson, Mark S. 72–74, 82
Murphy, Eddie 201

narcissism 125–126, 130
National Committee for the Defense of Political Prisoners 80, 83–86
National Medical Association 22
naturalism 1, 7–8
Nelson, Dana 208n1
neodomestic 156
neoliberalism 157–159, 168, 170n9, 171n13
New Criticism 1, 10–11
The New Masses 70–74, **77**, 80, 87
New Woman 46, 54n18
The Nigger of the Narcissus 50, 54n21
Noble, Marianne 63
Norris, Frank 7
North, Joseph 79–82

Oscar Wilde 127
otherness 134, 135, 136, 138, 142, 149

Page, Thomas Nelson 17
Pamela 112
Penfold-Mounce, Ruth 157
Perry, Tyler 190–210; earnings 190; as Madea 191, 193–201, 205

Person, Leland 3
photography 127–128
plantation fiction 17
Poole, Ernest 71, 87n2
postmodernism 7, 152, 156, 169
postsentimentalism 17–18, 25–25, 28–30, 31
Pound, Ezra 56, 66n1
Precious 135, 137, 149n2
Prodigal Son 185
prostitution 110–112
Push 135, 137–149
Pynchon, Thomas 178

Rabinowitz, Paula 85
A Raisin in the Sun 200
rape 139, 140, 142, 144, 148; *see also* abuse
realism 1, 7–8, 68n2, 72, 87, 152–153, 156–157, 159, 165, 167–168; and sentimentalism 156–157, 167, 167–168
Reed, Ishmael 135, 136
Reynolds, David S. 154
Richardson, Samuel 112
Rideout, Walter 71–72
The Rise of Silas Lapham 57
Roberts, David J. 159, 171n13
romanticism 7
Rosenberg, Alyssa 209n6
Rowson, Susanna 8, 112
Ruth Hall 3, 196
Ryan, Barbara 17

St. Augustine 125
Samuels, Shirley 4–6
Schaub, Joseph Christopher 157
Schiller, Friedrich 37–38
Scholes, Robert 80
Scott, James 68n2
Scottsboro Boys 74, 80–83, **82**, 86
Sedgwick, Eve Kosofsky 141, 145
segregation *see* Jim Crow laws
self-control 42–43, 91, 97, 103, 110
serialized literature 151–152, 165, 170n6
"servant problem" 16–17, 33n1
Sex 108, 112
Shakespeare, William 131, 158
shame 134–137, 141–148
She Done Him Wrong (film) 108
She Done Him Wrong (novel) 107, 112, 113, 115, 119
Shephard, Thomas 178
Silko, Leslie 178
Simon, David 152, 158–159, 171n12
Sinclair, Upton 71–72, 77–78
Sister Carrie 7
60 Minutes 207

slavery 154–160, 163, 166, 169n1, 171n11; *see also* abolition
Smith, Adam 17, 33n3
social mobility 17–18
socialism 2, 71, 73
Stern, Julia 7
Stevenson, Robert Louis 15, 27
Stowe, Harriet Beecher 5, 17, 18, 33n4, 60–63, 65, 110, 151–174, 176, 181, 186, 188, 192–193
The Strange Case of Dr. Jekyll and Mr. Hyde 15, 27
Strychacz, Thomas 90
Swedenborg, Emanuel 122, 126, 128, 129; Swedenborgianism 121–133
sympathy 4–6, 10–11, 17, 28–31, 33, 36–37, 41–44, 47, 61, 64–65, 77–78, 83–84, 94, 98, 101, 104–105, 111, 130, 137, 138, 141, 152, 154, 164–165, 167, 169–170, 175–176, 179, 191; and abolitionism 175–176, 179; and the anti-sentimental 130, 137–138, 141; and Enlightenment philosophy 17; as ironic strategy 36–37, 41–44, 47; and Leftist politics 77–78, 83–84; and race 28–31

Tanner, Laura E. 178
Tassie, Keisha 204–205, 208n5
theosophy 124
Ticknor, William B. 3, 190
Todd, Janice 91
Tompkins, Jane 5–8, 11, 110, 181, 198, 206
Tompkins, Silvan 141–144, 147–148
transcendentalism 122
trauma 58–60, 62–63, 66–68, 68n2

Uncle Tom's Cabin 17, 18, 51, 60–63, 65, 81, 87n2, 110, 151–174, 176

Van Vechten, Carl 51–52
vaudeville 108
Veblen, Thorstein 115
vernacular writing 41–45
Vest, Jason P. 166
violence 195; domestic 136, 140, 141, 148, 194–195, 198–200, 201, 203
virginity 60

Walker, Alice 149n3, 199
Walker, David 181
Wall Street crash 115
Wallace, Frank 108
Wanzo, Rebecca 75, 77, 81, 157, 159
Warner, Susan 109, 192
Warren, Diane 68n5

Warren, Joyce 191
Washington, Denzel 193
Weinstein, Cindy 96, 109, 113, 192, 194, 208n1
Weld, Theodore 180
Wharton, Edith 54n22
What Dreams May Come 122
What Katy Did 65
Why Did I Get Married? 191, 201–207, 208n4
The Wicked Age 108

The Wide, Wide World 109, 161
Williams, Mamie 86–87
Williams, Raymond 52n3
Wilmington Race Riot 18–19, 33n6
Wilson, David 158–159
Wilson, Marq 136, 137
The Wire 151–174
Wolfe, George C. 200
women's labor 48–49
Workers Monthly 73–74, 87n7

www.ingramcontent.com/pod-product-compliance
Lightning Source LLC
Chambersburg PA
CBHW032054300426
44116CB00007B/739